How to plan advertising

Edited by
Don Cowley

CASSELL
in association with the Account Planning Group

Hardback edition first published 1987 by **Cassell Educational Limited**
Villiers House, 41–47 Strand, London WC2N 5JE

Paperback edition, with new Introduction, first published 1989
Reprinted 1990

British Library Cataloguing in Publication Data
How to plan advertising
1. Advertising
I. Cowley, Don
659.1 HF5823

ISBN 0-304-37121-7

Typeset by Chapterhouse, The Cloisters, Formby, L37 3PX

Printed and bound in Great Britain by The Bath Press

Contents

Notes on the contributors

DON COWLEY was a media man and account handler before becoming an account planner in 1973. He was a founder member of the Account Planning Group in the late 1970s during his time as Planning Director of FCB, London. That job in an American-owned agency allowed him to get a close view of how an American agency set about developing advertising.

Desire to have a greater say in how an agency operates took him to Kirkwood and Partners as a partner in 1983. With the same end in view, in late 1986 he joined the agency that very shortly afterwards became Slaymaker Cowley White, where he is Planning Director and a management partner.

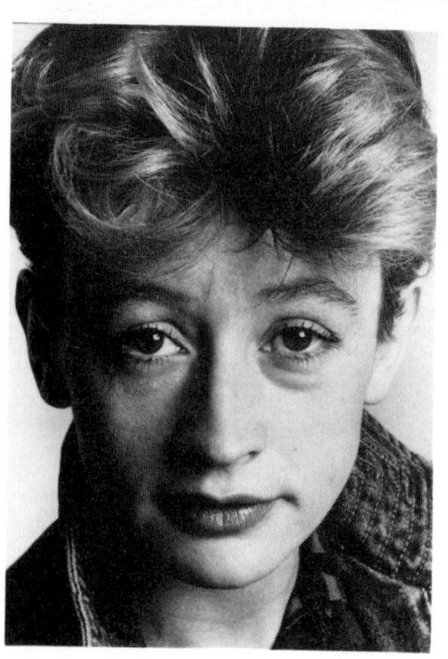

KAY SCORAH graduated from London University with an honours degree in Biochemistry, and went straight into market research with NOP Market Research Limited. From there she moved to MIL Research before succumbing to the attractions of a career in advertising.

She joined Boase Massimi Pollitt as an account planner in 1979, and then moved to SJIP/BBDO, before setting up her own company, rather creatively dubbed Holder & Scorah, with researcher Susan Holder in 1982. Two years later she was drawn back into mainstream advertising as Planning Director of BBDO and, in January 1986, moved on to Ted Bates as Executive Head of Planning. Kay now has a programme production company, as well as acting as a freelance advertising consultant.

SEV D'SOUZA's professional contact with advertising began in 1972, as a founder member of BJM Research. In 1974, he joined the BBDO agency—involved mainly with advertising research. By 1977, account planning was becoming more widely practised, and he joined Ayer Barker as a planner. Here he worked under planning luminary, Charles Channon, until, five years later, he was invited to become Head of Planning at SSCB:Lintas. His brief: to develop a planning function in a traditionally-structured agency.

In 1983, Sev joined the board of up-and-coming agency, Hedger Mitchell Stark, as their first Planning Director. Following the takeover of this agency, he joined other colleagues in starting their own agency in 1985. In only two years they had twenty-one clients, and the agency with the longest name in the business, Still Price Court Twivy D'Souza, has achieved a high profile in UK advertising.

Sev D'Souza has been a committee member of the Account Planning Group since 1982, and in this capacity he wrote the *What is Account Planning*? booklet published by the APG.

DAVID COWAN was one of the team who took Boase Massimi Pollitt to its top ten position.

He was Stanley Pollitt's first graduate trainee when account planning began at Pritchard Wood & Partners in 1966. He joined Stephen King at J. Walter Thompson shortly after account planning started there in 1968. After two years he rejoined his former PWP colleagues at the newly formed Boase Massimi Pollitt.

David was at BMP for sixteen years, fourteen of them as Head of Account Planning. He built up the department to be the biggest and most prestigious in London; many ex-trainees of this period are now account planning heads of major agencies. In 1987 he left BMP to found his own management consultancy company based on the ideas of account planning.

David is one of account planning's leading thinkers. He has spoken on many public platforms in the UK, United States, Europe and Australia. He is a graduate of University College London, and alumnus of the Harvard Business School.

JOHN WARD entered advertising in 1969 when (to quote his father) he 'threw away sixteen years of education', to become a copywriter. After two years of a career less than meteoric, with his art director going catatonic, Ward switched to advertising research. In

an outstanding act of philanthropy, J. Walter Thompson offered him a job in their Creative Research Unit in 1971, where he rose without trace for three years.

From 1974 until 1980 John worked at CDP in a variety of roles including researcher, dogsbody, entrepreneur, lunch-ticket, new business pitcher and, ultimately, Group Planning Director. He left to enjoy a brief spell of spectacular success as Deputy Managing Director of McCormicks, followed by an equally brief spell of spectacular failure in his own agency Weinreich Walsh Ward.

Having been one of the founders of CDP/Aspect in 1978, John returned to the newly independent Aspect in 1983 and remained until 1986, when he joined Doyle Dane Bernbach as Marketing Director. He is now Managing Director of Yellowhammer.

DAMIAN O'MALLEY was born and brought up in Wolverhampton. After an undistinguished grammar-school education, he arrived at Wadham College, Oxford, to study Psychology.

His love of mankind undiminished by this terrible experience, he entered the glamorous world of advertising. Five happy years ensued at Boase Massimi Pollitt, where he discovered the joys of fine wine and long motorway journeys, before being lured away to fledgling Gold Greenlees Trott by the promise of a new Alfa Romeo. He was made Planning Director in 1983 and deputy Managing Director in early 1987.

Damian has won two first prizes in the IPA Advertising Effectiveness Awards and speaks and writes extensively on advertising topics.

In July 1987 he set up his own agency, Woollams Moira O'Malley.

LESLIE BUTTERFIELD graduated from Lancaster University in 1975 with a BA in Business Studies, and an MA in Marketing. In the same year, he joined Boase Massimi Pollittt as an account planner working on Courage, Ferrero (Tic Tac) and Chefaro Proprietaries, and in 1979 was made an Associate Director. His accounts inluded Johnson & Johnson, Tjaereborg, Halfords, Cussons, Toyota and CPC (Hellmans and Mazola).

Leslie joined Abbott Mead Vickers in 1980 as Planning Director and main Board member with the brief of setting up what came to be one of the most highly regarded planning departments in London. His accounts there included Seagram UK Limited,

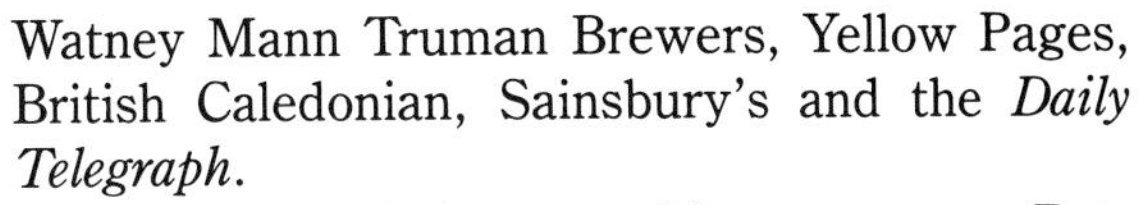

Watney Mann Truman Brewers, Yellow Pages, British Caledonian, Sainsbury's and the *Daily Telegraph*.

In January 1987 he set up his own agency, Butterfield Day Devito Hockney, already acclaimed as the most successful recent agency 'start up' and the first of what many believe is the 'third wave' of UK agencies.

He has been an active member of both the IPA Education and Training Committee (twice chairing their Campaign Planning Course) and of the APG, as a committee member and as convenor of the 1983 One Day Event and since January 1987 as Chairman of the APG.

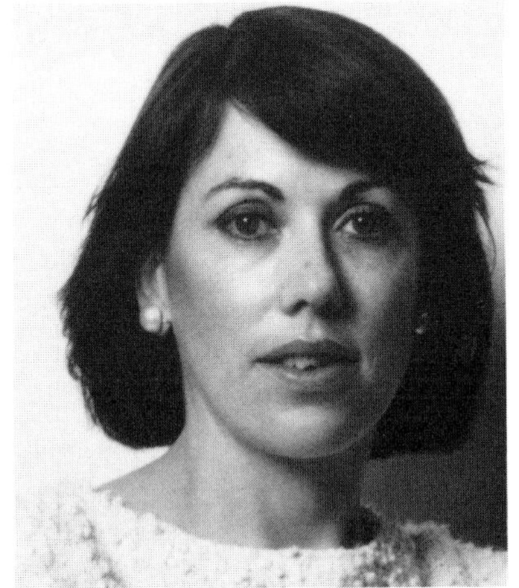

On graduating from Girton College, Cambridge, MARY STEWART-HUNTER received her basic research training at Marplan. She then went on to gain advertising agency experience at Grey and FCB, before joining Davidson Pearce as Director of Planning in 1979. In addition to her agency responsibilities, Mary serves on two IPA Committees: the Advertising Effectiveness Awards and Publications and Marketing Appraisals groups.

JEREMY ELLIOTT was educated in France, Spain and England. With a Cambridge degree in languages, Jeremy did not take the obvious course of joining the diplomatic service but (after sundry jobs as a teacher, a print buyer and a writer of instruction manuals) joined J. Walter Thompson instead, originally in the media department.

He later became a founder member of the first account planning department, set up by JWT in 1968, and spent eighteen years there as an active planner. During that time, Jeremy worked on most things from breakfast cereals to bedtime drinks, and from banking to wrist-watches. He also confesses (but only very quietly) to having planned the public information campaigns that launched decimal currency and VAT.

He became involved in developing the use of computers as part of the planning process, and has been particularly interested in analysing and evaluating the effects of advertising by different techniques, including market modelling (a term he prefers to the more pompous 'econometrics'). This interest led to no fewer than six IPA Advertising Effectiveness awards in the four competitions to date, the latest being the 1986 Grand Prix for his paper on the TSB Youth Market.

He is married with four grown-up children whom he regards as even more satisfactory awards.

Jeremy is now a freelance consultant.

Acknowledgements

Liz Watts for an enormous amount of behind-the-scenes work.

Sev D'Souza for helping me with the editing as well as writing a chapter.

The Commercials Trading Company, for providing us with high quality stills from commercials.

Introduction

Don Cowley

We wrote this book for account planners. It is about the craft of planning advertising in advertising agencies, which is what account planners do for a living.

We expected interest in this craft book to extend to other job functions that participate in the advertising planning process, such as researcher, account management and brand management. We also hoped to reach advertising people outside the UK who were interested in applying the disciplines of account planning to their own advertising needs; but we were surprised by the level of interest from people who are not connected with the advertising business, particularly students, both those studying business as a subject and those wishing to know more about the practice of advertising, presumably with some career intention.

Most of the people in our business who needed a copy of our book have already acquired one (probably paid for by their company), so it is with the wider audience in mind that our publishers have agreed to produce this paperback edition.

WHAT KIND OF PLANNING?

This book does not fit into the category of a 'good read'. It is not full of airy generalizations about what makes good advertising, there is no name dropping and only a modicum of self-promotion. It has not been written by people who write for a living: the authors were chosen for their skill as planners. Their style is intended to communicate, not impress. It is a description of how to do something put together by people who have done it every day for some years. Nor is it a theoretical tract. It describes activities which go on every day in advertising agencies now! That's its strength.

One point needs to be made clear up-front. This book did not set out to review the different ways in which the planning of advertising has been approached over the years. It does not offer you a choice. Its intention is to provide a straightforward guide to the principles and methodologies applied by account planners, that group of strategy specialists who have emerged over the last twenty years to change the way in which advertising is developed in British advertising agencies.

The profound difference that account planning brought to the process was a method which is consumer-led. Since advertisements are supposedly designed wholly and inescapably to influence the consumption behaviour of members of the public, you might be forgiven for thinking that this is not much of a breakthrough. But surprisingly enough it was, and still is for many parts of the advertising world, a revolutionary and controversial philosophy.

The history of advertising philosophies traditionally involved a conflict between a manufacturer-led view and an artistic view. For the manufacturer the advertising development framework was built around the question of 'How do we construct an ad which most effectively registers our product messages?' The artistic or creative viewpoint was driven by a desire to make the advertisement itself less stereotyped, banal and irritating, and to clothe the inevitable product message in such a way that the audience become willing participants in the persuasion process. The high priest of this creative movement was an American named Bill Bernbach from the agency DDB. Bernbach invented modern creative advertising and some of the DDB advertisements of the 1950s and 1960s, particularly for Volkswagen, are still among the most celebrated of all time.

But the manufacturers' approach held all the aces. Not only was it their own view and their own money, they had another secret weapon called research. The early 1970s saw a substantial upsurge in numerically based techniques, which set out to measure the effectiveness of advertisements. The typical research evaluation methods concentrated on measuring the registration of the product message, rather than collecting impressions of the advertisement itself and assessing how these might affect people's overall response to the product. So Bill Bernbach's inspired revolution petered out and the mainstream of American advertising returned to tried and tested formulae like the side-by-side comparison, the celebrity presenter, the non-celebrity presenter and so on.

The British experience has been rather different. Bill Bernbach's work inspired a generation of British creative people who began to apply the same kind of approach in the UK just at the time that the clouds were closing in on the American scene. The creative initiative in Britain, though, coincided with the widespread emergence of account planning as a discipline. Whilst the tools of the account planners' trade were the methodologies of market research, the techniques that they used were more qualitative than quantitative. The methods they favoured were smaller in sample size than the methods normally applied in the USA, but broader in scope. Also, they were less bound by the literal findings of the research and more intuitive in their interpretations. Account Planning proved a natural partner for this new strand of creative insight. Instead of ignoring or emasculating executional values, the account planners' data identified the enormous importance of imaginative executions in developing effective advertising.

As the skills of planners developed, so their consumer's eye view of the world began to prove its worth as a means of providing new types of strategies and expressions of strategy, which are more helpful to the people who have to write the advertisements. Planning began to show how a straightforward consumer benefit could be enhanced by an involving and original advertising expression. The *relevant and unexpected* began to represent an ideal.

During the late 1970s and early 1980s, the disciplines of account planning spread to the majority of large UK agencies, and in more recent years out-posts in Australia and the USA have been established. In this time, there has been a very great change in the type of advertising that we normally see. There are fewer formula executions than in earlier decades. Many more advertisements use humour or set out to beguile and entertain as the means of registering the sales message, rather than assert and insist, as in the traditional manufacturer-led style. The result has been a sea-change in the relationship between advertising and the public. Attitudinal data tracked over time show a lessening of the dislike and suspicion of advertising and a growing recognition that it is an art form that can rival TV programmes and magazine editorial for dramatic and imaginative entertainment. This is a benefit that all advertisers can potentially share in, since it works to create a more demanding but ultimately more receptive audience.

So a point has been reached in UK advertising where, through the process of planning described in this book, the instincts of creative people to produce surprising and imaginative advertising have found a natural interpreter, constantly reminding advertisers of the values that the *consumer* demands, if she/he is to be a willing participant in the game.

THE STRUCTURE OF THE BOOK

If you are already working in advertising or marketing, then the relevance of this volume is obvious. If you are a student or an interested outsider then a word of explanation is required. The book is pitched at an advertising agency audience and it explicitly recognizes that some of the real-life difficulties account planners face are organizational. These are the inevitable consequences of working in advertising agencies. Since agencies are a mixture of different skills, there is unavoidably some level of conflict between the outlooks of these different skills. This is something that is worth knowing if you are contemplating a career in advertising. If not, perhaps you could ignore these somewhat parochial considerations and concentrate on the main theme of the book, which is a highly informative guide to the craft skills involved in planning advertising.

The plan of the book is a simple one: it follows the sequence of tasks a planner has to be concerned with as a campaign is developed. This is usually referred to as the 'planning cycle' because it is in effect a continuous process where the last part of planning one campaign—the evaluation stage—is also the first stage of planning the next campaign.

The book starts with a view of the context in which planners find themselves operating, both the very particular atmosphere of advertising agencies, where details of advertisements can assume huge importance, and the world of consumers, where the advertisements are used, absorbed and enjoyed but represent to most consumers a peripheral element in their lives.

After that come three chapters dealing with the analytical and research processes fundamental to the development of strategy. The first tackles the conceptual problems of the role of advertising. It illustrates that, although the motivation of the advertiser is to sell his product or his point of view, the way in which advertising will help him do it can vary a great deal, according to the particular circumstances. The next is designed to show how research can be used in strategic development and demonstrates the most important point about commissioning research—that the right research will only be done if the question it is trying to answer is fully understood. The third concerns one of the planner's most fundamental tasks: brand positioning. Nearly all advertisers find themselves in competitive markets, and this chapter looks at the various ways the planner can find an effective position for the brand in the minds of the consumers.

Of the final four chapters, two deal with areas where account planning has made its greatest mark—creative briefing and creative development research—both of which depend on getting the active co-operation of creative people. The next chapter deals with the subject of pre-testing advertisements, with the author trying to make sense of an area noted more for prejudice than thought. The last chapter (or the first if you like) deals with campaign evaluation, trying to bring objectivity to an area where the subjectivity of people closely involved in the advertising is likely to be very great.

And now a final note on behalf of the authors: we certainly would not claim that these chapters have been written in a uniform style or have been designed to dovetail exactly with preceding or succeeding chapters. Each of the subjects has been handled by the author in his or her own way. However, they are all experienced and well-known planners. If you are interested in the art of planning advertising, I hope you will read all of the chapters in order and learn much that will prove of value.

Don Cowley 1989

1 *The planning context*

Kay Scorah

PLANNING AND THE AGENCY—THE 'HOW TO' OF ACCOUNT PLANNING

> 'We no longer had to work with producers who said "You can't do that, they won't understand it in Bradford" '
>
> John Cleese on the making of *Monty Python*.

Account planning within the advertising agency should contribute to far more than advertising development.

In considering the wider aspects of the account planning function we need to look at:

1 The role of the planning director.
2 Planning the agency and its business.
3 Planning the client's advertising.

THE ROLE OF THE PLANNING DIRECTOR

As with any department head there are the obvious personnel duties—maintaining standards, morale, and in particular relationships with other departments on both an

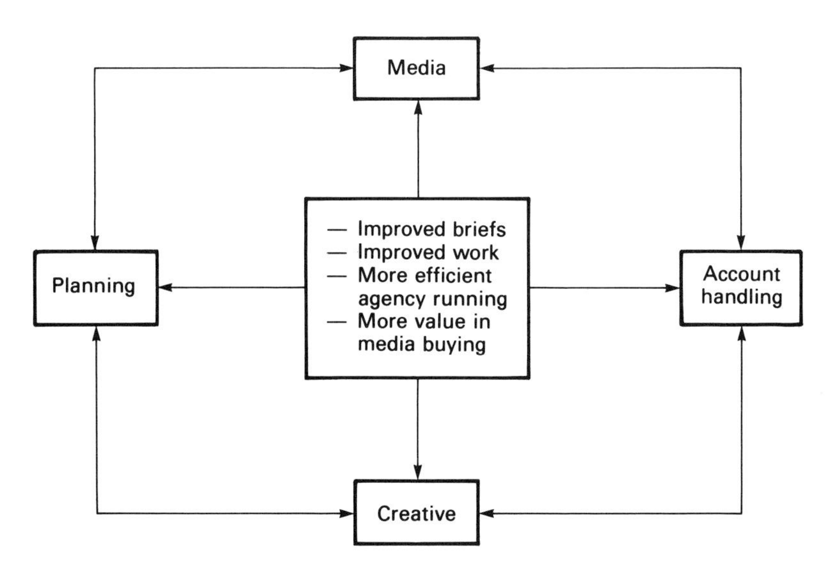

Figure 1: Inter-departmental relationships

individual and departmental basis. Inter-departmental relationships (Figure 1) are important since all agency functions can benefit from an exchange of views and knowledge. Media departments can benefit from the planners' background qualitative knowledge of how the various media are used and viewed by the consumer. Creative departments can benefit from the planners' insight into trends and attitudes to fashion and style, and from the media departments' knowledge of new media opportunities. Perhaps the most important function of inter-departmental discussions is to improve constantly on the individual agency's briefing system—both for creative and media. On an in*tra*-departmental basis the planning director should also be the source of knowledge on developments in advertising thinking, research techniques, and so on.

PLANNING THE AGENCY AND ITS BUSINESS

The skills and techniques used by account planners in briefing and evaluating a client's advertising are rarely used internally. However, those same skills can and should be used, in conjunction with the rest of the agency team, to plan the agency's business, its advertising and its future.

The levels on which planning can contribute to an agency's (and its clients') business development are as follows:

1. Identifying new opportunities for advertising.
2. Identifying new opportunities for existing clients.
3. New business opportunities.
4. Agency positioning and advertising.

IDENTIFYING NEW OPPORTUNITIES FOR ADVERTISING, that is, sectors in which advertising spending is buoyant, or likely to increase considerably in the near future. This knowledge arises not only from social and consumer-based trends but also from trends within the financial and business community.

Developing 'general' new business presentations in these areas which show an understanding of the consumers' attitudes in these new or newly public product fields, the brands within them and their advertising (if any).

IDENTIFYING NEW OPPORTUNITIES FOR EXISTING CLIENTS New product development projects for existing clients very rarely result in an advertised new product launch, and even more rarely result in an established brand. However, these projects, to which planning skills are ideally suited, also forge close relationships with the client, often at senior level. (Not to mention the fee income potential on new product development projects!)

NEW BUSINESS OPPORTUNITIES The old adage that 'good creative work wins new business, poor account handling loses it', could be amended to read 'good planning and creative work wins new business, poor planning and account handling loses it'.

Planning so often provides the extra insight into the client's business at the credentials or actual pitch stage which persuades a client that this agency team really has something to offer. The danger lies in the planning complacency which can set in once the pitch is won. The belief that the planning which took place in the three weeks leading up to the pitch is all that is needed is an arrogant and dangerous one. A new business presentation allows planning to demonstrate the *kind of* insights and creative direction it is capable of providing; it rarely produces the fully thought-out solution. Even if it does, because the consumer's life is constantly changing, then the brand is constantly changing—planning is a continuous process which should not stop once the pitch is won or the advertising strategy approved.

AGENCY POSITIONING AND ADVERTISING Advertising agencies produce among the worst advertising around for their own service. They simply do not adhere to the disciplines they enforce on their own clients. They produce advertising which is based only on the way that they perceive their brand from the inside and on how they would like it to be perceived on the outside. The planner's role in the production of 'house' strategies and advertisements should be identical to that in the production of client strategies and advertisements, i.e. to establish:

- Who is the target audience? (client, potential client, other agencies, suppliers, staff) and what are they like?
- How does that target audience feel about the product field (advertising agencies, consultancies or other sources of the service in question)?
- How does the target audience feel about our brand in relation to others?
- How does the target audience feel about advertising in this product field and, in particular, our advertising?

PLANNING THE CLIENT'S ADVERTISING

The processes involved in this, the most important planning function, are discussed at length in the remainder of this book. Here we look only at the relationships and dynamics within the account group in which the planner operates.

We shall assume here that planning *does* operate within an account group, and that the development of advertising on any brand is the responsibility of a core partnership between account handler and planner, in close association with the creative team, media planner and client. Without these close and often difficult relationships, planning cannot operate.

Examining each of the relationships in detail, and then looking at the overall picture:

ACCOUNT PLANNER/ACCOUNT HANDLER

Access to the client This relationship is vital to the effective operation of account planning within any advertising agency. The account handler is ultimately responsible to the client for the smooth, effective running of the business. The account planner should accept that the closest of the client's relationships in the agency must be with account management. However, the account handler should also accept that without direct access to the client team the planner often misses out on information vital to the planning function. The account handler must ensure that the planner has sufficient access to the client both to *receive* information in the form of market research data, sales data, product information or even company gossip and to *impart* information and ideas. The smart account planner/handler team manages the client relationship extremely effectively by allowing the planner enough access to be an informed but impartial expert, but not so much that the planner becomes indistinguishable from the handler in terms of their aims for the client's brands and the agency.

The 'marriage' The exact nature of this relationship obviously depends on the skills and personality of the individuals concerned. Irrespective of individual peculiarities, however, the team should be as close as an art director/copywriter team (the difference being that they may not always work together across all their brands). Like a writer/art director team the two perform different functions, with the planner responsible for the commissioning, analysis or interpretation of consumer data. However, in the same way as writer and art director bring together their different skills to formulate and produce advertising ideas, the planner and account handler together formulate brand strategies, advertising strategies, creative and media briefs (see Figure 2).

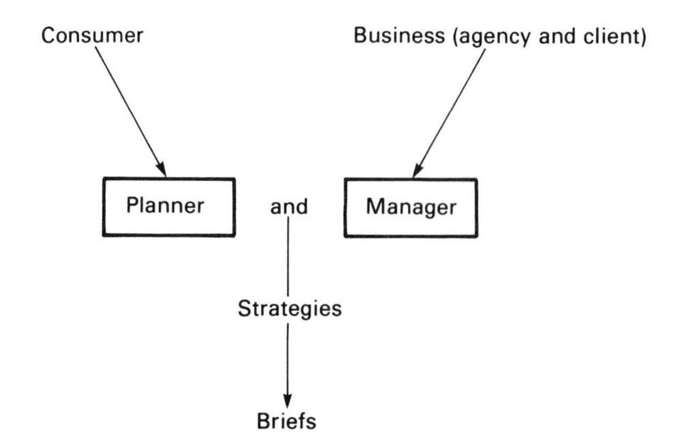

Figure 2: The account planner/account handler relationship

While the account handler is the nerve centre of the account in terms of client contact and simply getting things done, the planner is the account conscience. The planner is the unbiased point of contact with the outside world.

Disagreements in this relationship normally stem from arguments over territory (who should be at the client meeting, who should brief the creative team) rather than philosophy. They really need to be resolved at the individual level (with the example set by the agency 'elders').

ACCOUNT PLANNER/CREATIVE TEAM

Creative teams view account planners on a spectrum ranging from the unsympathetic hurdle over which their precious idea must leap before it even reaches the client, to the malleable boffin who will always side with them against the account man.

In an ideal world, the creative team should see the planner as a source of clear briefs, telling them exactly what aspect of the product is most motivating to the target audience and why. They should also see the planner as an objective sounding board for ideas, representing the likely consumer reaction but also going beyond that to analyse and develop embryonic creative routes.

From the planner's point of view, the creative team must be treated as intellectual equals. All too often planners treat creative people either as dangerous unguided missiles who do not understand words of more than one syllable, or as sensitive creative flowers who should not be upset by an open discussion. Perhaps the most fundamental rule within this relationship is to be *honest* but thoughtful.

If the creative team thinks the brief stinks then they should be prepared to say so, and why. If the planner thinks the work is wrong then he or she should say so, and why, at the first possible opportunity. Likewise, if the work seems to be *right*. The worst thing either side can say is 'I don't know why, I just don't like it'.

Harmonious planning/creative relationships are not about getting drunk together or wearing the same kinds of clothes, they are about mutual respect which must be *earned* on both sides.

ACCOUNT PLANNER/MEDIA PLANNER

This is one of the most underestimated relationships in the agency team. If you think it is difficult to get a creative team along to a research debrief, try getting the media planner!

Account planning can contribute an enormous amount to media planning, by putting even half as much effort into a media brief as that which goes into a creative brief.

There is more to media briefing than telling the media planner the regionality and seasonality of the brand sales and the demographics of the target audience. As media choices became more diverse, and target audience more tightly defined and precisely targeted, media arguments begin to move away from cost and towards value and environment. The account planner can help here, not only by providing quantitative and qualitative data on the consumers' usage of and attitudes to the brand, but also on usage of and attitudes to the various media available.

Within any agency, the media department is inclined to feel isolated from the advertising process. This is often the fault of the media department itself, but more likely the result of the rest of the team's lack of awareness of the benefits of a closer working relationship with media.

For the account planner, the relationship with the media planner can be a fruitful and very powerful one—not least because it is less likely to be fraught with emotional and power struggles than the other two! In the interest of developing the planner as a total advertising person as opposed to a kind of irresponsible guru, the media relationship is of key importance since it gives the account planner a more realistic view of the harsh commercial realities of the advertising business—like relative costs per thousand.

THE OVERALL TEAM PICTURE

There is no doubt that the best way to achieve real team work is to understand at least something of the other members' jobs. This can be achieved in a variety of ways, and obviously sheer experience of life in an agency helps. However, this process can be speeded up and facilitated by the simple method of spending a few weeks as an acting account handler/copywriter/media planner. The investment of a small amount of time in this exercise almost always pays off. Alternatively, role reversal courses—either within or outside the agency—prove extremely valuable.

In summary, the overall team picture should look like Figure 3:

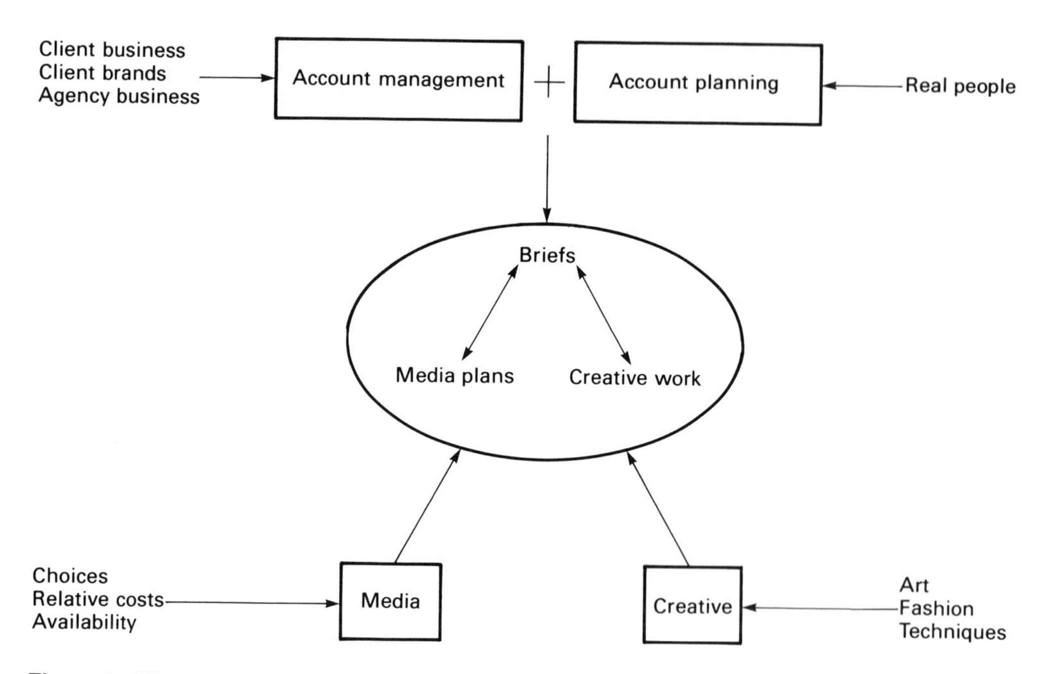

Figure 3: The agency team picture

It is most important to remember that an advertising agency's product is *advertising*, placed somewhere where the target audience can see it. The account planner's contribution to that is the *brief*. The thickest, most intelligent planning document does not compensate for a poor brief; it only serves to justify a good one.

PLANNING AND THE OUTSIDE WORLD—THE 'WHY' OF ACCOUNT PLANNING

> 'I had grown up, audiences had grown up, films had stayed in inertia'.
>
> Michael Powell, Film Director.

Most advertising is planned and created in relatively plush offices in major city centres, by people who are paid well above the average wage. These people tend to marry later than the average, and have their children later in life. They are more likely than average to get divorced. They are unlikely to watch the most popular TV programmes of the day, or read the popular newspapers. The vast majority come from middle-class homes and are university educated. In 1984–5, 3.05% of 16–24-year olds were in universities and new recruits into advertising are being taken from this tiny minority.

Despite the fact that these people are in no way representative of, or even in touch with, the majority of the population they are expected to be able to communicate in a meaningful and motivating way with all those not lucky enough to be among the chosen few destined to work in an advertising agency.

The fact that advertising agency employees are a small and fairly homogeneous minority ensures that the chances of producing advertising which means anything to the rest of the population are remote. To make matters worse, most advertising agency employees believe that they, their families and friends *are* quite typical of the population as a whole. When asked to produce advertising for women, they will write for their mother, wife or themselves. When writing for teenagers they write for themselves (no one in advertising ever admits that they are no longer in touch with youth culture!)

The world of advertising is small, élite and restricted. For advertising agency employees, even travel rarely broadens the mind; we travel in the company of our own kind, and when in foreign parts tend to gravitate towards those most similar to ourselves. The client's world is somewhat broader: client company employees are often involved with the manufacturing process. They may also be directly involved with the end consumer of their product or service. However, this contact is often restricted to the place of work and rarely extends to social life where, like the agency employees, they too tend to gravitate towards those most similar to themselves.

Most of this book is concerned with relationships and dynamics within the advertising development and evaluation process. It covers the consumer/product field interface, the brand status, the creative briefing and development process and the search for advertising evaluation. There is a world outside the advertising agency, and within that world the consumer receives, processes and reacts to advertising stimulus. An account planner should know as much about the market and the brand as anyone. The most sophisticated techniques can be used in developing and evaluating the advertising, but without knowledge and understanding of the real world all this brand knowledge and technology could be wasted.

Within an advertising agency—and on a smaller scale within an account group—it is the responsibility of the planner to keep in touch with the real world. In many cases, other members of the team have a good understanding of the context in which advertising is received, but the planners' access to social and demographic trend data, and direct access to consumers through quantitative and qualitative research enables them to provide the agency and account team with a (hopefully) objective view of the world outside.

This essential background knowledge can be considered at two quite distinct levels, as follows:

1 What is life like out there, and how is it changing?
2 How do people (in particular, the target audience) feel about their lives?

However, all too often, planners start the planning process from the level of product field or even brand without taking into account the fact that there is life beyond that particular product field.

While we would warn against the narrow-mindedness of starting the account planning process at the product field level, it is important to remember that however much we learn about life on a broader scale the knowledge is academic unless we understand how this affects our target audience's attitude to the product field, the brand and its advertising. The role of advertising is not to reflect people's real lives, nor is it to reflect their problems or aspirations. The role of advertising is simply to contribute to the selling of a product or service.

If we accept that there is more to account planning than those processes directly related to the brand and its advertising described in the remainder of this book, then it seems appropriate to describe here some of the processes and sources which help us to retain our sense of perspective.

WHAT IS LIFE LIKE OUT THERE AND HOW IS IT CHANGING?

The study of 'life out there' can be divided into macro factors and micro factors.

MACRO FACTORS include the really important, lasting trends which affect peoples lives. The kind of homes they live in, the amount of money they earn, their chances of being employed or unemployed, the chances of their marriage breaking up or their children taking drugs.

The sources of information here are diverse and very detailed. Assuming that we all have better things to do with our lives than produce a social and demographic history of our particular country then we have to exercise judgement over the amount of detail we go into.

Much of the basic data is collected and collated by civil servants; it is therefore usually out of date and presented in the most confusing manner, as one would expect from people who also bring you income tax and social security forms. However, more action-oriented organizations, including market research companies, marketing consultants and the advertising industry, often produce summaries of government statistics which are generally sufficient for the planners' needs.

A well-organized planning department will have its own reference book of key social and demographic facts. One of the greatest wastes of planning time and effort is to reanalyse government statistics for each new business presentation.

Understanding the nature of the society in which we operate is an essential element of the planner's task, and one of the reasons why the exportation of UK planning talent is not always an unequivocal success. However, there is more to knowing the country than knowing the number of households, what people own, what they choose to spend their money on, and where they go when they're not at home.

Neither is it sufficient to take a snapshot of life as it is today. It is vital to understand where these people have come from, how experiences in their formative years may have affected the way they now think and behave, in order to place their behaviour with respect to your brand in the context of their overall behaviour. These observations are important not only to the content of our advertising, but also the context in which it is set.

It is becoming increasingly important for the account planner to contribute to the media planning process. As targeting becomes more precise with the introduction of new media, so the psychographic nature of a medium's audience, and the frame of mind of that audience, become important factors.

In those glorious days of the 1970s when the English were actually good at football, an advertisement in a break during a televised football match was sure to reach an enormous number of enthusiastic males of all ages, social classes and types. In 1986 there is a wide range of televised sports available to the media buyer. Some of these appear to have similar viewer profiles but in fact the audience may differ considerably depending on the sport. The kind of man who enjoys American football (unheard of in the UK in the 1970s) may be very different from the one who enjoys English soccer, and may be in a very different frame of mind when watching it.

In the 1940s, a pair of shoes was likely to cost a young, fashion-conscious woman the best part of two weeks' wages. Buying a pair of shoes was, for her, a pretty exciting but possibly traumatic event. The same woman in the 1980s can buy a good pair of shoes for considerably less than her average weekly income, but she has not shaken off the feeling that a pair of shoes is a pleasurable and important purchase. What she wants to know, and how she wants to feel about those shoes, or indeed the retailer she buys them from, is very different from the requirements of a 30-year-old for whom shoes are a far more casual purchase.

MICRO FACTORS are the short-term trends, fads and fashions, particularly important to a young target audience, which can be used tactically to great effect in advertising (cf. Bartle Bogle Hegarty's use of the 1960s music revival in their 1986 Levi's 501 commercial).

Simply looking at the amount of time and money that consumers spend in a particular product field tells us something about how interesting and important that product field is to them. Looking at the order in which households acquire certain durables tells us not only something about the importance of those durables in their everyday lives, but something about their priorities and attitudes.

One of the failings of the account planning discipline is that it has tended to result in 'lifestyle' advertising, which draws on the planners' interpretation of the nature of the target audience but fails to talk about the product. Understanding the context in which advertising is received enables us to present those aspects of our product or service which are most motivating or appealing to our target audience, and in a way which is both interesting and sympathetic.

To achieve this optimum presentation we need to understand our *product* fully. We must know everything about it, *as well as understanding our consumers' lives* both within and outside their need for and use of the product field in question. Effective advertising is created out of a good balance of knowledge of the product and consumer among the advertising agency team.

Knowing what life is like does not mean that we have to reflect that life in our advertising. If anything, the more thorough our knowledge of our country's population, the more we realize the difference between individuals.

The tendency to invent and label population sub-sectors can be dangerous, since we may ascribe identical behavioural characteristics to them when in fact they are generally characterized by being only 'more likely' than other people to behave in a certain way *in a given area*. These sub-sectors often take on a group personality. To take a recent example, the 'yuppy' is seen as being materialistic, ambitious and superficial, and yet millions of people fall into this group. Is it really likely that there is not a philosophical, caring individual among them?

HOW DO PEOPLE FEEL ABOUT THEIR LIVES?

More important than reflecting the way people are, or the way we think they are, is to reflect their aspirations and feelings. In the 1960s 'Katy' made Oxo synonymous with family cooking, and the brand became part of family life. In 1986, J. Walter Thompson's Oxo Family campaign was voted the most popular advertising campaign by TV viewers.

Katy and Philip in the 1950s and today's Oxo Family (see Storyboard 1) do not really reflect everyone's daily life. We know that the occasions on which families sit down together to eat are increasingly rare. The strength of the Oxo campaign is in *evoking*, not *reflecting*, the warmth and humour of those rare occasions when the family *does* get together, even if they are not all on the best of terms. Similarly, in the 1960s Katy and Philip evoked feelings of security and success that the target audience hoped—and in those days believed—they could achieve.

To take another example, in the Hofmeister lager commercials the bear provides a device through which to show the Hofmeister drinker. His personality and behaviour are an exaggerated representation of the 'jack the lad' present in any group of young men in a pub. The fact that he is dressed as a bear is not only an entertaining branding device, but it conveniently allows Boase Massimi Pollitt to avoid showing the 'real' target audience in too much detail. The commercials are about the *dynamics* within a group of mates in a pub, rather than about the people themselves.

This understanding of real life situations, group dynamics and consumer aspirations should be drawn by the account planner from three of the most under-used data sources in the planning armoury:

1 Background quantitative data from industry data sources and account-specific quantitative studies.
2 Warm-up sessions during group discussions.
3 Walking around with eyes and ears wide open.

BACKGROUND QUANTITATIVE DATA collected from TGI or NRS questionnaires and other quantitative studies helps us to understand how other people live. It can tell us, for example, how often women visit the shops and how often they do so in the company of men. From this we can estimate how often our advertising message for, say, a packaged product is likely to be reinforced by seeing the brand on the shelf, and whether the male partner is likely to influence brand choice.

Also, we can find out from established sources how often people go on holiday, and where they go, and hence draw some conclusions as to how their behaviour and attitudes may be influenced by other cultures.

WARM-UP SESSIONS DURING GROUP DISCUSSIONS These are woefully under-used. The warm-up, as well as the group discussion itself, gives us an opportunity to find out a little about how our target audiences really feel about their lives. We may know, for example, that most of our target audience is employed in manual labour. What we do not know is how they feel about their jobs, what goes on in their place of work, how they behave with their friends and workmates and, extremely important, how interested they are in advertising, which are their favourite advertisements and why.

PRODUCT: OXO

TITLE: EXAM RESULTS

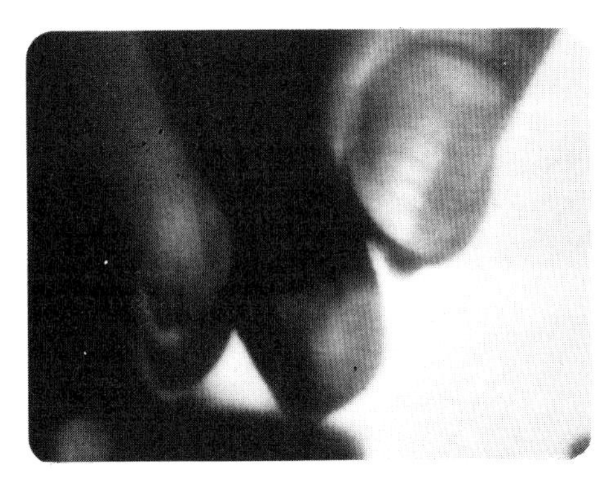

MUM: Leave it alone! BOY: Only looking. DAD: Hello love. Is he back with his results yet?

MUM: He only left an hour ago. BOY: Exams are rubbish. He won't have passed anyway.

GIRL: What do you know? . . . Is that Nick? What if he hasn't passed? . . . Here he comes.

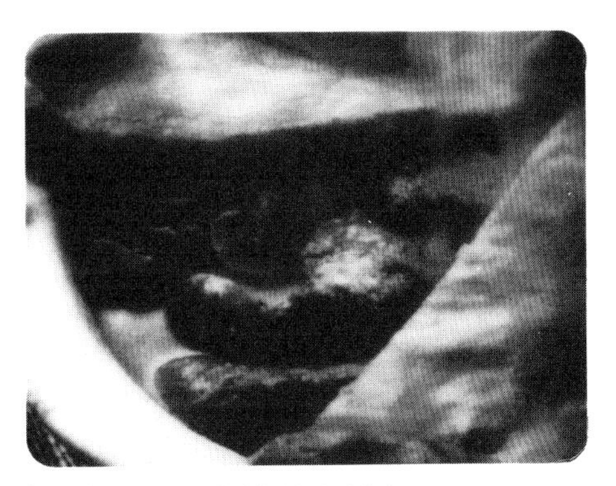

(SFX. *Door latch*). DAD: Hello Nick.

NICK: Sorry I'm late . . .

. . . Easy as pie.

Storyboard 1

All of this information should not be regarded simply as a means of 'breaking the ice' in group discussions, but should be used in developing creative briefs and helping us to understand the way in which advertising is received.

WALKING AROUND WITH EYES AND EARS OPEN As discussed earlier, the chances are that, as middle-class advertising executives, we do not usually travel by public transport, read the popular press or watch the highest rating TV soap operas. The account planner should listen to conversations on the street and in pubs, not only to hear what people talk about and what interests them but also to hear how they talk.

The planner should also observe short-term trends in fashion, music, vocabulary—the 'micro' trends referred to earlier.

This responsibility for setting advertising in its real-life context is what differentiates the account planner from, on the one hand, the market researcher and, on the other hand, the account handler.

The market researcher is there to *answer* questions, the planner is there to ask them and to interpret the answers. The researchers' role is to design the best possible sample, questionnaire and overall market research technique. The questions they are required to answer are about the product field, the brand or the advertising. Unlike the social researchers, they are not generally required to provide answers to questions about the context in which those products and advertisements are received. The account handler is responsible for the well-being of the client's business, and for the agency's product and profitability.

2 The roles of advertising

Sev D'Souza

WHY ADVERTISE?

It pays to advertise. The old cliché is truer than most people, even in advertising, realize.

Those who undervalue the role of advertising tend to be pragmatists who perceive it as a *cost* to be justified by sales return in the fiscal year. The more enlightened users value advertising as a brand-building *investment*—rather like capital expenditure on plant and machinery—to provide a long-term return.

Investments have to be justified, and advertising is no exception. Accountability here is multi-dimensional, dependent on the role and intended effects of the advertising, which vary enormously in different markets and different competitive conditions.

In most advertising strategies there will be a section on campaign objectives. Inevitably it will include some of these tasks:

- Make an impact.
- Create awareness.
- Communicate messages.
- Evoke an immediate response (sell off the page or get more information).
- Create favourable impressions.
- Remind consumers.
- Fulfil needs.
- Change perceptions (mental repositioning or overcome prejudice).
- Reinforce attitudes.
- Consolidate a position.
- Enthuse the staff and the trade.
- Encourage trial.

These objectives are valid but bland. Complex markets and sophisticated consumers demand that recognition and appreciation of the roles for advertising need fuller examination. This will be done through various theories and examples of what advertising can achieve. Hopefully, an enhanced view of advertising will result from being sensitive to the following issues:

- Appreciate how consumers' predisposition towards advertising can affect its roles.
- Consider not only the explicit objectives but, more importantly, the implicit roles of advertising that reflect the growing importance of emotional effects in today's highly competitive advertising environment.
- Realize how the media environment in which an advertisement appears can affect its role.
- Understand how roles vary depending on the different stages of a brand's development.
- Recognize when different roles apply, depending on the type of advertising.

HOW CONSUMER PREDISPOSITIONS AFFECT THE ROLES OF ADVERTISING

The majority of the British public likes advertising in spite of agreeing that it raises prices. Buying can provide a great deal of emotional satisfaction, and advertising contributes to this. At a basic level consumers look at advertising for information, ideas, entertainment, challenge, stimulation and reassurance.

What follows is a deeper look at some of the less obvious functions that advertising performs:

BRANDING ROLE

This is not about the size of the logo. It is about long-term branding in terms of identifying a reputation with a name, and the role that advertising plays in creating or reinforcing that reputation. To understand how advertising can enhance the desirability of a brand, it is necessary to examine why branding, as a concept, works.

People like buying brands that give them satisfaction over and above their basic function. They buy certain brands as a symbolic gesture—'shows I care'—or to make a social statement—'I've made it'.

Advertising is part of the language that brands use to 'talk' to their consumers. Thus, in addition to its mechanistic role of communicating rational reasons for buying, advertising can add value by building an image and personality for the brand.

Examples abound of how advertising has added to the meaning and richness of brands—Persil, Andrex, Levis, Guinness, to name a few. In all these cases, advertising worked through the brand's own qualities to provide added values in markets where any product differences were not enough. These added values emanate largely from the tone of voice and the style of the advertising. The lager market in the UK also provides an excellent example of how to develop brand values.

Much ingenuity is needed to stay ahead in this increasingly competitive market. The most successful brands provide, through their advertising, product quality clues as well as distinct brand identities. Identity can stem from the country of origin, the genuineness/authenticity, or a statement about the drinker's social status. The role of the advertising is to make the brand respected and sought after, using values such as heritage, wit, humour, masculinity, street credibility, fashionability, sociability and strength.

In this way, advertising is helping to build 'equity' that has short-term *and long-term* value in the brand. Thus Coca-Cola has a large measure of 'brand equity', and its sales today are as much in response to cumulative build-up over the years as in its current investment in advertising.

Another way of looking at this concept is through the analogy of a current account and an interest-gaining deposit account at a bank. So, by all means, consider the short-term needs but bear in mind that advertising can protect future sales as well.

BMW cars also provide an excellent example of maximizing 'brand equity'. The 'yuppie' image has developed more by word of mouth, and the advertising cleverly builds on the quality and style of the product. The intelligent, witty advertising focuses on BMW as being 'The Ultimate Driving Machine'. Yet their current agency has admitted to making a mistake with their first advertising for the marque, which showed Kirk Douglas enjoying the trappings of success, including a BMW. The introduction of a planner on the account helped them to tap the right emotions in a more subtle manner.

PERSUASION ROLE: HARD SELL VERSUS SOFT SELL

There are big cultural differences in attitudes to selling between Britain and, say, the US. The British have traditionally regarded selling as being slightly vulgar. On the other hand hard sell is very much part of the American way of life. This is an important underlying principle in understanding the consumer relationship to advertising and the broader issues at stake in determining its roles.

Consumers are consciously aware that the purpose of advertising is to sell them something. However there is a subtle difference between 'being sold' and 'making people want to buy'. The 'trickster theory' can be applied to advertising. The 'trickster' in politics knows how to heighten consciousness of a cause and raise an audience to a state of frenzy and conviction. In a sophisticated democracy people are aware of this kind of indoctrination, and are not frightened to be at the receiving end of it because they are confident of their ability to control their actions.

At the sharp end of selling, watch the 'trickster' at work in a street market. The crowd builds up, perhaps out of curiosity, perhaps to play a 'persuasion game'. The vendor still has to rely on his product messages to make a sale, but his success depends more on his presentation and his personality.

Consumers want to be charmed into buying through cleverness, humour and honesty. They expect advertising to exaggerate, sing praises, transform products. They find good advertisements fascinating and compelling. Enjoying the art of persuasion, they 'recognize' marketing strategy, appreciate production values, and are becoming more skilled at judging advertisements. They can differentiate between claims that call for a value judgement—'Refreshes the parts other beers cannot reach'—and factual claims—'9 out of 10 cats preferred it'. Consumers understand the rules of the game and confidently seek to play.

Thus, certain advertisements which do not appear to be selling anything can often leave consumers mystified. They wonder why, for example, the Electricity Council needs to advertise when there is no perceived competition. Indeed most corporate advertising, aimed at creating 'nice warm feelings', can potentially be ineffective unless it carries a *selling* proposition.

DISARMING ROLE

Modern society knows that advertising has to be truthful. This does not prevent consumers from being sceptical about product claims. They feel they have the right to be critical, to argue, to reject. This brings sharply into focus an often overlooked role for advertising: *the disarming function*.

There are certain areas of marketing where a cynical attitude prevails among consumers:

- Addressing a male audience with technical claims.
- Addressing secretaries with claims about what an employment agency will do for them.
- Making financial investment claims.
- Making public services like British Rail seem efficient.

In situations like this, rational claim is often met with counter-rational argument: 'Not in my experience' or 'I have a friend who . . .'. One has to disarm such an audience so that the underlying cynicism doesn't surface. If British Rail told commuters in their advertising that 90 per cent of trains run on time it would attract the cynical response of 'So what? Mine's always late.' Instead, British Rail talked about the magnitude of their task, and the fact that each morning's rush hour into London was equivalent to a movement of people three times the size of the D-Day evacuation. In this way they could evoke public sympathy and toleration.

As another example, insurance companies are second only to second-hand car salesmen when it comes to mistrust. One innovative advertiser, Legal & General, turned this problem on its head. They took an honest line and showed investments they failed in, but with the rider that 99 per cent of the time they were successful in increasing policy holders' money.

The trick is to charm people into believing, and the best way to alter opinions is not by confrontation and belligerence but by gentle persuasion—making people *want* to believe.

REASSURANCE ROLE

This is probably one of the most important, and most under-estimated roles of advertising. There are several aspects of the reassurance role:

- Big safe brands *advertise more* than small untried ones and consequently provide more reassurance. Having different advertisements reinforces this role.
- Expensively produced advertisements can lend *status and respectability* in markets where this is relevant, e.g. cars and airlines. It is irrelevant whether the Superman/Superwoman advertisements for British Airways are credible or not. What is significant is the statement the advertisements make: that BA are taking this market seriously; that they are big and popular.
- *Justifying a premium price* Witness the growth of the premium sector in many markets—food, lager, clothes, cars, etc.—which suggests that people want to buy expensive things. The advertising can help them to justify paying the price, e.g. BMW cars.
- *Justifying a lower price* On the other side of the coin advertising can provide reassurance that a lower price does not necessarily mean lower quality. Examples are the themes for Sainsbury's: 'Good food costs less when it's Sainsbury's', and for Virgin Atlantic airlines: 'We cut fares not corners.'
- *Solving consumer problems*, as opposed to inward-looking listing of product features,

can be very reassuring. The problem-solving role has served organizations well. When British Rail launched their Gatwick Express service they resisted the temptation of listing attributes like faster service, more frequent service, air-conditioned coaches and special luggage racks. Instead, they identified the biggest problem as anxiety about getting to the airport on time. The resultant advertising showed a flying BR logo with the reassuring tag-line 'Catch the train and you've caught the plane.'

- *Providing quality clues* In markets where there is little differentiation and the emphasis is on brand image, minor product references can provide rational reassurance. There are good examples in the lager market: 'All the sugar turns to alcohol' (Holsten) and 'Amber Nectar' (Foster's)

SOCIAL TARGETING ROLE

Here, the role of advertising is to link a brand with a particular consumer target. Advertising thus provides a means of social identity. It can also provide public expression of social superiority. This is manifest in the advertisements for luxury cars—where owners are the most avid readers.

A much debated issue is whether you have to show the appropriate people consuming the product in order that the target audience can identify with the brand. Consumers who are more skilled at judging advertisements will see through this and prefer an advertising style (say one that is mentally challenging or has classy art direction) that they can identify as appealing to people like them. However, when the advertising idea is based on the relationship between characters, then casting and setting take on a more important identification role.

Advertising, like all art forms, has the ability to arouse human emotions. Of particular relevance here is the vicarious pleasure that can be derived from relationships depicted in advertisements. In recent years the lifestyle advertisements for Renault have been particularly good at building driver/car relationships, as well as showing the cars fitting into inter-personal relationships. Consider also the emotional situations in the finely observed *Yellow Pages* advertising series (Storyboard 1), or the sending up of social stereotypes like the mother-in-law in the hugely funny 'Tefal' series (Storyboard 2). Another excellent example of emotional release is the Foster's lager advertising in which Paul Hogan misunderstands the British way of life. The Foster's drinker gets particular pleasure from seeing 'stuffed shirts' and upper classes taken down a peg or two.

WISH-FULFILMENT ROLE

Products do not exist in a vacuum; they fit into people's lives. The symbolic value of brands has been referred to before. It is important therefore to understand the *role of the product category*. How is it used? What do people want out of it? How do they feel when they are using it?

This examination leads inevitably to the issue of realism and fantasy in advertising.

PRODUCT: *YELLOW PAGES*

TITLE: DAD'S BIRTHDAY/ SIGNAL BOX

MUSIC/BOY: No, oh! Well thanks very much anyway—goodbye. (SFX. *Telephone ringing*). SHOPKEEPER: Townsends.

BOY: Hello, you know the Hornby double 'O' model railway. SHOPKEEPER: Yes. BOY: Do you have an

R186 signal box? SHOPKEEPER: Well, let's see. Yes, I've got one left. BOY: Great! . . . They've got one, Mum.

(SFX: *Coins rattling*). MVO: Good old *Yellow Pages*. We're not just there for the nasty things in life like a

blocked drain or a broken window.

BOY: Happy Birthday, Dad.
DAD: Laughs.

Storyboard 1

PRODUCT: TEFAL

TITLE: CHUNKY KEVIN

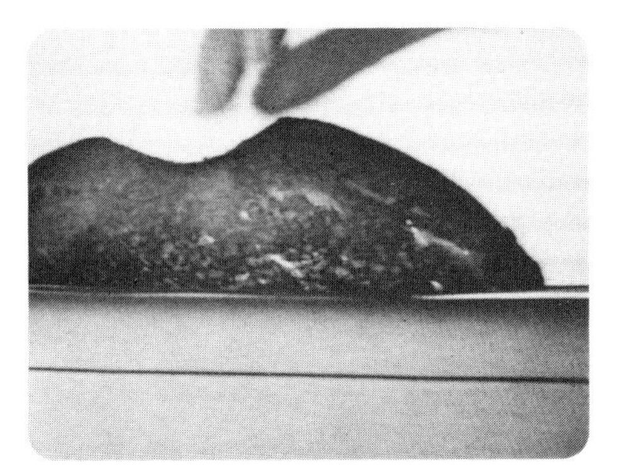

(SFX: *Boing*). WOMAN: Isn't it nice to have Mum to stay, Kevin. We can show off our lovely new Tefal Thick

'n' Thin toaster. Look, Mum, with this level it can grip any sized slice and brown it all nice and even.

From big chunky doorsteps for my big chunky Kevin

to little slices for me.

Well go on dearest, cut Mum a slice. (SFX: *Cutting*).

(SFX: *Crunch*). MVO: The Thick 'n' Thin toaster from Tefal.

Storyboard 2

People need *both* in their lives.This explains why 'slice of life' soap operas on TV like *Coronation Street* and *EastEnders* are popular at the same time as fantasy ones like *Dallas* and *Dynasty*. The real consideration facing the role of advertisements is to ask which approach is appropriate for the product. With certain products their psychological role is to give the user a feeling of luxury and indulgence. This is why the makers of perfume and boxed chocolates resort to aspirational fantasy. An everyday food product, however, has a different role to perform and the advertising should reflect this. In 1986 a public poll showed that the best-loved advertising was the campaign for Oxo, which depicts realistic family life—warts and all (Storyboard 3).

NON-CONDESCENDING ROLE

Consumers like to be treated as equals by the advertiser. They do not want their intelligence insulted. Yet many advertisers misunderstand this fundamental role. The biggest offenders are certain coffee and detergent brands. These advertisements are met with derision because of the assumption that consumers sit around discussing coffee beans and dirty washing, as if they have nothing better to do.

Neither do consumers deserve to be patronized. This consideration is often overlooked, judging by the amount of advertising that is set in a 'never never land'. Airline advertising in general is fairly typical of this patronizing approach. Many airlines assume people have never flown and glamorize their advertising on the basis of subservient service, cuisine, seat comfort. The truth is most air travellers find the experience boring, the service as plastic as the food, and no conventional seat really comfortable on a long flight. Consequently, advertising hyperbole and marginal differences in product are treated with scorn.

PIONEERING ROLE

One of the more innovative advertisements in 1986 was the 'Double Indemnity' film for Pirelli tyres in which the advertising *is* the brand (Storyboard 4). There are numerous other examples, usually in low-interest markets with similarity of product and brand images. Inevitably, this implies developing new styles in advertising which place consumers in something of a dilemma. On the one hand they want their imaginations stretched; on the other their innate conservatism leads them to believe that the normal is right and the unusual is wrong. It all depends on execution and a balanced approach to creative development.

Particular sensitivity is required when researching innovative advertisements. Consumers sometimes respond over-literally and judgements are often based on an historical framework. The advertising for Cointreau failed in initial research but the campaign went on to become one of the most enduring and endearing of all in spirits advertising. Better-known cases are those for Benson & Hedges and Heineken, which also failed in research. The agency and clients, at the time, believing that research could not predict the cumulative effect of the advertising, deserve credit for the risk they took and their conviction that consumers needed time to adjust.

Nowadays consumers show a more open acceptance of unconventional styles, and the planner should encourage movement away from the safe option.

PRODUCT: OXO

TITLE: REMEMBER PRESTON

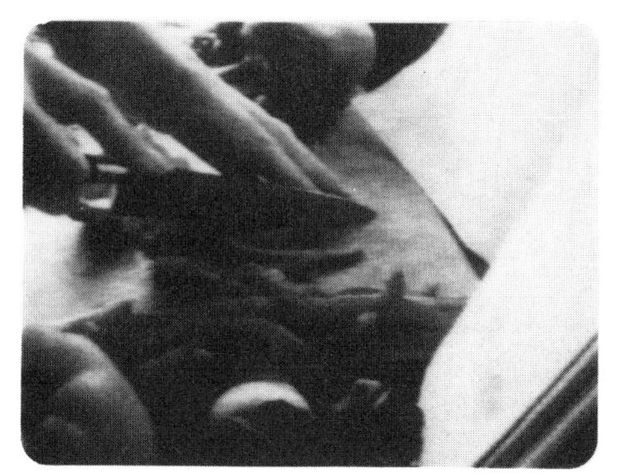

(SFX: *Chopping*).
JASON: What's that?
(SFX: *Sniff*).

NICK: Uh! (SFX: *Muttering*).

WOMAN: Yes, it is a surprise. No, I haven't cooked it before. Yes, it is foreign.

No, Jason, it is not a hamburger.

Yes, Alison, dolly will love it. No, Nick, no garlic,

and Michael, remember Preston?

Storyboard 3

PRODUCT: PIRELLI TYRES

TITLE: DOUBLE INDEMNITY

MUSIC/WOMAN: It's done, hurry. Ciao.

MAN: Should only be a couple of days.

WOMAN: Take care. Ciao.
(SFX: *Car engine*).

ECHO: Ciao, Ciao, Ciao.
(SFX: *Tyres screeching*).

WOMAN: Humming.
(SFX: *Suitcase dropping*).

(SFX: *Car engine*).

Storyboard 4

STYLISTIC ROLE

Consumers nowadays are 'advertising literate'. They feel that if advertisements can intrude through their television, radio or daily paper, then they in turn have every right to criticize the advertising. The paying customer has every right to comment on the performance. Thus, making a likeable advertisement is as important to the audience as communicating a relevant message. More and more it is becoming a case of the style is the advertisement; and *how* the effect is achieved is becoming more important than *what* is actually said. This does not mean that 'slice of life' advertisements, for example, are automatically boring. It depends on execution. For example, the advertisement for Persil, which depicts a teenage boy trying to use a washing machine, is done with much observational wit.

It is characteristic, therefore, in the current environment, for the public to 'consume' advertisements. One notices from qualitative research that consumers recognize fashions in advertising. More and more they judge advertising style as this factor becomes an increasingly important discriminator.

In a recent group discussion with men and women aged over 45, respondents asked the moderator 'Do you want us to tell you which advertisement we like best or which will be most effective in the market?' They went on to expound on which would stand repeated watching, which would stick in the mind, and so on. Advertisement 'experting' has taken on a new dimension and relevance, though the degree to which this takes place varies across the population. Research on advertisements which rely heavily on style values will be more constructive if carried out among 'appreciators of advertising'.

It is also worth the planner looking at the issues that different advertising styles can raise since it will help to define the role of advertising in more depth, and alert the creative team to the potential risks involved. For example, if nostalgia is the chosen style, then the key issue that may cloud communication is whether it is relevant today. The use of personalities can lead to credibility issues. The depiction of healthy lifestyle can be seen as 'jumping on the bandwagon'. A 'Golf GTI and cocktails' imagery can be seen as transparent and obvious.

HOW ADVERTISING ROLES INTER-RELATE WITH MEDIA CHOICE

The medium is the message. All good media planners work on the basis that *where* an advertisement appears is as important as the actual message. The *Sun* newspaper reaches more upmarket people than the *Times* but each title makes very different statements about the reader and the potential users of the product. Appearing on TV gives a brand the status of being big, confident, reassuring and available to the whole population. Contrast this with direct mail, which can give the impression of a private communication.

Media choice is therefore influenced by the overall objectives of the advertising campaign. The planner needs to take account of the *environment* in which the advertisement is seen or heard. Radio is a passive or background medium. Cinema has a captive audience of younger members of the public in a mood to be entertained. Women's magazines are part of a woman's private world. Therefore where an advertisement is seen affects the response it arouses.

In defining the role of advertising there is a need to take account of the context of the advertisement. The *context* is as much a part of the communication as the *content*. This has implications for the media brief, which should include a statement of what role the advertising has to play in a given context.

Media choice will, of course, be influenced by several other factors but it should stem from a basic understanding of how the advertising is meant to work in a given circumstance. Thus if the role of advertising is to provide an *aspirational* context it might lead to the choice of one medium rather than another, although both might be equally efficient in coverage terms against a set audience.

The roles for advertising and media choice can vary within a campaign. A good illustration of this is the advertising campaign for Virgin Atlantic Airways where the media used included TV, radio, cinema, local press, underground posters, 48-sheet posters, magazines, business press and trade press. In each case the advertising had a different role and the context in which the advertisements were seen also varied. The advertising message and style were tailored to suit each individual role and context.

HOW ROLES CHANGE DEPENDING ON BRAND CYCLE

There are three critical stages in the development of a brand:

- The launch stage.
- The mid-cycle stage.
- The mature, established stage.

THE LAUNCH STAGE

It is important that consumers recognize the product for what it is and does, where it is positioned *vis-à-vis* other brands, and the emotional values attached to it. Consider the launch of Swan Special Light lager into the UK. Low-alcohol lagers had not met with great success owing to their puritanical image and inferior taste. They were a compromise choice for limited occasions. The advertising role was defined on the following basis:

RECOGNITION To establish Swan Special Light as a lifestyle lager brand based on its authentic Australian heritage, its success in Western Australia, and its association with the celebrated Swan Premium Export.

PERFORMANCE VALUES Swan Special Light is real, mainstream lager with a light palatable flavour (the result of brewing expertise and low-alcohol properties). Thus it is a positive, regular choice.

EMOTIONAL FRAMEWORK Alcohol-free lagers had to date been presented without a genuine brewing heritage. Importantly, they were sold purely on their alcohol-free property, creating a separate (and small) segment with connotations of drink/drive benefits. Thus they were drunk for negative reasons.

However, the success of Swan Special Light in Australia—a credible source where they know about good lager—is testimony to its palatability and social acceptability. To maximize its appeal, it was decided to combine Swan Special Light in the advertising with Swan Premium Export which was already respected as a strong lager with a cult following in certain parts of the country. The benefits were two-fold:

- The Light product was imbued with a genuine brewing pedigree.
- The use of the end line, 'Swan Lager. One Taste Two Strengths', reassured consumers and gave a positive reason for choosing both.

MID-CYCLE AND LATER

When a brand develops into the mid-cycle stage, emotional benefits begin to come more to the fore. In the *mature, established stage* the brand needs revitalizing and interest can be added via the advertising itself. Polo mints provide a classic example of a correctly defined role in relation to brand cycle.

HOW ROLES CHANGE DEPENDING ON TYPE OF ADVERTISING

DIRECT ADVERTISING

The role of this category of advertising is to achieve an immediate response—to clip a coupon, to phone a number or to send away for goods by post. By definition this kind of advertising has to be hard-sell and very product-oriented, rather like the proverbial brush salesman trying to get a foot in the door. Elegance and high-production advertising values are usually missing.

However, it is disappointing to see the lack of creativity and ingenuity in this advertising category; many of these advertisements look like a page out of a catalogue. The formula seems to be to show or identify the product and list the features. This clearly works in terms of immediately measurable response, but the selling role could be further improved with a single-minded proposition-based approach.

RETAILER ADVERTISING

During the last decade there has been a big upsurge in retailer advertising. Its main role has been to generate store traffic with the promise of sale bargains and cheaper prices. Generally speaking, the advertisements have not been among the best loved by consumers. The form on TV has tended to be loud, brash and irritating; the content has invariably been about prices.

One food retailer, Sainsbury's, pioneered a whole new approach to retailer advertising.

They built an image through elegant and stylish press advertisements to an extent that the 'Sainsbury shopper' took on a social meaning and Sainsbury's became a *brand* in its own right. (see Sainsbury's press advertisement opposite).

To an extent the decor and ambience of the shop make a more powerful statement about the retailer image, e.g. Harrods, Habitat, Next, Benetton. However, many retailers are missing a trick in perceiving their advertisements as only having a short-term role of 'getting them in through the door'. The longer-term role of building the store image as 'a place I'd like to shop at' should not be overlooked. Tesco, as an example, successfully broadened their image from the 'pile 'em high, sell 'em cheap' doctrine into a quality-based food store.

Retailers pose a serious threat to consumer food and durable marketing and advertising by virtue of the increased buying power that stems from mergers and takeovers. By forcing prices down and their own profit margins up, retailers have put pressure on the advertising budget of consumer brands. It is true that, in turn, the retailers are advertising those brands they stock, but the important issue is that they are inevitably sold on price rather than the more emotionally-based brand values.

Defining the role of retailer advertising is not easy. There has to be a careful balance between selling the store image and selling the products within the store. At the present time the bias is towards the latter, and planners should try to enlighten these companies to the long-term implications. Retail shops can engender the same sort of social meanings as brands.

ADVERTISING TO THE TRADE

The primary role of trade press advertising is to give advance information of new product launches and new advertising campaigns in order to motivate the trade to stock a product. As a rule, not a great deal of time and attention is devoted to this form of advertising and it shows. The cliché-ridden route of 'massive TV campaign nationally will get your tills ringing' has become advertising 'wallpaper'.

What is required is a more imaginative approach with a much broader role for the advertising. This type of advertising should take on an educative role, perhaps using advertorial to build a two-way relationship. Communicate your competitive positioning and the research that showed your brand being preferred by the consumer. This will enable the trade to make a business decision that is not just based on automatically stocking the brand leader.

There is the question also of advertising *for* the trade rather than *to* the trade. The only way some (new) brands can achieve distribution is by buying it, with the promise of consumer advertising mentioning the retail outlet. When Krups wanted to launch their coffee-makers in the UK, the department stores were in no frame of mind to stock yet another make. Anxious to create a unique premium position in the kitchen appliance market, Krups invested in a TV campaign that forced the stores to reconsider their earlier stance. Krups is now well established in department stores for their coffee-makers—the results of clearly defining one of the roles for the advertising as forcing distribution.

ADVERTISING THE MEDIA

Conventional wisdom would lead one to believe that the role of advertising here is to sell the contents, i.e. specific issues or specific programmes. Examples would be *The Sun*, *Woman's Own*, Thames TV, etc.

Once again there is evidence here of a narrow view of the role of advertising. It has two serious shortcomings:

- There is only a short-term effect with no contribution to subsequent issues or programmes.
- The content of competitive newspapers or magazines is much the same.

The more enlightened media owners have seen the role of advertising as building a long-term image for their brands. They have recognized that contents for women's magazines or quality newspapers do not vary too much; that what is more significant is the *way* in which the contents are communicated and what statement is made about the user.

The best examples of this differentiated role for media advertisers are *The Guardian*, whose strategy is based on the paper's independent and unbiased stance; and *Options* magazine, which says something about the lifestyle aspirations and intelligence of its readers.

SELLING A RANGE

This is a difficult role for advertising to perform because consumers rarely buy a whole range. The intention is to sell everything, but the effect is usually to sell nothing.

While it is true that company image can be enhanced by working through its various products, it is much more effective to use flagship brands to sell the rest of the company's range. Thus the advertising for the BMW 7 series must help to give their 3 series a lift as well. In situations like this it is important to be conscious of the broader role for the advertised product, i.e. to draw out certain corporate values that apply to other brands in the range.

ADVERTISING A SERVICE

Friendly smiling faces are indistinguishable between one company and another. Making a differentiated statement on the other hand can result in credibility problems. Achieving the right balance is critical.

The public find it hard to differentiate on service between banks, between hotels, between airlines, between insurance companies, between building societies, etc. They are often confused as to the target of the advertising: is it aimed at the public or is it aimed at the staff, to set a standard they must live up to? The confusion is understandable if it bears no resemblance to real life. Thus customer care programmes that have been the focus of advertising can potentially elicit a cynical consumer response of: 'I haven't found that myself.'

In contrast, the advertising for Commercial Union—'We won't make a drama out of a crisis'—evoked a feeling that this insurance company was different: a sympathetic and understanding one (Storyboard 5).

ADVERTISING A COMPANY

Often referred to as corporate advertising, the role has been to improve the climate of opinion surrounding a company's business affairs. Consider the following case history:

BP used to be seen by the public as a large, rather cold company, not communicative about its activities, and rather anonymous among the host of multi-national oil companies. Nothing was known of BP's increasing diversity in fields other than oil. The role of advertising was to improve awareness and to sharpen BP's corporate image with the public and employees. The humorous and challenging commercials, based on the theme of 'BP. Britain at its best', achieved spectacular success in improving the company's image in all the planned dimensions.

What was important about the role of advertising in this case was that the criteria for success was *change in attitudes* rather than increased sales. It is therefore an expense that is hard to justify in the balance sheet, and this probably explains why companies do it retrospectively to address a problem rather than as a positive or preventive measure. An exceptional case is the Cadbury-Schweppes advertising (see the press advertisement on page 30). They eschewed the formula of just listing brands owned by the company. Instead, working through a single-minded theme of 'Management proven in the market

PRODUCT: COMMERCIAL UNION

TITLE: OVER THE TOP/A G-CANE

(SFX: *Seagulls*). MVO: On the 4th January 1980, Andrew Gratten-Cane set out with his wife and mother for a stroll

along the beach. It was a bright and breezy day, nippy enough to send him back to the car for his scarf.

Though he said he'd only be gone a minute, his family thought he was gone for good (SFX: *Crash*!). Thankfully it

was only his new car that was blown away. After the tide had 'rubbed salt into its wounds' we went out of our

way to find another new car, identical right down to the last mud flap. You see with our Gold Key Policy, Mr Gratten-Cane had nothing to lose not even his

no claims bonus.
(SFX: *Engine*).
Commercial Union, we won't make a drama out of a crisis.

Storyboard 5

When Cadbury Schweppes acquired the great American company Mott's, they were told "apples is apples."

They responded with a raspberry.

The news of Cadbury Schweppes' acquisition in America of the famous Mott's apple company was greeted with raised eye-brows in both Wall Street and Throgmorton Street.

Mott's boasted a range of apple products. But the consumer did not consider this range to be either interesting or exciting enough. Cadbury Schweppes had to devise a strategy to tempt American taste buds.

Mixing your drinks.

The 're-invention' of Mott's Apple Juice began with a ploy to make it not taste just like apple juice. Fruits such as raspberry, grape and cranberry were partnered with it to achieve this effect. The result was an immediate move out of the ranks of invisible commodities.

Next some clever product manoeuvring was called for. Moving Mott's juice out of the home meant it could capitalise on the huge potential of the leisure food and drink market.

A cranberry.

If Cadbury Schweppes' plan was to be successful, Mott's Apple Juice had to be repositioned as a single serve 'soft drink'.

This transformation was achieved by introducing convenient juice pak cartons and cans for sale in vending machines.

A grape.

Ultimately Mott's had, through these shrewd tactics, given themselves the chance to penetrate many previously untapped markets such as schools and health clubs.

A snack a day.

Mott's other major product, apple sauce, was ripe for similar treatment.

Here again the potential for growth lay outside the home market, where there was a growing demand for healthy snacks.

Cadbury Schweppes identified two distinct consumer categories for the sauce. First, the 'baby-boomer', or 'yuppie', a fitness conscious group who 'graze' while working, rather than eat formal meals.

They demand natural as well as convenient snacks. Secondly, health-conscious mothers who want a natural addition to their children's packed lunch.

These offspring have a loyalty to burgers and fries that is legendary.

The key to satisfying both these appetites lay in the introduction of a convenient 6 pak of single serve Mott's Apple Sauce.

Raise a glass.

To say the re-launch of the Mott's apple was a success would be a gross understatement. Sales literally went bananas.

Since 1982 Mott's juice sales have jumped from 4 million cases a year to 8 million. Its market share has leapt by 25%. And the vending programme has proved a real winner. The juice was definitely on the loose.

Not to be outdone, the 6 pak of sauce is already selling at a rate of almost a million cases a year and increasing Mott's Apple Sauce volume by a healthy 20%.

So the objectives of adding value to the apple and creating a differentiated brand were fulfilled.

As Jim Schadt, President of Cadbury Schweppes U.S., says, "We have successfully extended usage of the Mott's brand from the home into the growing leisure food and drink market – further evidence of our commitment to seek out new consumer opportunities and exploit them effectively in the market place."

And a touch of sauce.

Cadbury Schweppes

MANAGEMENT PROVEN IN THE MARKET PLACE

place', they produced a variety of case histories to demonstrate their marketing ingenuity. If the role of the advertising is to influence the financial community and shareholders, then one suspects the campaign is effective.

For many years in the UK there was a reduced level of corporate advertising, until the merger mania of the mid-1980s. Then for the first time the UK advertising world witnessed some aggressive tactical manoeuvres to influence shareholders. Many would question the value of advertising in these instances. Certainly it should not be viewed as the only weapon, but rather as a complement to a skilful PR campaign. The value of advertising here is two-fold: to control the message, and simplify the argument.

Burton's takeover advertising for Debenhams was successful, not only in terms of the end result, but also for the single-minded strategy of pushing the expertise of two well-known and respected managers. In contrast the Argyll–Distillers fight involved more fragmented communication and was full of tit-for-tat aggression, which must have left shareholders in a state of bewilderment.

In a sense it is asking a great deal of this kind of advertising to provide corporate identity as well as tactical takeover rationale. It points to the fact that most companies lack good corporate communications, otherwise they would not have had the identity problem in the first place.

A new development in the UK advertising scene has been the public flotation campaigns of nationalized industries like British Telecom, Trustee Savings Bank and British Gas. They all faced complex communications problems in trying to persuade millions of people to buy shares for the first time, while adhering to the strict legal code covering securities. Inevitably, they ended up being bland, generic and somewhat condescending, yet successful as publicity campaigns rather than as advertising in the true marketing sense.

The British Gas flotation campaign attracted the most criticism. Many people were put off by the sheer expense of the campaign (reported at £20 million) and the banal nature of it. The results might have been good for British Gas/the British government and the advertising agency involved, but one suspects that damage was done to the image of advertising itself. Was the role of advertising properly judged in this instance?

FINANCIAL MARKETS

Having referred to the importance of style and production values in creating advertising effects, it is interesting to consider the rather dull and staid press advertisements for saving and investments. Do they work? Coupon receipts enable immediate judgement on effectiveness to be made, and clearly these advertisements *do* work.

Grabbing attention is less important for people with money to invest, and who are looking avidly for financial opportunities. All they need is enough information and reassurance to write out a cheque. However, as financial markets become more competitive following deregulation in October 1986, one feels that this type of direct response advertising is going to need a proposition and a more distinctive style.

In this regard the Alliance & Leicester Building Society is leading the way in broadening the role of its advertising. Its advertisement (see page 32, top) could be open to criticism about the relevance of the fashion model; but in another regard it could appeal to a more sophisticated segment who find the 'common touch' in most building society advertisements off-putting.

Even insurance companies are now looking to TV advertising to achieve some of the effects that fast-moving consumer brands have enjoyed for years. This broadened role for financial advertising has been appreciated particularly by companies like Prudential who are eager to change their old-fashioned, down-market image. The company uses comedian Griff Rhys Jones in a style of advertising that would not have seemed possible for a financial institution a few years ago. The advertiser recognized that creative style can make a powerful, implied statement about the company.

There is, however, always the danger that style becomes an indulgence which confuses the role for the advertising. Take the extravagant surreal advertising for Barclays Bank, shot by top film director Ridley Scott to a mega-budget. At a literal level the problem depicted is hard to identify with, but people often respond literally when they have not been touched emotionally. One suspects that the overall effect is to reinforce the dynamic and progressive image of the bank, rather than the caring one intended.

An important role for financial image advertising is to develop a long-term relationship with customers. Readers can make their own judgements about which financial advertisers are more successful at achieving this.

ADVERTISING SOCIAL AND POLITICAL ISSUES

The role for political advertising has changed from being purely informative to being more emotive and persuasive. Following the dramatic impact of Conservative Party advertising, other parties turned to the adman's craft to sell their ideas with the same

NOW IT'S
8·25% INTEREST
ON JUST
£500 SAVINGS;
DON'T
SAY WE DIDN'T
TELL YOU.
The Premium Plus Account
Save as little as £500
Get a full 8.25%
3 months notice or 90 days
loss of interest
Save as much as £10,000
Get 8.5%
Immediate access on balances
over £10,000
Available at any branch of
the Alliance & Leicester
ALLIANCE LEICESTER
Building Society

IMAGINE WHAT
LONDON WILL BE LIKE RUN
BY WHITEHALL.
SAY NO TO NO SAY.

slickness of a consumer brand. The GLC took anti-government sentiment to new heights with their powerful advertising in 1984 and 1985 (see opposite, below).

The advertising role for social issues is to change public attitudes and behaviour. This type of advertising has often used shock tactics to motivate people, for example, to save energy; stop drinking and driving; prevent burglary; stop drug addiction.

The shock tactic is also used effectively by charities like Oxfam and Greenpeace. The latter's advertising took away the 'loony' perception, and influenced decision-makers by making their cause respectable.

The campaign for the Royal College of Nursing broke new ground for trade union advertising. It had a clearly defined role: to draw the public's attention to changes in hospital management that were undermining the nurses' responsibility, and having detrimental effects on patients. Decision-makers, who are influenced by public opinion, will be much more impressed by a case well made publicly than they would be if the same points were made privately.

BUSINESS-TO-BUSINESS ADVERTISING

The role of business-to-business advertising is often misunderstood. The common mistake is to assume professional interest and reaction to the advertising; and to create advertisements that are little different from a page in a catalogue in terms of product features.

The role of advertising must take note of the fact that businessmen are first and foremost human beings, and therefore in need of emotional as well as rational benefits. It is ludicrous to think that the businessman changes from being an ordinary consumer into a different person whenever a business advertisement comes up.

Epsons is one office automation supplier that has judged its advertising role perfectly. The selling feature in its printer advertisement (see page 34) is communicated in an involving and witty fashion.

Financial protection is another area where businessmen are sceptical. London Life, keen to target small businesses, found a way to provide important information in a human and engaging way, through animation and symbolism (Storyboard 6).

TRADITIONAL MARKETS

This section refers to the categories of advertising where adherence to a particular look or message is expected.

The whisky market is arguably one of the most conservative male markets around. Word-of-mouth reputation is more important than advertising in this market. Once brands become members of the exclusive whisky club, e.g. Bells, Teachers, Famous Grouse, they do not need to try too hard with glossy advertising. The role of advertising here is to be seen as a 'handshake from an old friend'—thus the inevitable bottle and glass treatment with all the ambience of a gentleman's club.

Recruitment advertising is another traditional area. There is almost a total absence of creativity, yet there is so much scope for integration with a company's mainstream advertising theme for greater effectiveness. One recruitment agency, Brook Street

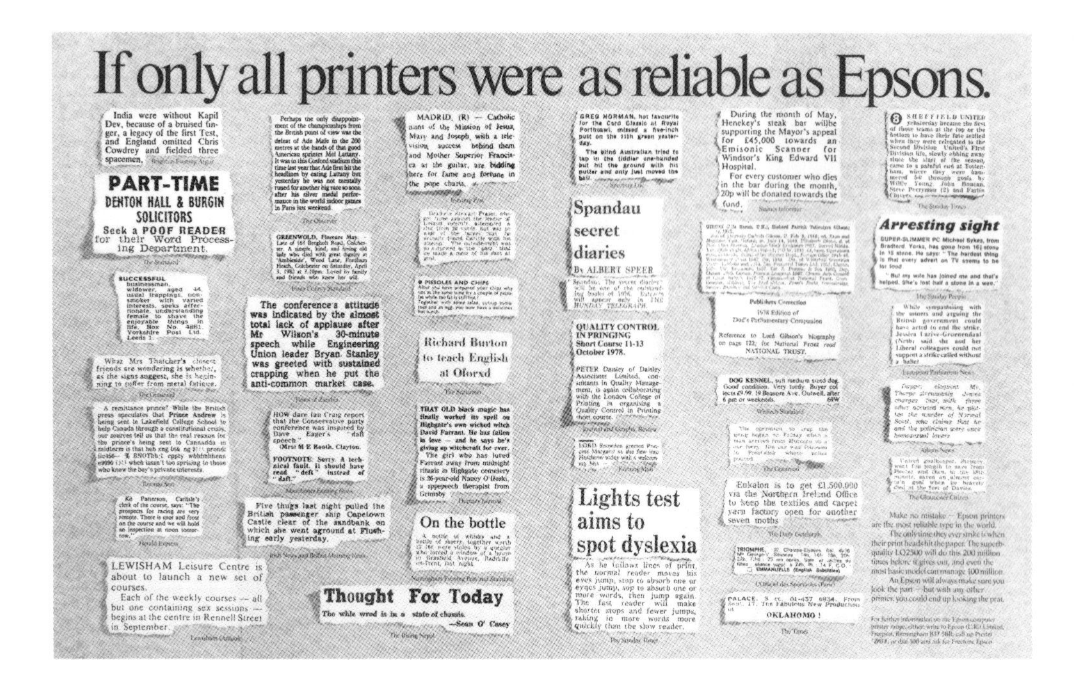

Bureau, managed to introduce an element of creativity within the confines of advertising secretarial jobs. The advertisement (see opposite) manages to communicate the traditional messages *and* make a corporate statement—without resorting to the clichéd look of the genre.

POSITIONING OR REPOSITIONING BRANDS

This is an area which demands a great deal of strategic sensitivity and skill in order to avoid the inevitable pitfalls.

For the Skin Fitness Company to avoid effeminate associations with their male moisturizing cream, they had to prevent the problem from surfacing. An important role for their advertising was therefore to associate usage with the masculine act of shaving. By positioning the product as an After Shaving Moisturizer, with stylish masculine packaging, the brand gained acceptability among men.

P&O were keen to change the rather negative image of cruise holidays among younger people, and reposition a Canberra cruise to compete with other holidays. Their advertising (Storyboard 7) challenged existing perceptions by showing some of the unexpected pleasures of a Canberra holiday.

In the case of Dylon's advertising, the company set out to reposition the brand in order to correct the old-fashioned cheapskate imagery that was linked with dyeing household fabrics. The role of the advertising was to interest young girls in the idea of dyeing their clothes with the new season's fashion colours. For such a radical change in emphasis to work, the advertising must be capable of making the consumer do a double-take. The

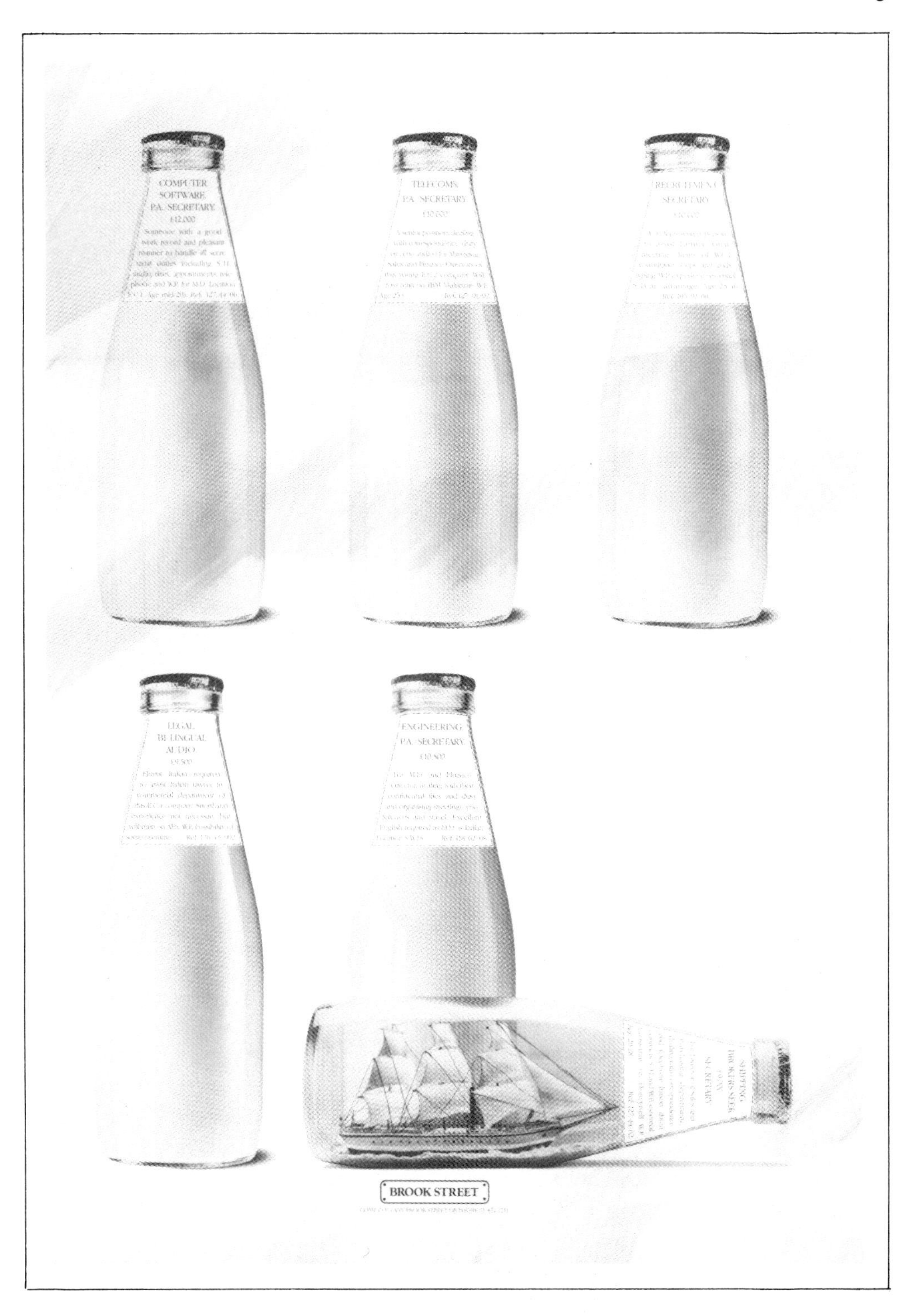
COMPUTER
SOFTWARE
P.A. SECRETARY
£12,000
TELECOMS
P.A. SECRETARY
RECRUITMENT
SECRETARY
LEGAL
BI-LINGUAL
AUDIO
£9,500
ENGINEERING
P.A. SECRETARY
£10,500
BROOK STREET

PRODUCT: LONDON LIFE

TITLE: GLASS

MAN 1: So London Life are an insurance company. MAN 2: That's right. Established in 1806.

MAN 1: And as well as insuring your business they've given you a tailor-made

plan that lets your business grow by using your company pension scheme to provide money. MAN 2: Yes.

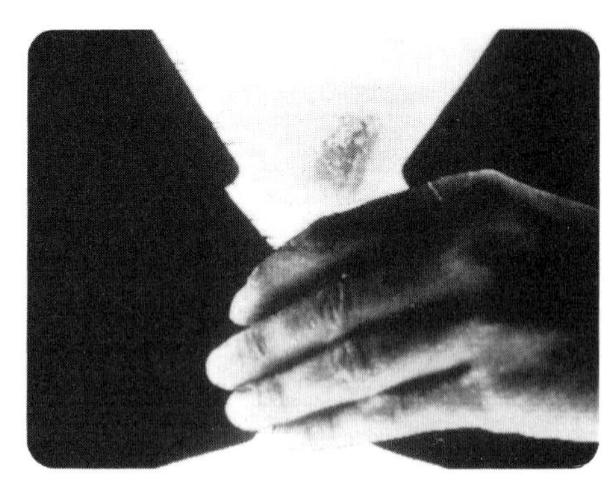

MAN 1: Why do they think they give such good advice? MAN 2: Because their salesmen are trained to

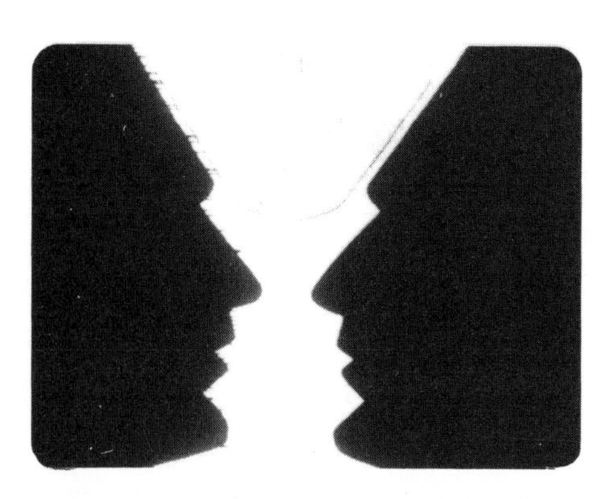

understand the problem of growing businesses. MAN 1: Well, you certainly seem to have done all right out of it. (SFX: *Champagne cork popping/Pouring into glass*).

MAN 1: Oh! Thanks. MAN 2: Cheers. (SFX: *Clink!*) MVO: London Life. Good advice for your business. Good for you. MAN 1: Er, have you got their number? MAN 2: Just phone 01-200-0200.

Storyboard 6

PRODUCT: P & O CANBERRA

TITLE: THE FIRST RESORT

DISCO MUSIC/MVO: From frantic, to romantic. From piggy (SFX: *Swallow*),

to gourmet. From after dinner ports to unforgettable ports.

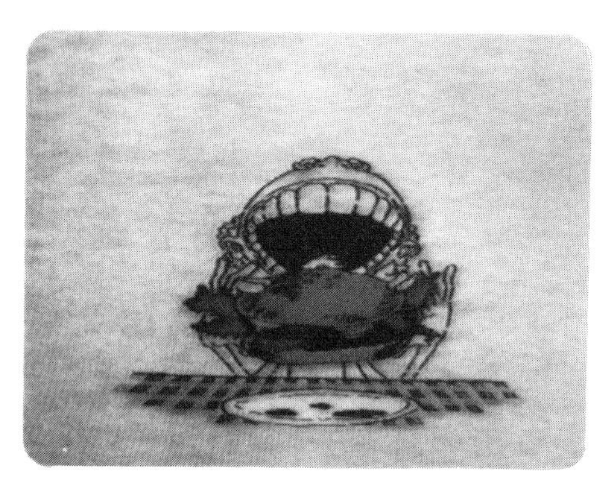

(SFX: *Camera*). A Canberra Cruise, is every

holiday you've ever wanted

in one. Canberra the first resort.

Call 01–200–0200 for your brochure.

Storyboard 7

PRODUCT: DYLON

TITLE: MAKE-UP FOR CLOTHES

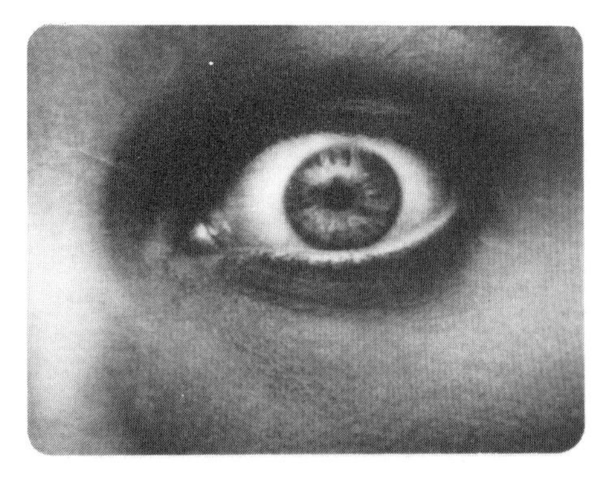

MUSIC/FVO: You know how good

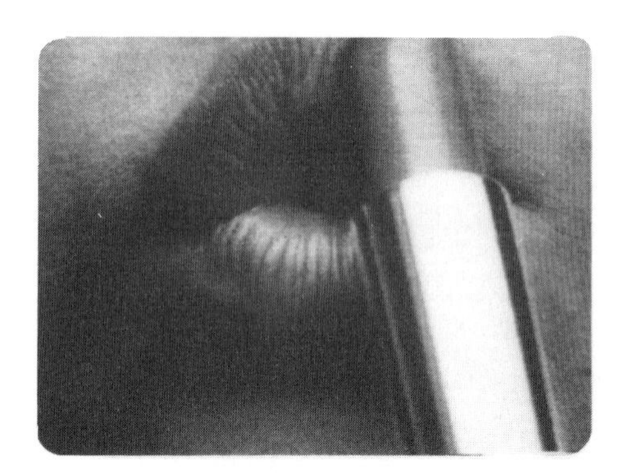

make-up can make you feel. Now Dylon

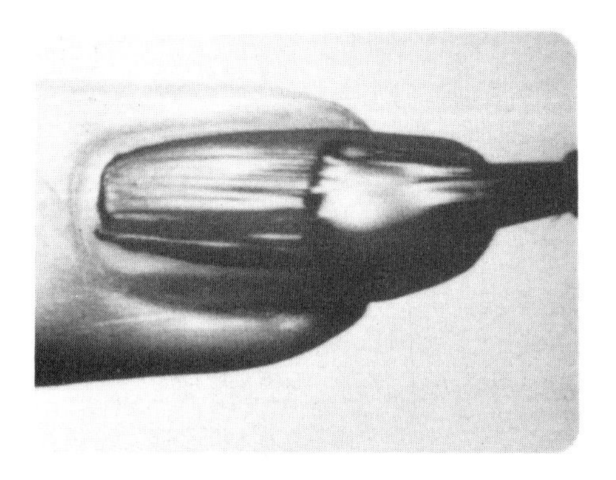

can make your clothes feel the same way.

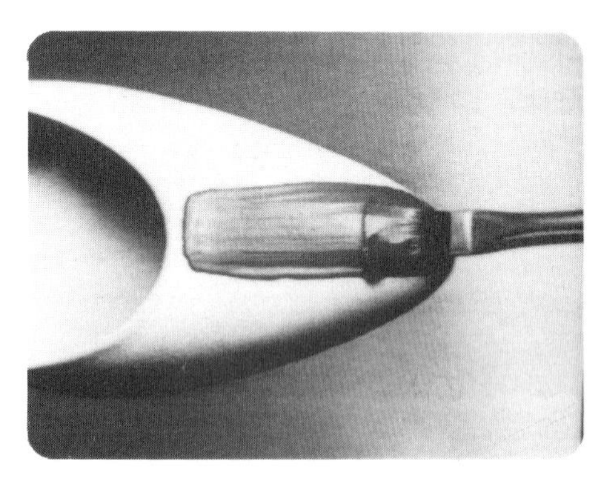

Dylon is as versatile as make-up, as simple to use

as make-up, as individual as make-up.

That's why we call it make-up for clothes.

Storyboard 8

PRODUCT: BROOKE BOND RED MOUNTAIN

TITLE: SFX/DINNER PARTY

(SFX: *Background chatting*). MVO: Because we thought making filter coffee

was sometimes a bit of an effort, WOMAN: (*Impersonating coffee-percolator*).

MVO: we made Brooke Bond Red Mountain.

WOMAN: Hiss-ss-ss! MVO: Specially freeze-dried to stay fresh and richly roasted.

GUEST: Mmm. Lovely coffee. Anyway . . .

MVO: It's like ground coffee taste without the grind.

Storyboard 9

creative solution was to portray dyeing as analogous to make-up. Their striking commercial (Storyboard 8) refers to Dylon as 'Make-up for Clothes'.

When perception lags reality advertising can be a very effective tool to counteract prejudice and negative predispositions towards a brand. Offering rational facts tends to be met with counter-arguments. The crucial role for such advertising is two-fold:

- It has to disarm the audience by some appropriate means—gentle humour and charm usually works.
- The advertising has to provide some basis for re-evaluating the brand.

A case to illustrate this point is Brooke Bond Red Mountain coffee. First launched with advertising reminiscent of 'Marlboro Country', the cowboy situation led to down-market association, and a feeling that the product was too strong and bitter. Over the years the product formulation was improved and the advertising changed, but the consumer had still not caught up with the reality in terms of quality and positioning. Their agency tackled the problem with a clearly defined advertising role: to appeal to a young, up-market audience, to give the brand social acceptability, and to reposition the brand in taste terms as being better than Nescafé and more accessible than Gold Blend. The advertising idea, encapsulated in the end-line, 'Ground coffee taste without the grind', showed Red Mountain passing for filter coffee (Storyboard 9).

IN CONCLUSION

To maximize the investment value of advertising it is essential to recognize its full capabilities in different situations. The *ultimate* aim of commercial advertising must be to make a brand desirable, and this is more likely to happen if the following guidelines are borne in mind:

- Consumers are not learning machines. Identify the most potent message, then communicate it simply and consistently.
- Consumers are not as interested in advertising as you might be. An advertisement will therefore work harder if it is inextricably linked with a brand, and has a competitive edge.
- Consumers are very sensitive to tone of voice. Treat them as equals, don't patronize them.
- Advertising style can be the main discriminator between different brands and different target audiences. Consumers like executions that involve, where appropriate, a degree of originality, humour, entertainment, cleverness and honesty.
- Most importantly, show an understanding of the consumer psychology involved in the persuasion process. Do not overlook the implicit, emotional roles of advertising.

3 *Research for strategic development*

David Cowan

ADVERTISING STRATEGY

The advertiser has an objective and the advertising strategy is the means by which advertising helps the attainment of that objective.

Advertising strategy has two parts, the target group and the creative objective. The creative objective is what the advertising should 'say' to the target group; it is also how we wish the brand, issue or whatever it is we are advertising to be perceived.

The advertising strategy in effect says that if the advertising aims at this target (or targets) and communicates so that they perceive the brand in this particular way then the objective will be achieved.

To the advertiser, the advertising strategy is the logic of *how* his objective will be achieved while, for the creative department, the advertising strategy is the definition of their objectives.

The reason for needing market research is that the objectives, target group and creative objectives are usually not clear. The role of market research is to clarify them.

USING MARKET RESEARCH

Market research is a tool for answering questions. It has many techniques:

- Retail audits.
- Consumer panels.
- Questionnaires to ask about product performance, attitudes and usage behaviour.
- Group discussions.
- In-depth interviews, and so on.

Each technique has numerous sub-techniques or ways in which they can be used.

Advertising also presents a bewildering variety of different things to advertise:

- Grocery brands.
- Retail outlets.
- Campaigns against drug abuse.
- Campaigns for political parties, and so forth.

This variety makes it difficult to give general prescriptions of how to use market research to help set advertising strategy. A starting point is to remember that market research is a tool for asking questions and it will only be of value if we ask the right questions. To frame the right questions two disciplines are helpful:

- To remember that our task is to clarify the *three key areas*
  (1) the advertiser's objective
  (2) the target group
  (3) the creative objective.
- To think about whether we have come across a similar problem before. (Similar problems have similar sub-sequences of questions which need to be answered and can reduce the time needed to think the problem through.)

When starting on a new advertising problem, we need to read all the existing company research as well as any general research which might exist, e.g. TGI, government statistics, research done by media owners.

Unfortunately, in my experience, having done all this, one rarely finds the answers to the three key questions. This is because the people who provide the information did not have your specific problem in mind when they set up their research. A good deal can be achieved by reanalysing existing data, as in the Ovaltine example (Box 2, page 46), but in almost all cases effective planning will necessitate setting up some specific research.

The variety of research techniques available is very wide and a number of different methods are referred to in this chapter. However, what I've tried to do is to illustrate how the planner should approach the problem of strategy development rather than describe particular research techniques.

SETTING A CLEAR OBJECTIVE

We must be clear about what it is that we want the advertising to do. Here are some questions you can ask:

- Is the advertising seeking to create awareness of a new brand or social issue?
- Is it seeking to reinforce existing attitudes and behaviour?
- Is it trying to change the way something is perceived, e.g. trying to reposition a brand?
- Is it seeking to expand the market by gaining new users or greater frequency of existing users?

Sometimes the objective is obvious, e.g. a new grocery product must get trial and then repeat purchase. Alternatively, we may find the advertiser's long-term commercial objective clearly implies the role advertising needs to play. For instance, a service company may wish to improve its staff behaviour towards customers. It may wish to advertise its customer care programme in the knowledge that this will reinforce good staff morale and encourage the public to reprimand wayward staff.

Research can help us set objectives by telling us where realistic opportunities may lie or by diagnosing the cause of problems.

FINDING AND ASSESSING OPPORTUNITIES

Opportunities may lie in getting new users or encouraging new types of usage.

NEW USERS In looking for new users, qualitative research should ask:

- Why is it that non-users are not using the brand?
- Is the reason influenceable by advertising?

In the case of Hellmans, the reason for non-use was influenceable by advertising but in the case of Butlins (discussed later) it was not.

The Hellmans' case history is written up in *Advertising Works 3*. It describes how Hellmans was perceived as a posh salad cream and that qualitative research showed that this poshness was deterring C2Ds from use. The reason users used Hellmans was taste not poshness. The reason that Hellmans was perceived as posh was because historically its advertising had consistently portrayed it as such. New advertising was therefore able to undo this perception and reposition Hellmans as a brand for everyone—sales rose 56% in two years.

NEW USES In looking for new uses we can learn from what minorities of consumers are doing with the brand. We can use research to ask:

- How are minorities using the brand?
- Why aren't others using it in this way?
- Do they have the same needs?
- Is there a role for advertising in encouraging these new uses?

Yellow Pages is predominantly used for calling mini-cabs or making emergency calls to plumbers when water pipes burst. Qualitative research among users shows that there are many other ways in which *minorities* are using *Yellow Pages*. For instance they use them for finding the name of a shop or restaurant whose location they know but whose name they have forgotten. They use it for drawing up visiting lists of car showrooms or furniture shops. These findings were quantified to show the proportion of people who ever had each need and the proportion who were aware that *Yellow Pages* could answer these needs. The group discussions showed that the only reason the *majority* of *Yellow Pages* users don't use them in these ways is lack of awareness. There is, therefore, a role for advertising.

REPOSITIONING A major opportunity may lie in repositioning a product. That is, selling it to different people for different reasons. For this to be possible we would expect some people to have discovered the 'new use' already. We can use research to ask:

- Are consumers already using the brand in the new way?

Lucozade is a good example of research answering this question. The first part of the Lucozade story (i.e. before Daley Thompson) is written up in *Advertising Works 1*. For years Lucozade was sold as a recuperative drink mainly for child sickness. It is now sold as a refreshing, energy-giving drink and has doubled its sales. To my mind the key research fact was contained in the following table in the case study:

Table 1: Lucozade Volume by Purpose

User	% Housewives	% Volume	Purpose
Heavy	5	50	Refreshing drink
Medium	39	32	Pick-me-up (minor sickness)
Light	46	18	In sickness

Source: *Advertising Works 1*

This meant that half the volume was *already* being consumed as a refreshing drink. Clearly an opportunity lay in this type of usage. In 1982 Beechams fully capitalized on this usage, riding the consumer trend towards healthy, active living.

DEFINING THE PROBLEM

At the outset of a problem research can be very helpful in describing the current situation.

SIMPLE AWARENESS AND ATTITUDE MEASURES can be very helpful. Thus when the GLC started to oppose abolition it was important to know that among London's population, 45% were unaware of the abolition plan, 32% were on the side of the GLC and only 10% agreed with the government. This told us that an important role of advertising was to get the issue on the perceptual map. It also encouraged us to believe that the battle for minds could be won.

CLARIFYING THE CLIENT'S BRIEF Client briefs to agencies are sometimes vague and we need to define what the problem is. In the case of the Texas Homecare Company (Box 1) the brief to the agency said, 'We want to build short-term sales targets and build an image for the store.'

DIAGNOSING THE CAUSE Research can be very useful in diagnosing the *cause* of a problem. We can then decide if there is a role for advertising in tackling this cause.

1 New product launches If a new product is failing we can use quantitative research to ask:

- What proportion of households have tried the product?
- What proportion have repeat purchased?

AGB and Mintel can give us norms which will help us decide whether the achieved levels are good or bad.

Qualitative research can tell us why these things are or are not happening. If the trial level is low the research agenda is:

BOX 1
Texas Homecare Company

The store sold decorating materials, DIY and furniture in equal proportions, but the company wanted to develop its furniture business. Qualitative research was done among people who had recently bought in these markets. It showed that the stores visited were chosen from a candidates' list and that Texas was strongly associated with decorating and DIY but less so with furniture. These findings were quantified and showed that while 33 per cent of Texas's sales were in furniture, only 18 per cent of Texas's image was in furniture.

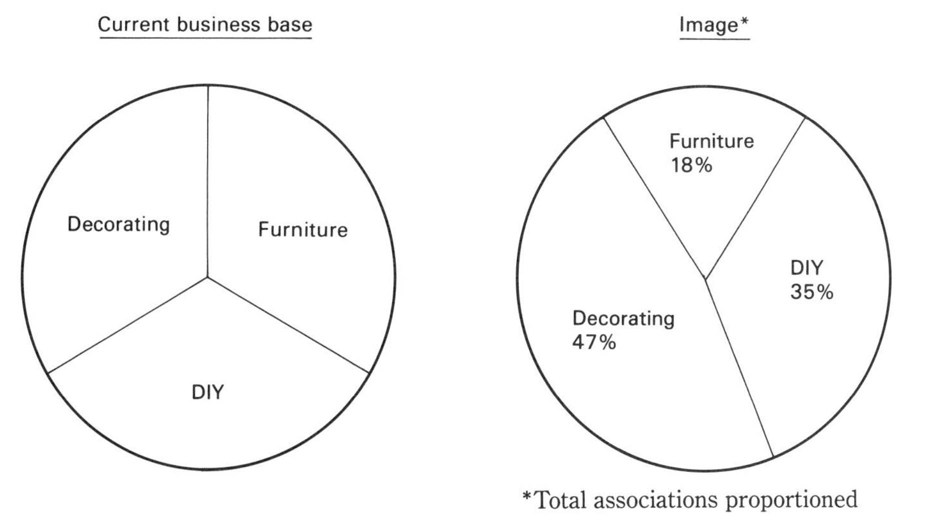

*Total associations proportioned

There was therefore a *mismatch* between the current business base and the consumer perception. This defined the 'image' building we needed to do.

- Recruit people who 'should' have tried the brand.
- Show them the advertising and packaging and let them try the product.
- Ask them why in real life they have not tried it.
- Decide if the cause of the problem is product, packaging or advertising.

2 ***Established brands*** The Ovaltine case study shows research diagnosing the cause of an existing brand's problem. It is given in detail because of the general applicability of the ideas behind it. It shows:

- Advertising objectives emerging from our understanding of the cause of the problem.
- Research tools used in combination.
- Consumer panel data showing *how* sales are being lost.
- Research eliminating possible explanations.
- Research checking and disproving an advertiser's assumption.
- The interpretation coming from the above *and* MEAL spend taken together with qualitative research assessments of the responses to the brand and its advertising.

BOX 2
Ovaltine

Between 1980 and 1983 Ovaltine sales fell by 18 per cent. This was entirely due to a decline in the traditional food drinks sector (Horlicks, Bournville, etc.). Ovaltine's share remained the same over the period. During this period the shares of Drinking Chocolate and Instant Horlicks grew so that the total market remained static.

The theories around at the time were:

- The traditional sector had lost to instant and drinking chocolate.
- The bedtime occasion was old-fashioned and on its way out.
- The future lay in repositioning Ovaltine for daytime use. It was thought that Instant Ovaltine would be the best product to do this with because Horlicks had advertised Seb Coe drinking Instant Horlicks for energy during the day.

Thus, so the argument went, the advertising money should be put behind Instant Ovaltine to be advertised as a daytime drink.

Several pieces of research and information completely changed the picture:

- Gains/loss analysis (a special AGB analysis which tracks the buying behaviour of individual households) showed that the rise of Instant bedtime drinks and Drinking Chocolate and the fall of traditional food drinks were unconnected.
- Instant Horlicks and Drinking Chocolate had both grown by getting new users, *not* switching users from traditional food drinks. Traditional food drinks had declined because users had dropped out of the sector completely.
- The National Drinks Survey showed no decline in the bedtime occasion and showed a loss of traditional food drink share to tea and coffee.
- A telephone survey linked to a sample of Instant Horlicks users located by the TGI showed that, despite the daytime advertising, over 90 per cent of Instant Horlicks was drunk after dark and that instant users had a very young profile.
- MEAL showed that the part of advertising food drinks spend which depicted the bedtime occasion had declined to 25 per cent of their 1980 weight. During this time tea and coffee advertising had doubled.
- Qualitative research among Ovaltine drinkers showed that users were very satisfied with the brand. They enjoyed the comforting, soothing, relaxing sleep benefits it offered. The Ovaltine advertising was very branded; it was advertising which talked about the heritage of the brand and did not evoke the benefits of drinking it.

The interpretations made from this were:

- The bedtime occasion was as large as ever, not in decline, and therefore did not need to be abandoned.
- The sales decline was due to sector share losses to tea and coffee caused firstly by the diversion of advertising funds to supporting the virtually non-existent daytime occasion, and secondly because the Ovaltine advertising was branded and not stimulating usage.
- The instant products had been totally misunderstood. They were bedtime not daytime products. They had succeeded in attracting young new users, which was a great strength, but Seb Coe's daytime use had not changed habits.

Thus there was no need to change perceptions of Ovaltine, using Instant as a vehicle. There might be a case for advertising Instant Ovaltine at bedtime until the trial period was over. But after this Instant and traditional Ovaltine could be advertised together, reinforcing the existing perceptions and benefits and in this way supporting the use of Ovaltine at bedtime.

In my experience, advertising problems are thought through by reference to multi-source information from which an understanding is built. Ovaltine (Box 2) illustrates this.

CHOOSING THE TARGET GROUP

The target group is one of the most important concepts in advertising. Sadly it is often trivialized with only lip service paid to it. Targets defined as ABC1 housewives are usually debased target group descriptions.

The target group choice is of vital importance firstly because it determines our behaviour/attitude objectives. For instance, to aim at new users we will have to *change* something to get them into usage. We may need to change their attitude or reassure by reducing the perceived risk. To aim at existing users we do not need to change anything. All we have to do is to reiterate what they already think and like about the brand. The target group also influences the advertising approach. Advertising aimed at mothers will be very different from that aimed at children. As we will see later, advertising aimed at the people that *do* the house painting is very different to that aimed at the people who *buy* the paint.

The target group choice is vital in a narrower sense as well, because the target we choose brings with it its audience characteristics—what they have in their minds about the product, brand and competition. Do they bring favourable or unfavourable attitudes? Do they have doubts, concerns, anxiety? Depending on our choice the target group will 'bring' different things to the advertising.

When faced with a new problem the first thing we need to ask is: who is the target? (When we know who they are we need to understand them.) To choose, we can ask ourselves some questions:

IS THE TARGET SELF EVIDENT? The target may have become evident from our analysis of the problem and our objectives. On other occasions the target is reasonably obvious, e.g. they must be people already in the market for what we are selling.

Sometimes we need to use our knowledge of how the world works to decide the targets for advertising. In the case of the GLC anti-abolition advertising the core target was the House of Lords. If they were to vote against it their Lordships needed to believe that abolition was an important issue which the public opposed. Therefore the advertising needed to create an issue among the public. But it was important that the media saw it as an issue as well. If they did, then editorial space would be devoted to it. Money would be spent on opinion polls which would be read by the public and members of the House of Lords. The targets for advertising were therefore peers, the public and the media.

CAN WE USE SURROGATES FOR THE TARGET? Often we do not know how to identify the target group but we are reasonably sure that they will be similar to the people who have already bought the product. Thus in the car market we may not know who is most predisposed to buy a particular make of car but we can get a good steer on them by talking to people who already have bought this car. Of course, we have to be careful with this way of thinking because the future of a brand may not lie with the people who bought it initially. There is an adage which alerts us to this danger: 'Who is the target today? Who is the target tomorrow?'

CAN WE IDENTIFY THE 'REAL' TARGET IN GROUP DISCUSSIONS? In qualitative research we often recruit users of the product field. It is sometimes evident that the real target group for the brand is a sub-group of these who are difficult to classify on recruitment questionnaires. We should focus on the attitudes of these people as they are our real market.

IS THE TARGET EXISTING USERS? Cumulative research experience tells us that well-advertised, high-awareness, high-trial brands are unlikely to get new users. Market experience tells us that existing users are likely to be tempted by competitors. This leads us to aim advertising at the brand's users to reinforce the loyalty. The questions for research are: Why do people use the brand; what do we need to say to reinforce loyalty?

DO WE NEED RESEARCH TO UNDERSTAND WHO INFLUENCES WHOM? In lots of situations there are interactions between different target groups. The GLC was an example of this. A commonly occurring situation is where the purchasers and consumers are different people. Research can help us sort out who influences whom. L'Aimant (Storyboard 1 and Box 3) is a good example:

CAN RESEARCH INTRODUCE SOME REALISM? Quite often an advertiser wishes to increase his sales by selling his existing product to new users. Research can tell us whether this is realistic or wishful thinking. The key research questions are:

- Why are non-users not using the product?
- Are the reasons for non-use influenceable by advertising?

Butlins furnishes a good example of this. Qualitative research showed that non-users of Butlins either want foreign or quiet English holidays. They correctly perceive Butlins as too crowded, regimented and offering standards of accommodation inferior to their own homes. They also think Butlins customers are down-market and vulgar. Unless the product changes significantly it is unrealistic to target advertising at the non-users with the expectation of winning them over.

DO WE NEED SOME LATERAL THINKING? Sometimes lateral thinking uncovers the target group and this has major effects on the advertising content and achieves the advertiser's objective.

Up until the early 1970s anti-smoking advertising had been aimed at the smoker with the objective of directly persuading them to give up because of cancer risk, worry to other family members, etc. The model was then changed to an indirect one. Instead of aiming at smokers, the advertising was aimed at non-smokers. Non-smokers were

PRODUCT: COTY

TITLE: L'AIMANT

MVO: A little French lesson.
MUSIC. La femme, the woman.

L'homme, the man.
Le parfum de L'Aimant.
Les yeux, the eyes.

Le parfum de L'Aimant
La bouche, the mouth.
Le parfum de L'Aimant

La chaise, the chair.
Le mari, oh, the husband.

Le conversation, the conversation

Do you speak L'Aimant.

Storyboard 1

BOX 3
L'Aimant

The perfume market is very seasonal; 55 per cent of sales are at Christmas. Advertising spending is even more biased to this time of year. But who really chooses the brand—the Christmas gift giver or the Christmas gift receiver?

- Qualitative research showed that the receiver often got the perfume they wanted. Sometimes the giver asked the receiver what they used but other times they were aware that the giver found out by means of detective work.
- Questions on an Omnibus Survey confirmed that in most cases the receiver effectively took the brand decision.

How are brands chosen?

Brand asked for by receiver	33
Brand currently used by receiver	41
Brand chosen by giver	26

The decision to aim the advertising at the receiver of the gift had several implications for advertising strategy:

- Since the receiver is the target the role for advertising is to build the L'Aimant brand among brand users in the knowledge that the more users the brand has the more it will be bought at Christmas as a gift. Thus the advertising reinforced existing perceptions portraying the L'Aimant user as a married woman in her early thirties who was still desirable to attractive men.
- Because the advertising was aimed at building the brand franchise it was possible to advertise at other times of the year when airtime was cheaper.

encouraged to express their disapproval of smoking. At the same time restrictions on smoking in public places were progressively introduced. Thus smokers were subject to personal and public statements that smoking was unacceptable behaviour. This strategy worked where the more direct approach had failed.

SETTING THE CREATIVE OBJECTIVE

The key thing we have to decide is what the advertising should 'say' to the target group. The answer can come from a number of different directions:

- It may arise quite obviously from the target group definition. There may be an obvious gap between the desired and the actual perceptions consumers have of a brand.
- We may need to put our finger on the motivation or use advertising to overcome demotivating attitudes.
- The answer may come from studying the point of sale.

- There are also occasions where creative insight is the best starting point. In this latter instance research makes its contribution in the creative development phase.

Different research agendas will uncover the creative objectives for different sorts of problem. Here are some questions you can ask yourself.

DO THE CREATIVE OBJECTIVES ARISE DIRECTLY FROM THE TARGET GROUP?

INITIAL POSITIONING In the most simple cases, the advertising makes people aware that what we already know they want is available.

John Smith Yorkshire Bitter is an example of this. The brand was introduced to the South of England because a segment of southern beer drinkers believed that northern beers were superior. John Smith's was aimed at this favourably disposed group. The creative objective was to present the brand as an authentic Yorkshire bitter and it emerged quite naturally from the product development research which gave rise to the brand in the first place.

EXISTING BRANDS As we discussed earlier, brands which have been around a long time often have their existing users as their target group. In this situation the research agenda is:

- Qualitative research among existing users.
- Find out how, where, when and, importantly, why they use the brand.
- What are the functional and emotional benefits?
- What is the brand 'essence'?
- Does existing advertising sum up this brand essence?

CLOSING THE GAP BETWEEN DESIRED AND ACTUAL PERCEPTIONS

It is often the advertiser's objective to do this. Hellmans and anti-smoking are successful examples. In these cases, defining the advertiser's objective and target group led quite naturally to the creative objectives.

Quite often when a brand is in trouble it is because the brand is not perceived in the desired way. Defining the desired perception defines the creative objective. The research agenda is:

- How is the brand perceived?
- How should it be perceived? (We can often answer this question by answering other, sub-questions: What do people want from the product field? Does anybody view the brand in the 'right' way? How do they perceive it? Could we get the rest of the target group to perceive it as they do?)
- Can advertising close the gap?
- What does advertising have to 'say' to close this gap?

PRODUCT: DULUX SOLID EMULSION

TITLE: CREAM CHEESE

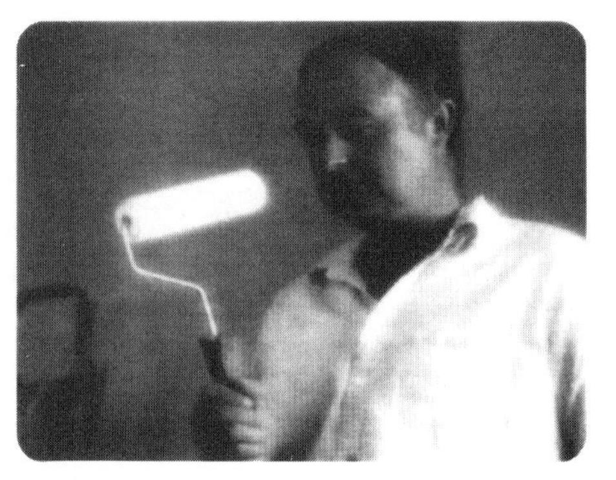

MUSIC/MVO: (DOG). Time they did this place up. Oh no. The dreaded roller.

Wait a minute, Dulux Solid Emulsion, funny looking paint. My mistake it's cream cheese.

And he's spreading it up the wall. Goes on nice and even though.

And not that splattery judging by his head. He's finished already . . . very good. Better check the finish. Good stuff this

cream cheese. MVO: Dulux Solid Emulsion in six shades of white.

The paints rollers have been waiting for.

Storyboard 2

BOX 4
Dulux

Dulux solid emulsion is solid paint in a tray. A major technological breakthrough.

Sales of the new product were disappointing. Quantitative research showed the product failed to get trial. However, those that did use it showed high satisfaction—and intention to repurchase. Quantified product tests showed that the product had the right characteristics and delivered opacity, coverage and durability.

The answer to the sales problem came from understanding:

- Who the targets were.
- What they wanted.
- How the advertising had turned them off.

From this we were able to see:

- How the brand should be perceived.
- What the advertising needed to say.

Previous qualitative research had shown that there are two types of people: *planners* and *appliers/doers*. Planning is concerned with the aesthetics, planners' only concern is that the transformation through choice of colour and finish will look good.

Both planners and appliers seek the best product in terms of perceived quality and reliability but appliers also seek a quite distinct value. They see painting as an act requiring their skill and their competence. Their reward is the gratification and pride in a job well done.

One commercial for Dulux's solid emulsion showed a suited man, complete with ladder and paint, enter a living room where the family were watching TV. He proceeded to paint the ceiling still in his suit while the family completely ignored him. The voice-over said how easy the job was, that solid emulsion would not drip, run or be a mess.

While *planners* thought convenience of the product made sense and liked the commercial, *appliers* gave this and other commercials a very negative reaction. The product was criticized as a 'gimmicky paint for the inexperienced'. No 'real painter' would come home and paint without preparation and precautions. In the commercial the painter was completely ignored and was given no rewards for his efforts. The commercial implied that because it was so easy, no recognition was appropriate!

It was clear that the commercial had mispositioned the product. It positioned it as a paint that any old fool could use and the appliers did not want to see their craft under-valued in this way.

The paint needs to be perceived as one which delivers 'applier satisfaction'. The convenience needs to be explained in a way that doesn't diminish the applier to a mindless, skilless cipher.

The emerging advertising seeks to reposition the paint from a 'gimmicky paint for the inexperienced' to 'the paint made for rolling'.

ICI Dulux (Storyboard 2 and Box 4) is a good illustration of using research to understand the gap between desired and actual perceptions. This way of using research occurs quite often. Qualitative research was used to identify the target and what they wanted from the product field. The brand was perceived as not offering the emotional rewards required. The existing advertising totally failed to address users' emotional needs and consequently was mispositioning the brand.

WHAT IS THE MOTIVATOR?

GENERIC MOTIVATORS If there is no other brand advertising, then the generic benefits of the product field are useable motivators. This is also the case if the product field is expanding. Research can tell us what the generic motivators are. The research agenda is:

- Why do people use the product field?
- What benefits or positives does the product field have compared with competing product fields?

CHOOSING BETWEEN MOTIVATORS In certain circumstances there are several possible motivators to choose from. Qualitative research using stimulus material can sort this out.

In the case of the GLC, research was needed to examine the pros and cons of various alternatives before deciding which approach would most motivate Tory voters, who were obviously the most difficult group to win over. Seven possible advertising approaches were shown in rough advertisement form to both Labour and Tory voters, before deciding that the loss of 'democratic freedom' would unite both poles of the political spectrum in opposition to the government.

IS THERE A DEMOTIVATOR?

Quite often the motivating benefits of a product are clear but consumers hold back because of unfamiliarity or perceived risk. Qualitative research can easily detect this reticence. The key question is:

- Why aren't target people using the brand?

When Smash launched, its 'instant' benefits were obvious. But housewives were concerned that the product would let them down in front of their families. The launch advertisement showed a 'slice of life' with Smash Instant Potato being eaten and nobody noticing that they were, in fact, eating Smash.

DOES UNDERSTANDING THE POINT OF PURCHASE GIVE US THE ANSWER?

Sometimes studying the point of purchase shows us the forces working on the consumer and can clarify what advertising needs to do to tip the balance in the brand's favour. The research agenda is:

- Qualitative or observational research to illuminate what happens at point of sale.
- How is the decision made at point of sale?
- What are the feelings, problems or trade-offs associated with the point of decision?
- If salesmen are involved, how do they behave?
- Given our understanding of all this, what is the role of advertising?

Unigate Farmer's Wife, detailed below, is a good example. It shows observational and qualitative research used in conjunction to understand how sales are influenced by what happens at POS. The creative objective arose directly out of this understanding. It is also a good example of advertising aimed at dual target groups and advertising fitting into the whole sales process. (Storyboard 3 and Box 5)

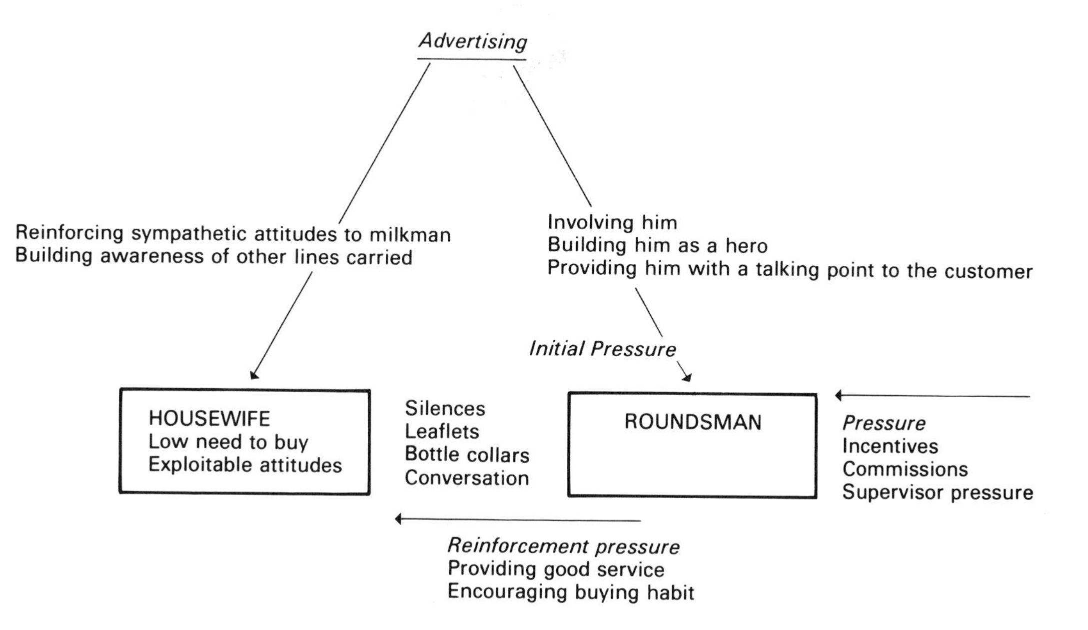

Figure 1: The role of advertising in the sales model

CREATIVE INSIGHT

The most difficult advertising problems are where 'there is nothing to say'. For instance, where a new brand is introduced into a crowded market with no differences or advantages.

In these situations there might be something to say if latent consumer-wants exist and advertising can effectively brand the product as satisfying them.

When working on this type of problem, it is difficult for the agency management team to set the creative objectives. Creative people are usually much better at seeing the potentiality for brand differentiation. When they have come up with a creative idea, then creative development research can make a contribution.

Hofmeister answers an identification need among young lager drinkers. John Webster had both the creative insight to spot this need and the creative talent to answer it—he created George the Bear. Research made a big contribution in the creative development stage.

PRODUCT: UNIGATE MILK

TITLE: FARMER'S WIFE FOODS

MUSIC. (SFX: *Alarm Clock*).

MVO: All over the country Unigate Milk men are getting up a little earlier because they've got more than just milk

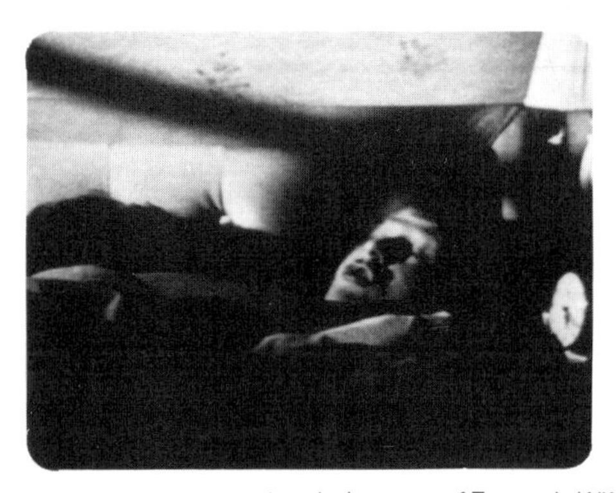

to deliver. They've got a whole range of Farmer's Wife Foods.

Eggs, butter and cream, real fruit, yoghurts and best-quality potatoes.

So have a word with your Unigate Milkman,

but softly, he was up early this morning.

Storyboard 3

BOX 5

Selling Farmer's Wife products from the milk float

Unigate's objective was to sell non-milk products, e.g. butter, cheese, potatoes, from the milk float to boost profitability.

Awareness of the products sold was high and qualitative research showed that the convenience of doorstep delivery was more than offset by the negative of higher prices, and the belief that the quick turnover of supermarket goods was a better guarantee of freshness.

The understanding of how this sales process worked, who to target the advertising at and what the advertising should 'say' emerged from understanding housewife attitudes and what happened at POS.

The amount of extra goods sold on milk rounds showed enormous variation:

- The top selling milkmen were selling extra goods to the value of 50 per cent of the milk sales.
- The bottom selling milkmen were selling virtually nothing.

These variations could not be accounted for by the demographic composition of the rounds.

Observation of how the top sellers did it was very illuminating: one in particular is illustrative. He already had high sales and we were interested to see how scrupulously he serviced his regular customers, sometimes making special trips to corner shops if he was out of stock. On several occasions he got new customers by the following method:

When the customer paid the weekly bill he stood facing her with non-milk goods in a handcrate and allowed silences to occur in the conversation. In one or two cases, the housewife broke the silence by asking for some butter or bread. He told us that next time he saw her he would ask if she wanted butter this week. It was clear that he had built his sales in this way and was determined to give good service so as not to break the habit.

The other side of this sales picture became clear from talking to housewives in qualitative research. While there were emergency reasons for buying products which had temporarily gone out of household stock it emerged that housewives had exploitable attitudes which the sales situation described was capitalizing on.

Housewives have some affection for the milkman:

- He does a good job. He delivers every day, in all weathers and is not well paid.
- The housewife is aware that the milkrounds are under financial pressure and sometimes milkmen will ask them to buy other goods because there is a promotion on. Sometimes the housewife is willing to help out.
- It can be embarrassing meeting him if there is nothing to say.

The sales occur because the milkman exploits the favourable attitudes. He sometimes chats the housewife up and asks her to buy his other goods. The tension of the meeting is exploited in the manner described earlier.

One of the advertisements in the campaign showed a milkman dreaming about a beautiful housewife only to be wakened by his alarm. The voice-over said that he was getting up earlier these days because he had fresh eggs, butter, cream and other goods to deliver. The last shot showed the milkman in front of a real housewife—he was looking glazed because he had been up so early.

When shown this commercial, housewives made jokes about their milkman and said they would pull his leg about it the next time they saw him. It was reinforcing their existing affection for him. The commercial also provided a talking point. The commercial built him into a hero.

When the commercial was shown to milkmen at their sales conference it had seven hundred of them on their feet cheering.

The diagram (page 55) shows who the advertising was targeted at and how it fits into the sales process.

CONCLUSION

Advertising strategy is our plan for using advertising to achieve the advertiser's objective. We have seen that, depending on the situation, research can make contributions to different parts of the strategy. The key question that we are always trying to answer is: How will advertising work in this situation? Or, putting it another way: What do we have to say in order that the target, having seen our campaign, be more inclined to do or think as we want them to?

Research can contribute to answering these questions by giving us an understanding of the situation. What opportunities exist? What are the causes of the problem or the causes of the unexploited opportunity? Can advertising affect the situation and what does it have to 'say'? We answer these questions by using all the relevant research tools in combination.

Before briefing the creative people it is very important to have a well-thought-through strategy as this keeps us pointing in the right direction and better able to make creative judgements and modifications to the plan as we go along.

4 *Brand positioning*

John Ward

ESTABLISHING AN IDENTITY

A brand needs to have 'positioning' in order to survive. A number of other words or phrases could be substituted for positioning—*raison d'être*, point of difference, justification of price, platform, territory, proposition—and still retain the flavour of what one means. Fundamentally, a positioning is an *identity*.

In a capitalist society consumers often have endless choices, and retailers always have limited shelf space. The combined pressure of these two factors upon a brand is enormous. On the other hand, a brand that has a clear identity, with strong relevance to a viable consumer segment, will not only be stocked and purchased: it will also command a higher price than much (if not all) of the competition.

SURVIVAL AND PROFIT

In my view, this literally represents the beginning and end of brand positioning's importance. And it is a reflection of this importance that in product fields where marketing professionals have a real influence, the majority of competitors have persisted over many years in the cultivation of a clear image. So much so, that it often seems there are no more left for the new boys. Advertising strategies are developed, executional platforms constructed and claims to superiority laid until even the most inventive account planners are stumped.

The UK automotive market (Figure 1) provides a notable example of a mature sector where most marques have decided what they stand for, and most consumers both recognize and understand this. Some brands over the years have failed, in the customer's eyes, to live up to these promises; or have decided to change the promise offered. The Italian marques in particular (notably Lancia and Alfa Romeo) have suffered by ignoring the brand heritage. But most marques, having established an identity, have wisely built upon it: Volkswagen and Volvo are classic examples.

When I first began speaking and writing about brand positioning some six or seven years ago, there were still two marques (and one whole country of origin) in the automotive market that had blurred images or a confused *raison d'être* in the consumer's mind: Audi, Renault and Japan. One platform—useful innovation through technology—was there for the taking. John Bartle has taken it for Audi. Renault have opted for 'high-quality finish', while Japanese marques like Mazda, Mitsubishi and Toyota now seem to be making a concerted effort to establish quality or reliability over and above the traditional Japanese 'good value' claim. They are wise to do so: selling cars on low price and a factory-fitted Teasmaid is no route to *survival and profits* in a market where every year the majors get bigger, and the import restrictions get tighter.

Over the next few years, the weaker brands who have under-invested in product and positioning will be shaken (or bought) out of the car market: indeed, this is already starting to happen. But this market is far from unique. It has never been more difficult, or more important, to find and capitalize upon an identity than it is in major markets today.

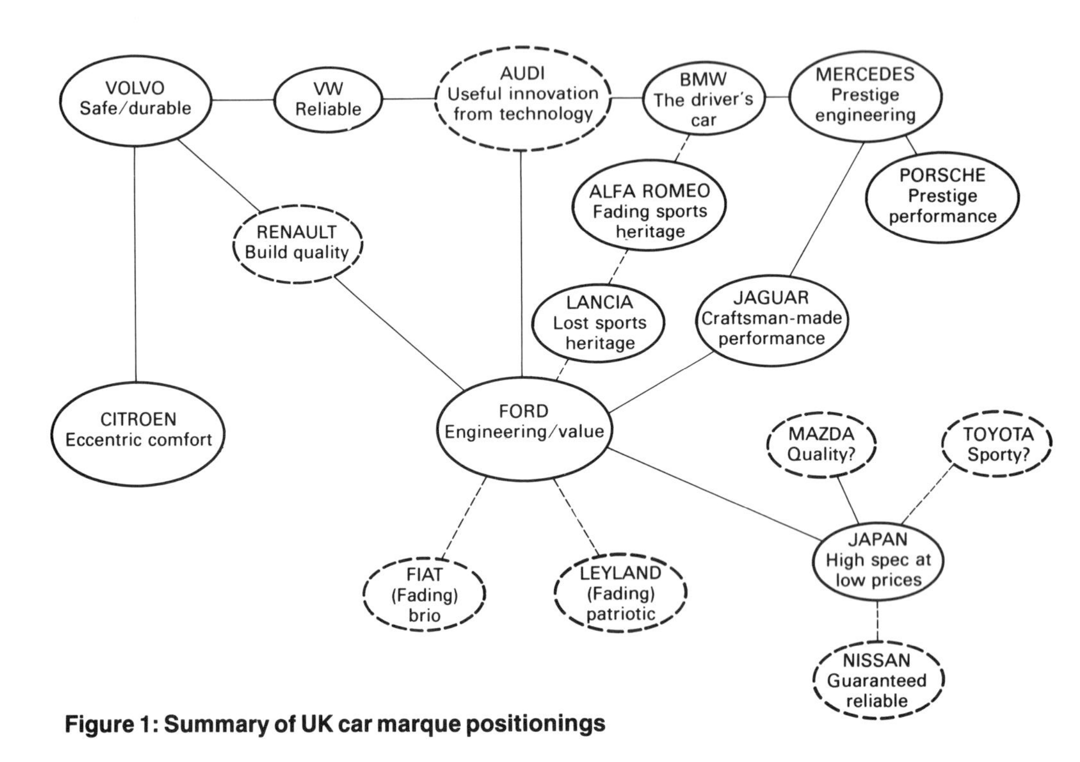

Figure 1: Summary of UK car marque positionings

In this context, the account planner should be a detective, hunting down this identity with flair and persistence. Flair will generate the theories and a persistent search through an eclectic range of client, trade, industry, government, continuous, *ad hoc*, quantitative and qualitative data will prove or disprove these theories.

Now this search for a positioning does not conform to scientific rules but it *is* a methodical craft, in that hard work and inspired design can produce stunning results. The knee-jerk 'let's do some groups' response is widely practised but far too narrow. However one goes about deciding where to 'put' a brand, there is usually a massive range of considerations to take into account, some of which are partly or even wholly removed from anything to do with the consumer. The main point of this chapter is to present guidelines on method and technique.

First, some basic principles, because unless some important 'ground rules' are agreed before the process of positioning analysis begins, many if not all of the recommendations you eventually make to account handlers, creative people and clients will have about as much practical effect as rearranging deckchairs on the *Titanic*.

FUNDAMENTAL PRINCIPLE 1

There is no point in deciding on a brand positioning in the first place if it seems unlikely that the consumer has a realistic chance of receiving and retaining the message. At the outset of being given a brand problem, remember that an advertised brand positioning can only be established with a visible execution built consistently over time on a realistic budget.

There are three key words in that observation:

VISIBLE Always resist the temptation to accept the first creative solution *just* because it appears to be on-strategy. Is it striking and memorable enough to work in the real world?

CONSISTENCY Always resist the temptation to change for change's sake when you take on a piece of business. If you inherit a strategy that is working, leave it alone.

REALISTIC Do a thorough analysis of competitive spends, the client's business objectives and what past history suggests it costs to achieve them in advertising terms.

It takes creativity, time and money to register a brand positioning via advertising. Often, the first task facing a planner is to persuade the account group of the need for time, and the client of the need for money.

FUNDAMENTAL PRINCIPLE 2

Do not confuse 'simple' with 'simplistic'. There may be more to a brand than its advertised identity, but people can remember one message seven times more easily than they can remember two. One of the central paradoxes of the advertising business is that while most marketing case histories are long and bitter, most advertising opportunities are short and sweet.

Over the years I have wasted many hours in meetings discussing nuances of difference and marginal 'changes of course' by 0.5 of a degree in the so-called 'fine tuning' process of positioning. The consumer (tracking studies usually show) ignores all this in favour of the hundreds of other things in his or her mind—all or most of which are probably more important in the stream of life than the client's brand.

This is hardly surprising considering the context within which advertisers operate: 30 seconds in an evening's entertainment, an opportunity to glimpse a poster at 35 miles per hour, an idle flick through a Sunday supplement, and so forth. Over-subtlety and over-complication in a brand positioning can lead to the same problems in the advertising of it. The consumer is unlikely to notice that the brand personality is now two years younger than it was in last year's planning document, if only because he has not read it. Equally, he probably does not have the time or interest to remember that the new Talbot Gaga V6i Cabriolet combines performance, reliability, economy and cat-like road-holding with sporty good looks yet room for a family of five.

In short, perhaps the main point about any brand positioning is that it should be quickly

Extra Strong Mints TV campaign

Mumm Champagne TV campaign

and easily understandable: Extra Strong Mints are *HOT*. Mumm Champagne is *PRECIOUS*. As their TV campaigns demonstrate (see above) this is easy to discern from the advertising.

FUNDAMENTAL PRINCIPLE 3

Bear in mind that the British public—on the whole an uncooperative and fairly intelligent bunch—are not always prepared to be squeezed into a target audience because it says they should in the Brand Plan. Do not be greedy; do not try to please all the people all the time.

Despite what many university lecturers, Tony Benn and Roy Hattersley want to believe, the average consumer is not a passive slave who can be manipulated according to scientifically predictable scales of reaction and behaviour by the all-powerful advertising Bogey Man. Defining the brand's *raison d'être* is infinitely preferable to an anarchic approach. But you cannot apply a slide rule to the process. Ultimately, a brand positioning is what you want the most common expression or the majority opinion of the brand to be in a given target audience. And it will not be universal, it cannot turn *everybody* on. No brand in this country has a monopoly; all have a niche. Whether that niche is 0.8 per cent or 80 per cent, there will always be some people who will just about never buy it. So decide who is in the viable target audience, and forget the rest.

INITIAL CONSIDERATIONS

Although one should accept the need for realism and simplicity, this will not stop a large and complex pile of data, amassed from various sources over several years, from landing upon your desk. To give the whole thing some kind of shape in one's mind on a first reading, it may be useful to keep an eye on the following key considerations with the accent on producing something distinctive, competitive and relevant at the end of the process.

1. WHAT CAN THE BRAND DELIVER? This means understanding everything from what the formulation actually produces as a result or end-benefit—and how this rates against the competition—right through in emotional terms to satisfaction believed by the consumer to be actually or potentially delivered by usage.

2. WHAT POSITIONINGS ARE 'OWNED' BY THE COMPETITION? That is to say, what claims, platforms and perceived end-benefits are overwhelmingly associated with a competitor's brand? It *is* possible in some cases to steal such a positioning for a brand: but you will need some pretty hard evidence of superior performance to do it, and usually you will be pushing water uphill if 'ownership' of the competitive position is long-established. A key purpose of analysing competitive 'ownership' is to try and isolate a relevant gap that has not previously been exploited.

3. IN ORDER TO KNOW WHETHER THE GAP IS WORTH FILLING AT ALL, you have to understand fully the consumer's *motivations*, and the criteria that he or she uses to distinguish between brands in the product field:

- What are the motivations in total?
- What usage and attitude evidence is there as to the relative importance of these motivations?

Of course, most motivation *hierarchies* are dynamic to some extent. Tar level was a relatively unimportant dimension in the cigarette market fifteen years ago. Clear positioning over that period, along with increasing social concern about smoking and health, has nevertheless made Silk Cut one of the major brands today. Not just social change, but advertising itself, can make a motivation more crucial. It is doubtful whether many parents cared about width fittings for their children's shoes before Clarks made it their brand property several decades ago; but largely because of it, Clarks are in an unassailable position in that sector.

Looking to the future, I would wager that the first major over-the-counter pharmaceutical, medicinal or specialist food brand to put some serious money behind a homoeopathic range of natural remedies will reap the benefit of what will probably be an explosion of interest in this area over the next decade.

What the brand can deliver, what the competition is claiming, what the consumer does (or might) want are not only key considerations; in many well-documented cases—even in surprisingly mature markets—they have helped both agency and client analysts to spot very quickly the right positioning to adopt. It is curious that the most obvious gap can be the one that everyone misses.

Collett Dickenson Pearce produced the famous 'refreshes the parts' lager campaign for Heineken from an excellent planning brief pointing out—in one paragraph devoid of waffle—that lager was refreshing, drinkers often wanted a refreshing change from bitter, and no other brand was claiming the ability to refresh.

Considering that refreshment was the top motivation for purchase in the usage and attitude study available at the time, it is staggering that nobody spotted this earlier. Equally fascinating is the fact that Skol rapidly attempted to claim that 'In test after test, Skol refreshes you best.' But to be first is all-important. While nobody now recalls the

"After 100,000 miles, I have to admit to a little ignition trouble."
Mr Court of Marple, Stockport, Cheshire is a testing judge of motor cars.
He covers the length and breadth of the British Isles, travelling for a pet food company.
Not surprisingly, his 2½ year-old Golf GL has seen every type of road, from motorway to mountain pass.
Each week, it has delivered him safely home again. Without fail. Without fuss.
Well, almost. The cigarette lighter acted up at around 80,000 miles.
That aside, "The tyres didn't even need changing until 100,000 miles, which speaks for the suspension."
To be fair to Mr Court, it says as much for his skilful driving. Long may it continue.
Meanwhile, we await with interest the impressions of Mrs Court.
She's just bought a Polo.
Golf
VW

Skol version, twelve years and an agency change later, the Heineken refreshes campaign continues.

While most drinkers want a lager to be refreshing, everyone wants a reliable car. Yet before DDB created the various 'reliability' campaigns for Volkswagen (VW) starting in the 1960s, nobody had followed the reliability strategy. As a brand, VW *does* deliver on this claim, but any one of several brands could have tried for it. A recent advertisement demonstrates how well. The claim continues to interest (see opposite) twenty years later.

What both these stories represent are examples of 'generic' positionings: the claim is not unique, but the combination of being first and consistent has strongly associated claim and brand in the consumer's mind. Perhaps the most famous example of all was 'Guinness is Good for You'.

I would argue that there are two other types of positioning apart from 'generic':

- The 'discriminatory'.
- The 'emotive'.

WHEN A PLATFORM IS BASED ON DISCRIMINATION, one is saying that the brand is qualitatively different from other brands in that it has a unique feature other brands do not have, or a considerably more effective performance than anything else. For many years, in fact, the USP or Unique Selling Point approach to branding-via-advertising dominated thought in the field. Being necessarily very 'formulation-led' as an approach, it cannot be an all-embracing method of positioning brands.

Nevertheless, it is perhaps the easiest type to establish with the consumer, and to this end brands have been *developed* and invented—let alone advertised—with the sole purpose of highlighting a USP element. Explicitly or implicitly, examples of this type of claim have included Duracell's 'Nothing looks like it or lasts like it' and Levis' work about rivets and stitching.

THE ADOPTION BY BRANDS OF 'EMOTIVE' OR 'INVISIBLE' PLATFORMS occurs in many developed markets where both the generic *and* discriminatory 'rational' performance claims have been covered by all the brands that exist; or straightforward and 'visible' performance is not appropriate to the ends of the consumer in the first place.

I have never done a hard-data audit of every brand positioning that exists. Nevertheless, it has struck me for some years now that this latter sort of positioning is by far the most common. On such a basis it has been claimed that Pernod will 'Free the spirit'; that Schweppes have a secret called 'Schh . . .'; that Castrol oil puts liquid engineering in your engine; that Heinz soup is 'The one you love'; and Grant's whisky is 'The stuff that drams are made of' (see page 66).

Many of the claims are based on a consumer desire merely to be associated—or seen—with the brand; others upon an abstract satisfaction from using it; others still upon a perception of the type of people (by implication, smart people) perceived to use the brand.

In my experience, it is also the type of positioning which, when expressed in a brief, has the most potential to produce boring advertising. This is not because of how much or little talent the creative team might have; mainly it reflects the fact that this sort of posi-

tioning has often allowed those *not* of a creative bent to insist on 'slice of life' as a means of executing it. Often 'clues' are inserted into the execution (actors' clothes, kitchen set, type of dog, number of children, etc.) to ensure 'identification', the theory presumably being that consumers enjoy watching mirror images of themselves, minus only their sense of humour.

There is a lesson for all of us in this: however 'exact' the advertisement may be in reflecting the brand position, creative people are paid to produce an original, involving and memorable way into the message so let them get on with it. The Levi's television work for 501 jeans is an excellent example of how style will triumph over cardboard consumer cut-outs in the execution of an emotive positioning.

SUMMING UP

We have thought about the key considerations to bear in mind and the types of positioning available. Perhaps an initial reading of the data, trade visits, a chat with R&D and four explanatory groups will produce one shining option that fits neatly into the frame. Or perhaps (as I always seem to find at this point) there are about ten possibilities, directions and avenues.

WHAT DO YOU DO NOW? Sometimes, it is what somebody else does that matters, for good or ill. That is to say, it has not exactly been unknown for a creative person to say at this point, 'I've got this idea, about . . .'. This is particularly possible during new business pitches when time is short, but it can happen on any project, and why not?

Instinct and intuition are responsible for many discoveries: often a theory is proved *after* the intuition has delivered the hypothesis. This was true of the major theories expounded by Columbus, Copernicus, Einstein and others of great genius. So if a creative group has an idea, set out to prove it right or wrong, but do not dismiss it on the basis of bad timing. To prove or disprove this and other potential solutions, however, a systematic approach is required. If you are to choose between the front-runners and the non-starters for a long-term identity, a checklist becomes an indispensable aid.

THE DETAILED CHECKLIST

Data itself will not necessarily take you anywhere unless you ask of it the right questions. Here are ten I always ask:

- How developed is the market? Is it as old as bread or new as micro-computers?
- In that context: what stage has the brand cycle reached—how many people have ever tried it? How long has it been available? And so forth . . .
- How well has it used the length of its cycle to capture a share of the market—what is its current position?
- What media have been or could be used to advertise it?
- At what target audience or audiences is it aimed: what class, age and sex? What are they like as personalities? How and where do they live? What *sort* of positionings are likely to turn them on?
- Assuming they are interested in the product, what do they want from it—what will they use it for?
- What appeals have been made to that potential user in the past, and what results did they achieve?
- If you believe a particular positioning should be adopted, what obstacles can you foresee in the future to its continued existence?
- If there is a corporate or core brand from which the brand you are working on emanates, how will your sub-brand's platform reflect back on the core—and vice-versa?
- Are there any legal and social implications from the brand course you would wish to recommend adopting?

Now these may seem at first sight to be random thoughts, but in reality they are not. In sequence, asking these questions covers:

- The background to the brand.
- The nature of it.
- How people learn about it.
- Who they are and what they use it for.
- What factors have influenced—and still might influence—their attitudes and behaviour in relation to it.
- The final two are 'checking' areas to ensure that the conclusions reached on a course of action do not cut across corporate, social and legal considerations affecting the client.

MARKET DEVELOPMENT

The age of a market can often expand or restrict the positioning opportunities: is, for instance, the market young enough to build a brand on *trialists* of the product field? If so, attaching a generic dimension to the brand is probably a preferable route. Even if the market has reached adolescence, there may still be such generic platforms unclaimed. If so, consider claiming one, as Heineken did in the early years of the lager market.

Alternatively, some adolescent—and even older—markets have identified a consumer need without ever really perfecting the technology required *fully* to satisfy that need. So ask yourself—is there a product improvement correcting such a generic product-field failure, which lends itself to discriminatory platform? For instance, in the soup market, early instant soups managed to perform well on 'hot drink' dimensions, but not so well on 'real soup taste' criteria. Knorr Quick Soup represented an improvement in formulation terms and adopted the 'first instant soup to taste like real soup' claim. In turn, Heinz's low-calorie soup could deliver more taste-enjoyment than most slimming products, and chose the direction of 'at last a soup that treats slimmers like human beings'. And of late, the Kitchen Classics range of pasteurized ready meals has been claiming 'convenience food that doesn't taste convenient' with notable success.

Finally, in older markets and sectors where the competing brands are largely of 'egalitarian' performance, as I mentioned earlier the emotive type of benefit is a more likely option. The Benson & Hedges cigarette brand has for many years used the emotional association with a gold pack as its platform, the more recent surrealist campaign representing merely a modernization of the old version which used headlines punning the word 'gold'.

BRAND LIFE CYCLE

The picture could be complicated—but in most cases will be clarified—by asking yourself pointed questions about your own brand's stage in its cycle. A recently launched brand in a newer market points fairly clearly to building associations with a generic market motivation; whereas a new brand in an old market may be there, again, to correct a performance deficiency or capitalize on an emotional benefit. Abbey Life, for instance, has been successful in capitalizing on the savings deficiences of older-style life assurance plans, as one of its lead-ads (see opposite, above) demonstrates in a no-nonsense way.

On the other hand, you may inherit a brand that has built a sizeable reputation by the time it reaches adolescence—and needs to add a discriminatory advantage to broaden its appeal. This was done for the Greek Tourist Office (see opposite, below) by stressing that it is one of the few destinations that has high 'shoulder month' temperatures coupled with uncrowded beaches. Indeed, one medium—posters—was entirely devoted to the job of lengthening the season.

As a brand gets older, however, inevitably newer brands come in to threaten its position, people try those newer brands, and 'fashionability' alone may lose the older brand some users.

In this case, the older brand is usually well known for one thing already, but this has less relevance as the nature of the market has changed over time. A new dimension has to be added to the identity which can appeal to the newer generation of users. An example of this was French wine, known for quality over many years but facing a threat

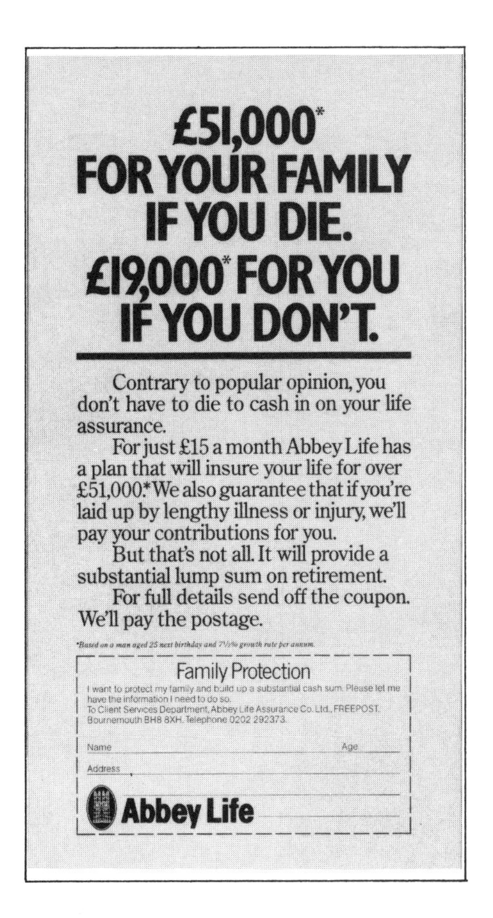
£51,000*
FOR YOUR FAMILY
IF YOU DIE.
£19,000* FOR YOU
IF YOU DON'T.
Contrary to popular opinion, you don't have to die to cash in on your life assurance.
For just £15 a month Abbey Life has a plan that will insure your life for over £51,000.* We also guarantee that if you're laid up by lengthy illness or injury, we'll pay your contributions for you.
But that's not all. It will provide a substantial lump sum on retirement.
For full details send off the coupon. We'll pay the postage.
*Based on a man aged 25 next birthday and 7½% growth rate per annum.
Family Protection
I want to protect my family and build up a substantial cash sum. Please let me have the information I need to do so.
To Client Services Department, Abbey Life Assurance Co. Ltd., FREEPOST, Bournemouth BH8 8XH. Telephone 0202 292373.
Name
Age
Address
Abbey Life

Visit the Gods. With fewer mortals.
GREECE
In the spring.
Spring temperatures in Greece. March 63° April 68° May 75°

Imagine the flavour of the
French countryside, in a wine glass.
Vin de Pays. The everyday
wine of France.
Make friends
with the wines
of France.

from the better known and less 'frightening' brands of German wine. Marcel Marceau's invitation to 'make friends' with French wine, and his mimes to make regions more familiar, have thus broadened the brand's image (see opposite).

Finally, a brand may literally be ancient, possibly operating in a dying or increasingly old-fashioned area of social behaviour, probably appealing to a shrinking target audience. Here, its life can be lengthened—holding real sales steady or slowing the decline—by capturing an increasingly larger share of remaining users with emotive reassurance. The Ovaltine drink, and the nostalgic advertising TBWA made to support it, probably represents as good an example of this as you will find.

MARKET SHARE

Closely connected with stage in the brand cycle is the *size or nature of business* position it has actually achieved in the market during that cycle. Is it on a rising trend from a small base, for instance? If so, there is a likelihood that it has a discriminatory appeal and this needs to be communicated to an ever wider audience. On the other hand, a brand's minority share may reflect a specialized usage; or the minority share may be based on premium price. This will lead naturally to some form of *justification* of the premium—either on a performance or emotive basis, or perhaps both.

Alternatively, the brand may be larger, find itself in second place after a number of years, but still up against the definitive brand that leads the market. In which case, you can opt to score discriminator points against that brand leader. In the car-hire market, for instance, Avis attacked the brand leader Hertz on the 'We're No. 2, therefore we have to try harder' platform; BCal's 'We never forget you have a choice' is another example; or alternatively, you could *reach* brand leadership by stressing emotive quality against own-label products where they are important—Robinson's soft drinks used the Wimbledon association and the line 'Anything else just isn't tennis' towards this end.

If the subject of your endeavours *is* brand leader, then think carefully before meddling with it: it has not got there for nothing, so probably you should aggressively ask yourself 'give me one good reason why I should change things'. Sometimes, however, there may be the option to re-express (in modern terms) or reinforce the discriminatory positioning that made it brand leader in the first place, but has perhaps been forgotten or neglected as an advertising point in previous years.

Dealing with a brand leader in a newer market also begs the same innately conservative question—'how did we get here, and why don't we just keep going?'—which will probably lead in turn to the conclusion (unless the client bolts on a clear product improvement) that you should stay close to the benefit you have.

MEDIA USE

Moving to media, mass-market products can afford television, minority products (unless they go for TV-AM or Channel 4) often cannot. In turn, some brands need—perhaps due to seasonality—one quick burst of TV and posters a year (for instance, Jif lemon juice and Pancake Day) others a continuous presence in the up-market or specialist press.

However, I have always felt that the rational or emotional nature of a brand claim should be influenced to some extent by the realistic media choices that are open to it; if only because all media are limited in length, style or type of message they can physically communicate. If, for market and target group reasons, it is essential to be in one or other medium, then the positioning should take account of the media limitations:

- Television is ideal for USP demonstration and 'mood' communication of emotive platforms.
- Mono press highlights key performance advantages in detail, or special offers.
- Colour press offers well-produced colour for emotional effect and carefully-written copy to tell a story.
- Posters can only really carry out a crisp, summary positioning.
- Radio produces, in my experience, its best results by providing tactical, informative promotional advertising that reflects the strategic platform.

TARGET AUDIENCE

The media used in turn relates closely (or should) to the type of audience. Is it a highly intelligent, introspective, 'self-image-as-rational-person' audience? (Good food costs less at Sainsbury's). Or more outgoing, emotional, family-oriented? (Milk's gotta lotta bottle).

Education/intelligence, social background/age and personality/psychographic factors will obviously affect whether technical knowledge or total ignorance, rationality or emotion, slick slogans or lengthy product explanations form the basis of the positioning. In recent years, Montagu Unit Trust Management has used the City cartoonist Calman to animate a television commercial aimed at the brokers and sophisticated investors who most appreciate Calman's specialism in City-biased subjects.

In short, ask yourself: this is my claim—given the nature of the audience, will they believe it, understand it or be interested in it? The point is that the tone and style of any positioning is bound to be crucially affected by what the product field in general is used for, and by whom. Beware, however, of the kind of shibboleths that can mythically develop over time and thus restrict creative execution unnecessarily. Too often, for instance, a target group's rational *self*-image is taken far too literally.

By this stage, several potential positionings may well have presented themselves, and as a rule, I find that until this point the list of possible platforms may still be quite long. The final considerations discussed below tend naturally to narrow the possibilities.

HISTORY OF PREVIOUS ENDEAVOURS

A thorough look at what has been tried in the past, for instance, often demonstrates the old adage that there is nothing new under the sun. Look through all the old reels, tear-sheet clippings of previous years; ask the older members of staff for their memories; and gather as much data as you can about what was achieved historically. Usually, this throws up the 'we tried that and it failed' syndrome, but occasionally, long-forgotten propositions may gain a new relevance via some recent quirk in the market.

Primarily, however, a cross-check between positionings historically followed and the latest U&A study is useful in that it may identify a point of relevance *never* used before.

POTENTIAL FOR COMPETITIVE RETALIATION

Next, look at your platform alternatives and gauge how safe they might be in the face of the future's often cruel fate. Can your positioning be questioned—or worse still, ridiculed—by the competition in their advertising? Of all the questions to ask, this must be one of the most fundamental. Nothing works harder than a strong, branded idea *that has remained unchanged for a long period of time.* It is therefore of central relevance to a strategist to check that the claim is neither the sort of trite 'weasel' that can be blown apart by knocking copy, nor a formulation advantage that can be easily matched and/or is unpatentable.

To claim generic things like 'refreshment' or 'goodness' is normally safe: *if* the product delivers on it to a discernible degree, or has no skeletons in its cupboard. But the world is littered with brands that took an ill-advised stance and then paid for it. For many years, the Philips electrical brand ran the base-line 'Simply Years Ahead'. That—whatever the real R&D situation may have been—was often the opposite of what the consumer observed in their product range. In another example, Hertz at one time claimed they were 'No. 1 in UK car hire'. Godfrey Davis, who had more outlets and a larger fleet, chose simply to run the Hertz line in advertisements with the words 'Oh no they're not' underneath.

Perhaps one of the more amusing examples in recent years was the British Rail claim that 'This is the Age of the Train'. In terms of the service available, and the travel-mode alternatives, most private and business travellers felt it certainly was not. The 'advance claim' is fine if there are signs of rapid improvement—indeed, it can of itself favourably influence staff behaviour.

When the BR claim first appeared, however, British Airways' agency FCB were quick off the mark. They took posters near or next to 'This is the Age of the Train' hoardings wherever possible, and ran 'This is the Time of the Plane'. Most people got the point. 'We're getting there', JWT's line for British Rail at the time of writing, is a more clever, credible and sympathetic positioning—especially as this time the product *is* beginning, bit by bit, to deliver on the claim.

CORE BRAND CONSIDERATIONS

Many brands are in reality a sub-brand of an overall corporate entity. It is therefore always worthwhile auditing what the original 'core' brand stands for. Positively, it can be used to enhance or 'rub off' on the sub-brand. Negatively, it is unwise to claim anything for the sub-brand that is out of keeping with the core: 'rub off' works both ways.

Certainly, it can become deliberate policy to do something 'atypical' with a sub-brand *in order to* change perceptions of the core manufacturer. But as often as not, the new brand has been developed by the client in the first place with this end in mind. An example of this in the car market would be the launch of Fuego from Renault: in other words, first and foremost a product strategy behind which the advertising naturally fell into place. In the middle-market coupé sector, it forced many consumers to revise their opinion of the core 'Renault' marque as making only 'sensible' cars.

It is more common on the whole for sub-brands to complement, rather than jar with, the parent brand. When Clarks launched the Clarksport brand in the late 1970s, for instance, they did so with a unique 'foot health' strategy to justify premium price. This reflected their reputation for foot health developed, in the children's sector of the market, for many years previous to the Clarksport launch.

SOCIAL AND LEGAL IMPLICATIONS

There are any number of social, professional, legal and industry self-disciplinary factors that can reduce a positioning's relevance, or even make it necessary to reject it entirely.

The most obvious market where this occurs is tobacco, but there are many others. The brewing industry is one where there are ASA/CAP guidelines as well as an industry body, the Brewers Society, that has to be taken into account. In turn, many public companies across a number of product fields have to gauge City reactions to the claims and general tone in their advertising. And similarly, most larger client companies have a union element to take into account. If that union deals with the public on behalf of the brand, the union reaction becomes of paramount importance. Anybody who has ever tried to develop a positioning for a brand of clearing bank or airline will know that this usually involves a claim about staff behaviour: 'We'll take more care of you' and so forth. The trade union—or whoever acts on behalf of the staff—will be centrally interested in what is likely to be asked of them. It is not uncommon for them to apply pressure, formally and informally, if they feel they cannot live up to the claim—as they usually do in my experience.

In the current political climate, it could be argued that union power has been reduced in such matters. While this is possibly true, one social group whose power will only ever increase is that which houses politicians and civil servants.

Large areas of industry are still directly or indirectly nationalized, and the Commons/Whitehall reaction is therefore crucially relevant in a remarkably broad range of manufacturing, service, institutional and administrative areas. Some examples—such as police and army recruitment—are obvious, others less so. I once achieved the dubious double of having a local Gas Board positioning proposal turned down (a) because the Union would not wear it and (b) Mrs Thatcher would not like it.

In the end, we live in a far from perfect world, and this should be recognized by those who are about to brief creative people, and use up their valuable time, to communicate a positioning that, for political reasons, is unlikely to ever see the light of day as a message in the media.

AD HOC PROPOSITION TESTING

Having been right through the checklist—and probably during the process having already conducted some qualitative research to get a personal 'feel' for consumer attitudes—there is still usually room for doubt about the best positioning. Further qualitative research will nearly always be useful at this stage.

This process is often referred to as 'concept testing' but, personally, I always think of a concept as—at least to some extent—a creative idea. More accurately, I believe at this stage you are in the business of testing a *proposition* or a claim: and this presents you with a difficulty. Because somehow you have to get a clear reading as to the appeal of the positioning, rather than the method of communicating it.

My belief is that, first and foremost, you have to separate the claim from the execution. I prefer at this stage not to confuse the issue with a 'rough ad' expression. This could easily bias the response and, no matter how many times you tell respondents in a group that such a presentation is *not* an advertisement, they are still likely to judge it as one.

In short: strive for a neutral rendition of the proposition. How do you do this? Basically, by typing a statement and projecting it on to a screen or 'blowing up' the typed statement on to cardboard as a prompt. Having done this, and exposed it to reactions in a group discussion; however, you must still remember that the consumer is not a marketing consultant. I still cringe every time I attend a group and the psychologist says 'Here's an idea that such-and-such a manufacturer has had about what such-and-such a brand is or does—what do you think of it?' The point of the exercise is indeed to work out which alternative platform seems the most relevant and motivating but you are in difficulties the minute consumers realize they have the power to choose between alternatives. This may sound a derogatory—perhaps even fascist—thing to say, but remember we are observing and discussing relative levels of interest in these alternatives, *not* asking consumers to make strategic decisions *for* us.

The key to it all is to disguise, firstly, that the different statements are indeed alternatives; and secondly, that they are still on the drawing board. Awareness by respondents of either or both of these facts puts them (often willingly) into the position of guru—'I don't think that'll work' or 'People wouldn't be interested in that', and so forth. But it is their personal needs, rather than their self-taught marketing opinions, you want.

So: consider using projective techniques to establish those personal needs as clearly as possible, to make the propositions you present 'real'.

There are many ways you can use such techniques. My two personal favourites are to present the propositions as 'quotes from other respondents', the ubiquitous 'some people I was talking to last week' and their 'views' of a particular brand, within which the claim or platform is stated. Or to mock up each proposition as an article from a newspaper—'here you can see it has been reported in this magazine that such-and-such a brand is claiming such-and-such a thing'—and so forth. (This latter technique is particularly apposite to new product positioning research.)

Effectively, having read and interpreted the response from such qualitative work, the analysis process is now at an end. You may still find that two alternatives seem equally appealing. In which case—and here again I perhaps commit heresy—talk to the creative and marketing directors. Which one does the former think most likely to produce the most competitive advertising execution? And which does the latter think can be most comprehensively demonstrated by the brand?

Such a course of action is, of course, not scientific; but as I noted at the outset, advertising is not a science. When all else fails to produce a clear answer, rely on the judgement, common sense and experience of those around you.

CONCLUSIONS

A positioning or identity is an essential prerequisite of survival and profitability for the owner of a brand or brands. Every year, the competition for identity and *raison d'être* hots up, rendering certain procedures mandatory for those who wish to remain in contention.

Visibility, realism and consistency in the advertising behind such a positioning are particularly crucial. Clarity is vital in the modern high-noise media environment. And disciplined identification of the niche or segment likely to be turned on to the positioning is equally important.

Much of commercial communication in general, and account planning in particular, involves the reduction of complexity to simplicity. In this context, the three key considerations are:

- What can the brand deliver?
- What are the competition up to?
- What does the consumer want?

There are, in turn, three basic types of positioning: *generic*, *discriminatory* and *emotive*. The last of these is probably by far the most common; to discover which is likely to work best for your brand in your market, there is a checklist one can work through. It is not foolproof and does not claim to be scientific, but it has the twin advantages of being both thorough, and conducive to narrowing the options generated by inspiration and hypothesis. However, even this process may not produce a definite solution. At this point, the gut feel or insight of senior creative and client personnel should never be ignored. Indeed, it is a foolish planner who has not carried both the writers (of the advertisement and the cheque) with him throughout the analysis process.

5 *Creative briefing*

Damian O'Malley

WHY WE HAVE CREATIVE BRIEFINGS

Reading through this book so far, you could be forgiven for thinking that you were the only person who worked in the agency. Of course you are not and this chapter is concerned with the way you interact with the most important department in the agency, the creative department.

Creatives are crucial to advertising agencies because they actually write the advertisements. What, you may sometimes have wondered, are we doing here at all? Why do creatives not deal direct with clients? There are several different reasons, some obvious, some unprintable, but the answer which most concerns us runs as follows.

Producing effective advertising is difficult, complex and demanding. Successful agencies use two contrasting styles of problem-solving in the search for effective advertising. One style is what psychologists call 'convergent thinking', the process of drawing deductive and logical conclusions from information. The second style is called 'divergent thinking'; it is lateral, moves from particular instances to generalizations, and there are no right or wrong answers. Advertising agencies are set up in a way which apparently distinguishes between these different thinking styles. Convergent style thinking is used by planners and account handlers to distill the essence of a problem and decide which particular piece of information or imagery will change consumer behaviour. Divergent style thinking is used by creative departments to devise advertising which will present that information or imagery in fresh new ways to catch the attention and excite interest in the proposition.

The creative briefing is the point at which one group of problem-solvers hands on the fruits of their labours to the next group.

This is a reasonable working explanation. It is perhaps unfortunate that people get identified with one thinking style or another, but this is a pervasive part of our culture, reinforced, for example, by our tertiary education system. One of the main themes of this chapter will be, however, that the more imaginatively, i.e. creatively, you approach the task of creative briefing the better and more effective the end results will be.

THE FUNCTION OF CREATIVE BRIEFING

We need to define some terms here. The 'creative briefing' is the meeting at which the creative team or teams are told what is required of them to solve a particular advertising task. The 'creative brief' generally circulated after that meeting is a piece of paper which contains all the essential information that the creative teams will need. In practice, the process of 'creative briefing' may involve several meetings, some formal, some just 'chats', but the actual briefing meeting is generally where the process is begun and we will concentrate on this meeting and the creative brief itself.

Creative briefing is the process by which the account team tell the creative team what it is they need to know to solve an advertising problem. This is, at bottom:

- Who it is they have to talk to and what it is they have to say to them to achieve the required behavioural shift.

Remembering, however, that the skill of the creative department is divergent thinking, and that you want to them to come up with fresh ideas, the creative briefing process has two further functions:

- It seeks to inspire creatives and give them an impetus towards the final solution.
- It must act as a means of quality control.

Creative people's understandable desire to embrace novel solutions to problems sometimes blinds them to the fact that a particular solution is not appropriate, or does not fulfil the requirements of the brief. In the interests of effective advertising, the account group may have to turn down the work if it is not on brief.

We can label these three functions of the creative briefing 'task definition', 'inspiration' and 'quality control'. As Figure 1 illustrates, the creative brief has a hand in all three, though not equally effectively. The creative briefing meeting has little use as quality control tool given the fallibility of human memory, but is vitally important, as we shall see, for inspiring creative teams.

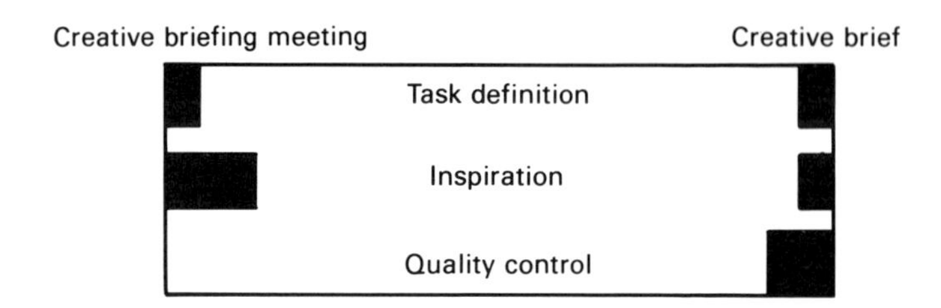

Figure 1: Function and utility

WHAT CREATIVE PEOPLE ARE LIKE

In all important respects creative people are just like anyone else: this means that they are lazy, get bored easily, have hangovers, periods, headaches, get confused easily, feel inadequate and defensive sometimes, are ambitious and often overworked.

You may be inclined to disagree. Surely, you may ask, creative people are more rude, aggressive and sullen than I am, they yawn and make stupid remarks in my briefings, they try to put me down.

This is how creative people may seem to you if you only ever meet them at formal internal meetings, but then imagine how clients and agency people must look to Nielsen presenters. Here I am a Nielsen presenter and I have spent hours drawing coloured lines on the overheads and still people yawn in my presentations. Some people look at their watches and doodle on their pads, some talk while I'm presenting, some even fall asleep!

To me clients seem rude, dull people, unable to respond to my enthusiasm for my charts on rate of sale and distribution.

You have to make sure that you are not like a Nielsen presenter as far as your creative teams are concerned. A relative stranger turning up at infrequent intervals and transmitting barely intelligible information. Get to know your creative teams so that you already have a relationship established when you come to brief them. You will find that you do actually have a lot in common. You go to the same movies, watch the same television, lust after the same men/women, witness the same travesties of justice in client meetings and awards ceremonies, hanker after similar cars, and so on.

Talk to them about their experiences of creative briefing, what they feel are good briefs, what they find unhelpful. This should not necessarily change the content of your briefs, just the way that you present them. It will, however, invariably improve the warmth with which they are received by your creative teams.

WHAT CREATIVE PEOPLE WANT FROM A CREATIVE BRIEF

When writing advertisements creatives often start by looking for a nugget of information, a spark, around which to build their idea. The spark can come from the product itself, the target market, the imagery of the brand or anywhere at all. The more such nuggets that your brief contains, the more helpful it will be. Moreover, the more concrete and vivid your expression of the ideas in your brief the more helpful it will be.

This was illustrated in a recent role reversal exercise run by the Account Planning Group in which delegates were required to spend some of the time as an account group writing a creative brief and briefing a creative team and the rest of the time as a creative team receiving a brief and writing work to it.

The syndicates were working on two problems—a sherry and a soft drink, and the advertising propositions produced by the four groups were as follows (Table 1).

Table 1

	Soft Drink	Sherry
1 Concrete	'Red and dangerous'	'The authentic sherry'
2 Abstract	'For kids who know their way around'	'A taste for the way you are today'

The syndicates who had to produce work to the two abstract briefs invariably found it hard to get started, hard to find their nugget, whereas the syndicates who were given the concrete propositions knew immediately where to start.

In this instance, and this is often the case, the most concrete propositions stemmed from the products themselves. This is not to say that good advertisements can only be written around product-based propositions, this is plainly not the case. We would submit, however, that if your brief is based on an image or lifestyle type of proposition both you and the creative department have to work much harder to glean concrete nuggets around which to build good advertisements. The later section on *Advertising proposition* (see page 83 ff.) develops this point.

SUMMARY

The previous four sections have outlined some general themes about the subject and it is worth summarizing these before we move on:

- The need for creative briefing has arisen *ipso facto* from the fact that we have different departments in the agency.
- Creative people are not 'different' types of people; they simply have a different job to do.
- We have drawn a distinction between the creative briefing meeting and the creative brief.
- We have asserted that creative briefing has three functions: task definition, inspiration and quality control. The creative brief makes an important contribution to all three; the creative briefing meeting has no role in quality control, but is very important for inspiration.
- By and large creative people are looking for nuggets of information to build advertising ideas around. Rather like an oyster needs a grain of sand to make a pearl.

THE CREATIVE BRIEF

We will start with a brief overview of the brief, then look at the different sections of the brief in more detail.

The sections of the brief (Figure 2) roughly mirror the three functions that we have already mentioned.

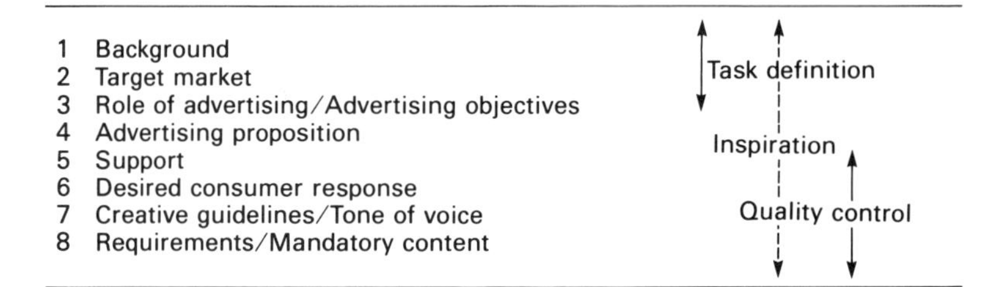

Figure 2: Typical sections of a creative briefing

The first three sections are principally concerned with 'task definition'. Why are we doing this advertising, what client problem are we helping to solve, who are we talking to in this advertising, what do they already know, think or feel about our product, what is the advertising trying to affect?

The next two sections are principally concerned with 'inspiration'. What is my grain of sand, my jumping-off point, what is the one point that if communicated will achieve my desired advertising objective, what evidence do we have to convince consumers? (As the dotted line suggests, creatives can—and often do—get inspiration from different sections of the brief than the ones you intended; sometimes this is a problem, sometimes it is not, and we will cover this in more detail later.)

The last three sections are principally concerned with 'quality control'. What should consumers think when they see this advertising, what sort of advertising should this be, what sort of advertising has worked well in the past, what information must be included in the advertisement, what media are we using, what space sizes, what time lengths, how many advertisements do we need, what production budget do we have?

When writing a brief we always have to create a balance between there being enough information, that creatives know what they are supposed to be doing, believe in what they are doing and have enough ammunition to actually write an advertisement, and there being so much information that they get confused, or, worse, are being asked to sort out their own communication priorities (which means that they are wasting their time doing your job for you).

In practice there are two areas—target market and support—where it is hard to give too much information; the rest should be the minimum possible.

We are now going to study each area in more detail. These sections and headings would gain wide consensus in the industry though individual agencies may have their own preferred headings; some agencies also have briefing formats and there is a section devoted to formats later in the chapter. There are some instances where you may wish to deviate from this format completely and we have included another section on *Exceptions and special cases*.

A final point about language and style. When writing briefs, please try to make them 'style-free'. In other words, write simple plain English: one thought to a sentence, no complex sub-clauses, no long words, active not passive voice, no redundant superlatives. If, when you have written something, you can read it out loud without stumbling or wincing then it is probably okay.

THE SECTIONS OF A CREATIVE BRIEF

1 BACKGROUND/INTRODUCTION/MARKET BACKGROUND

The function of the introduction is to give your creatives the information they need to understand and believe in the rest of the brief. Do not try to be comprehensive; give just the basic information.

Avoid the temptation to show off your knowledge of a particular market but do make sure that you are not assuming knowledge of, or an understanding of, jargon which your creative people may not have. If it is important that your audience grasp a certain concept to follow the rest of the brief then explain it fully; if it is not important then leave it out. Complex issues which nevertheless do need to be understood can be explained at length in an appendix. If the introduction is too long then creatives may not bother ploughing through to the end of it.

Do not copy marketing objectives and strategies out of a brand book; tailor your description of the market to the matter in hand. For example, if the brief is concerned with changing attitudes in a market then talk about the dynamics which underpin the market. Imagine that you are briefing a general on the state of a battle. If you are introducing a new brand to a market, picture the market as a map which you are using to describe the whereabouts of a particular town. Make the background as vivid and interesting as possible.

Your creative teams may have had previous experience of a market, or may themselves be consumers in a market and therefore have opinions about the products or brands in it. Though this may not affect what you write down in the brief it may lead to problems when actually briefing. It is as well to find out what opinions your creative people may have and anticipate conflicts or misunderstandings, making sure that you are clear in your own mind that your point of view is correct and that it is well defended.

One aspect of the market background that creatives are always interested in is what other advertising is going on in a market, what it is that they have to be different to and stand out from. Again, a full discussion of this may have to be relegated to the briefing or an appendix, although in some markets the advertising market is the only market that counts (see page 83 ff. under *Advertising proposition*).

The introduction is an appetizer. Make it interesting to whet the appetites of the creatives for the advertising struggle which lies ahead.

2 TARGET MARKET

There is no such thing as an 'average' person; averages are an invention of statistics. Statistical descriptions of the target market are very useful for understanding market trends, in defining the role of advertising and in intermedia decisions. However, when it comes to the advertisement itself, we have to appeal to the individuals who make up those statistics. Advertising is a private transaction between the individual consumer and the advertiser. It is only by influencing individuals that we can effect any change in a market place.

It follows from this that what creative people find most helpful is a vivid description of the types of individual to whom their advertising will be directed. Indeed many creatives actually like to picture someone in their mind's eye to whom they are addressing their advertisement.

This description of the key individuals should go much further than simple generalities. An average creative person can probably intuit the lifestyle of a 45-year-old housewife at least as well as you can (after all they had mothers too). Where you can help them is by describing, in detail, how your target market uses a particular group of products:

- What they know or think they know about a particular product category.
- How they feel about it.
- How interested they are in it.
- How they distinguish between different products.
- When they would use one rather than another and why.

And so on.

As advertising by and large works by changing what people know, think or feel about a product, the role for advertising will almost certainly be implicit in this section.

The target market definition is often a rich source of nuggets for creative people. Indeed, many advertising tasks are defined as one of identifying the brand with a particular target group. Consequently, we should aim to give creative people as much information as we can.

3 ADVERTISING OBJECTIVES/ROLE OF ADVERTISING

It is not the function of this chapter to tell you how to arrive at your advertising objectives. Suffice to say that there are different jobs that advertising can do, jobs it does well and jobs that it does badly. The creative brief needs to be explicit about what job the creatives are being asked to do: i.e. what we hope that this advertising will achieve.

Often, the role of advertising—or possible roles of advertising—will be obvious on reading the first two sections of the brief (if they are not then maybe you should think about rewriting them). In this section, however, we formally state what they are so that there can be no possible confusion. The list of objectives should be kept short, explicit and positively expressed; objectives which are self-evident ('to create impact') can be left out.

The advertising objectives are what we want to achieve; the advertising strategy is how we intend to achieve our objectives. In practice, the strategy is often obvious from the objectives. If it is not, it is made explicit by the advertising proposition. As the brief is an internal document rather than for client consumption in most instances a formal statement of the advertising strategy is unnecessary.

4 ADVERTISING PROPOSITION/BRAND PROMISE/POSITIONING STATEMENT

This section deserves a book in its own right. The whole advertising process hinges around this short sentence. Into it we must distill our learning about a brand in its market, about consumer behaviour and about advertising. From it must spring a fresh and original advertising idea.

Consumers can differentiate between brands in a market in three different ways:

- They can make decisions based on known factual product differences. Brand X is cheaper than Brand Y, Brand Z is the only one that has a strawberry flavour, and so on.
- Consumers can think that they perceive product differences even if in truth there are no real differences. These perceived differences between brands may arise because of historical product differences which have now disappeared, or because of advertising. Ironically consumers often ignore genuine product performance differences when choosing a brand in favour of perceived product differences; this is the sad fate of many second brands in a market!
- On the basis of how they feel about a brand, they may underpin this with product-based rationalizations but often consumers' prime reason for buying a particular brand is that the imagery of this brand fits better with their self-perception than any other. 'This perfume feels just right for me'; 'I'm getting too old to drive cars like that'.

When choosing an advertising proposition for your brand you need to know the chief way (or ways) that people use to discriminate between products in a particular market.

Surprisingly, there are fewer and fewer markets in which sustainable genuine product differences are available to advertisers to work with. In many markets what real product differences there are, are only available to a few brands (only one product can be the biggest, only one the cheapest, only one the fastest, etc.). If you have a sustainable and genuine product difference which the consumer finds motivating then you should use it in your advertising. If this is the case then the proposition practically writes itself. For example, 'Brand X is the cheapest brand in the market'.

Just because your brand does *not* have a genuine or sustainable product difference does not mean that we should not talk about product values in the proposition. If consumers believe that there *are* product differences even where none exist, then it is a good idea to appropriate a performance-based area of the market and try to make it your own. This is the classic marketing strategy of adding value, imbuing your brand with strength, flavour, reliability, care of manufacture, or whatever is credible and motivating.

Even if we cannot say that our brand is the cheapest in the market we can still say that it is cheap. Even if our brand is not cheap but we believe that price motivation is important, we can say that 'Brand X is good value for money'.

In many markets there are no actual or perceived product differences at all or the ones that exist are impossible for consumers to discern, or are trivial and not motivating to consumers. In this instance, you have to concentrate on building motivating imagery for the brand. Either identify feelings which consumers have about a brand and which may help to discriminate it from other brands (Brand X is more traditional) or present a brand to a particular group of consumers as a brand which is specifically for people like them (Brand X is for people who do not like fuss, Brand Z is for posh people).

Even in the latter case we must still be specific in the proposition about what it is in the brand that consumers are being asked to identify with.'The brand for people like you' is not enough.

In one or two markets, such as the lager market, advertising is used by consumers to discriminate between brands. Good advertising always forms part of a brand's personality, but there are as yet very few examples where all that a brand has to offer is its advertising. In markets where products are all the same, however, and where all conceivable product and emotional needs are already being catered for by the brands in the market this phenomenon will occur. As it becomes more common we will need to pay more systematic attention to the different styles of advertising that exist in a market and what these styles (form as opposed to content) communicate to consumers.

This analysis will help you to decide what sort of proposition you need, whether it should be purely factual, whether it should seek to influence what people believe about a brand or what they feel about a brand or in some rare instances about its advertising. Having decided what sort of proposition you need, here are some things you can do to help you find the actual proposition:

THE PRODUCT ITSELF Look at it, feel it, use it, talk about it with your mum and your friends. Visit the factory. Production people are often a mine of information.

- How is it made/how many quality control checks does it have?
- How long have they been making it?
- What is in it?
- Where do the ingredients come from?
- Who buys them?
- How are they bought?
- Where can you buy it?

- Is it exclusive?
- Who designed it?
- How is it packaged?

THE PRODUCT IN USE Some products, such as cars, jewellery and perfume, help define a person's 'lifestyle', both to themselves and to others; most products do not. As most people do not define their lifestyle in terms of, for example, which brand of bleach they use, they might find it hard to talk about it in depth in a group discussion.

- Get them to actually use the product in front of you and tell you what they think of it.
- Get people to compare products in product clinics.
- Go shopping with people and find out what goes through their mind when they are making a buying decision.

USER IMAGERY Here again, the right questions will tell you all you need to know:

- Who buys the product?
- What else do they buy?
- Where do they live?
- What sort of people are they?
- Does anyone famous use the product?
- Do most people buy it, or only a few?
- Do experts buy it?
- Can anyone buy it?
- Do people buy it for themselves as a treat, for sharing or as a gift?

MISCELLANEOUS To make sure you have covered every angle:

- Talk to an expert, a journalist.
- Read *Which* magazine.
- What would happen if this product did not exist anymore?
- What do other people say in their advertising?
- How do they advertise it abroad?
- Is it newsworthy or topical?

Brainstorm!

Once you have a proposition you should try to express it in a way which will propel your creative team towards a solution. A story will help illustrate what we mean.

You are no doubt familiar with the frescoes on the ceiling of the Sistine Chapel. They are one of the greatest works of art of all time, painted by the Renaissance genius, Michelangelo. We can imagine the briefs he might have been given for this work by his client, Pope Julius II, or the Pope's account man, Cardinal Alidosi.

(a) 'Please paint the ceiling.'

There is no doubt that this is what Michelangelo was being asked to do but this brief gives him no hint as to what the solution to the request might be. It leaves all the decisions and thinking to the artist before he can put paint to plaster.

(b) 'Please paint the ceiling using red, green and yellow paint.'

This brief is worse. Not only does it still not tell him what to paint, it gives him a number of restrictions without justification; restrictions which will inevitably prove irksome and which will distract him from his main task.

(c) 'We have got terrible problems with damp and cracks in the ceiling and we would be ever so grateful if you could just cover it up for us.'

This is much worse. It *still* does not tell him what to do, and it gives him irrelevant and depressing information which implies that no one is interested in what he paints because it will not be long before the ceiling falls in anyway. How much effort is he likely to put into it?

(d) 'Please paint biblical scenes on the ceiling incorporating some or all of the following: God, Adam, Angels, cupids, devils and saints'.

Better; now they are beginning to give Michelangelo a steer. They have not given him the full picture yet (if you will pardon the pun) but at least he knows the important elements. This is the sort of brief that most of us would have given. It contains everything the creatives need to know but it does not go that step beyond, towards an idea, towards a solution.

Here is the brief which Michelangelo was actually given, more or less . . .

'Please paint our ceiling, for the greater glory of God and as an inspiration and lesson to his people. Frescoes which depict the creation of the world, the Fall, mankind's degradation by sin, the divine wrath of the deluge and the preservation of Noah and his family'.

Now he knows what to do—and is inspired by the importance of the project—he can devote his attention to executing the detail of the brief in the best way he knows.

Words are like little bombs: the right ones can explode inside us demanding an original and exciting solution instead of a mediocre pedestrian one.

Always work very, very hard to find the right proposition and then even harder to find the words which express it in the least ambigious and most exciting way.

5 SUPPORT/REASON WHY

This section contains all the evidence which we have for our proposition. It provides a rich source of creative nuggets and it is legitimate to put in anything which could be used in an advertisement to demonstrate or communicate the proposition.

It will tend to include some or all of the following:

- Product information.
- Comparative product information.
- Product test results.
- Consumer perceptions of this and competing brands.

As well as simply listing points, the support section should explain why the points are significant (unless it is obvious). The richer and more dynamic the support section, the more the creatives have to work with and the easier it is for them to concentrate on producing original ideas.

If the support points are very complex or lengthy then it may be best to relegate them to an appendix, leaving a summary of them in the body of the brief. This gives the readers the choice of when and how deeply they immerse themselves in the support facts.

At the risk of becoming repetitious it is worth emphasizing that advertisements need to be about something; they need content. If your proposition is a mere assertion without any support then there is a danger that the advertisement will be thin and unconvincing. The more support you can give the better.

6 DESIRED CONSUMER RESPONSE

We are now moving into the area of the brief which is principally concerned with quality control. This section asks: 'What is it that we want consumers to know, think, feel or do as a result of seeing this advertisement?'

In many instances, from the creatives' point of view this section is redundant as it simply repeats material already given under target market, advertising objectives and proposition. Indeed, the same criticisms could be levelled at it that we levelled at 'advertising strategy' earlier.

However, it is a useful reminder of the fact that 'send' is not the same as 'receive' in advertising, and this section does enable senior management to look at an advertisement having looked at the 'desired consumer response' and decide if in their opinion the advertisement will succeed in achieving its effect.

Moreover, in certain complex markets where perhaps the consumer is more knowledgeable about the product field than the creative team it does help explain to them how the proposition is intended to achieve its effect.

7 CREATIVE GUIDELINES/TONE OF VOICE

This section often leads to problems between the account group and creative teams, particularly if the account group use it as an opportunity to pontificate about what is and is not good advertising, or waste precious time stating the obvious.

Too many guidelines simply restricts and frustrates the creative team. It leaves them worrying so much about what they cannot do that they devote less energy towards what they can do. Of course, there are instances when you have to make some restrictions for legal or CAP code reasons, or because clients impose certain disciplines on their agencies.

However, do creatives really need to be told that advertisements for haircare products should show beautiful shots of hair (oh, I was going to show horrible hair), or that advertisements for Sanpro products should be handled with tact and delicacy? How products are presented in advertising is their expertise and should be left to their discretion as much as possible. Avoid at all costs lists of ambiguous generalizations like: warm, soft, quality, reassuring, gentle, fashionable, etc.

There are instances in which you believe that you have made a genuine breakthrough in understanding of some aspect of consumer behaviour which merits incorporation into the advertisement. One way of expressing this is as an 'account man ad'. It may be a naff idea but if it provides something for creatives to react to then it has achieved its purpose. (Only you can decide if your relationship with your creative team is trusting enough to let you get away with this; if it is *not* then work it over in the pub.)

8 REQUIREMENTS/MANDATORY CONTENTS

In this section we tell the creatives exactly what sort of advertisement is needed:

- Is it TV, cinema, colour press, black and white press, posters or radio?
- What sizes or time lengths can they play with, how fixed is this?
- What production budget do they have?
- Is the advertisement a one-off or is it part of a campaign?
- Are there any existing end-lines or branding devices which they have to use?
- What are the rules on use of the company logo?
- Does the advertisement have to contain a coupon, a phone number or other response mechanism?
- If the advertisement is in the press, what sort of titles is it going in, what quality of paper, how much time do they have?

9 FORMATTED BRIEFS

As we said earlier, the typical sections of the brief that we have outlined would gain wide consensus in the industry even if they were not always called the same things. Some agencies, however, do not just rely on their staff knowing the information that should go into a brief; they make it easier for them by printing creative brief formats.

Formats usually stem from one or both of two basic motivations:

- A belief that there is a theoretical approach to creating better advertising which is manifested in a creative brief format.
- The desire to create uniformity and a minimum standard of briefing which everyone understands and can achieve, quality control pure and simple.

A criticism often levelled at formats is that they encourage people to believe that as long as they have 'filled in the boxes' on the brief then they have done their job. This is not, of course, a criticism of formats at all but rather a criticism of the way in which they are used. We could equally say that the size of restriction of a poster site engenders a belief among creatives that all they have to do is 'fill in the box'.

As long as people writing the briefs understand what they are doing, the briefing format is sensible and the system is well policed by senior agency executives, then there are no problems with formatted briefs *per se*.

Some advertising tasks may require a totally different form of briefing to that outlined on the form (see next section), but it is in the nature of all systems that there are exceptions.

Bad briefing formats, however, will lead to bad briefs, so if you are being asked to work with a form which does not allow you to execute briefs which agree, at least in principle, with what we have written in this chapter, raise the matter with your management. If what we have written is true, then you should find that the creative department will be your main ally in the campaign to change the brief!

We use a 'summmary briefing' format which does not replace the longer brief but is used as a quality control device by senior management and the traffic department. An example is shown below:

BRIEF SUMMARY

<table>
<tr><td colspan="3">CLIENT</td><td colspan="4">JOB</td></tr>
<tr><td colspan="7">WHAT JOB IS THIS AD TRYING TO DO?</td></tr>
<tr><td colspan="7">WHO IS IT TALKING TO?</td></tr>
<tr><td colspan="7">WHAT SHOULD THEY THINK WHEN THEY SEE IT?</td></tr>
<tr><td colspan="7">AGREED PROPOSITION</td></tr>
<tr><td colspan="7">WHAT SUPPORT DO WE HAVE?</td></tr>
<tr><td colspan="7">CREATIVE GUIDELINES</td></tr>
<tr><td colspan="4">MEDIA
PRESS/POSTERS
Size: Position
Ins: Stock:
Budget:</td><td colspan="3">TV/RADIO
Length: Budget:
Nat: Small
Reg: Medium
Lon: Large</td></tr>
<tr><td>Traffic</td><td>Creative Director</td><td>Management Supervisor</td><td>Planning Director</td><td>Account Director</td><td>Account Planner</td><td>Media</td></tr>
<tr><td></td><td></td><td></td><td></td><td></td><td></td><td></td></tr>
</table>

One other example worth showing is the briefing 'system' produced by Saatchi & Saatchi which separates key information on the market, the brand and competitive activity—of interest to both the creative and media departments—from the specific creative and media briefs.

Section 1.

SAATCHI & SAATCHI COMPTON

BACKGROUND TO CREATIVE AND MEDIA BRIEF

CLIENT	BRAND	SWO No.
		DATE

Account Group	Creative Group	Media Group	Traffic Group

KEY CHARACTERISTICS OF THE BRAND
Physical and emotional

MARKET AND BRAND PERFORMANCE
and reasons for performance

COMPETITIVE ANALYSIS
Who are they? How are they positioned? How are they different?
(Remember to show competitive ads.)

PREVIOUS ADVERTISING ACTIVITY
When, where, how much, for us and competitors

CAP/ITCA AND OTHER RESTRICTIONS

MAKE SURE YOU ATTACH CREATIVE AND/OR MEDIA BRIEF

Section 2.

SAATCHI & SAATCHI COMPTON

CREATIVE BRIEF

CLIENT	BRAND	SWO No.
		DATE

CAMPAIGN REQUIREMENT
Campaign, one off ad., no. of ads.

THE TARGET AUDIENCE
Demographics, lifestyle, product usage/attitudes

WHAT IS THIS ADVERTISING INTENDED TO ACHIEVE?

THE SINGLE-MINDED PROPOSITION

SUBSTANTIATION FOR THE PROPOSITION

MANDATORY INCLUSIONS
Stockists, logos, phone numbers etc.

DESIRED BRAND IMAGE
Friendly, sophisticated, contemporary etc.

TIMING OF CREATIVE WORK To Account Group To Client	GROUP ACCOUNT DIRECTOR SIGNATURE

MAKE SURE YOU ATTACH THE BACKGROUND AND MEDIA BRIEF

Section 3.

SAATCHI & SAATCHI COMPTON

MEDIA BRIEF

CLIENT	BRAND	SWO No.
		DATE

TARGET AUDIENCE Demographics, lifestyle, product usage/attitudes
SUGGESTED MEDIA Medium, length/size, number of executions
BUDGET Media and production
REGIONALITY
SEASONALITY
TIMING OF CAMPAIGN

TIMING OF PROPOSAL To Account Group To Client	GROUP ACCOUNT DIRECTOR SIGNATURE

MAKE SURE YOU ATTACH THE BACKGROUND AND CREATIVE BRIEF

10 EXCEPTIONS AND SPECIAL CASES

If your agency does not insist that you use a certain format (and even if it does) there may be instances in which you wish to ignore totally the guidelines you have been given in this chapter. You are the best judge of when it is appropriate to do that; it is your brand, your problem, your relationship with the creative team. We can think of a number of occasions on which you may wish to do this.

When the brief is for an advertisement in a long-running campaign What would the brief be for the next Heineken advertisement? 'Another one, please'. If there is a great deal of knowledge already shared or assumed about a campaign then it is fatuous to write it all down in a brief.

If it is a new team, then it is worth pointing out subtle nuances of the idea which may not be obvious to an outsider; it may also be worth pointing out to everyone from time to time the basic purpose of the campaign. Usually, however, the brief can restrict itself to actual requirements and any new learning or directions which the account group would like to exploit.

Highly directional briefings The concept of the briefing that we have kept in our minds when writing this chapter is a dialogue between the creative team and the account team. Sometimes it saves time and effort to couch the brief as an order, particularly for low-interest subjects like trade advertisements, cut-downs of television commercials and so on. Just tell the creative team exactly what they need to know to achieve the job satisfactorily in the minimum amount of time.

Creative pitches, creative concept development There are occasions when we find ourselves briefing when not in full possession of the facts. This is typically the case in a pitch, or when exploring a new market in which your agency has no previous experience and therefore cannot prejudge what sort of advertising messages will work, or in new product development.

The trick here is to be reasonably explicit about the situation you are in and what you want. For example: 'We don't know much about this yet, but here are a few areas we have been looking at and it would be handy to have some sort of advertising expression of these for research. What do you think?... and by the way you have got four days.'

The creative department's input as to what makes sense in advertising terms may help make your decision for you (it often does in pitches!). If you are not in a position to make a decision and have no prospect of making one in the near future, then do not hang around. Write the options down and enlist the help of the creative department.

One situation which is emphatically *not* an excuse for a brief which has not been very well thought through is the so-called 'big idea' brief. This is the one where we say 'Oh, there is not much to say about this brand, so we need a big idea, OK?'

If, after reading this book, you still cannot find anything to say about a brand which will motivate the consumer then you are in the rare situation in which advertising itself is the only discriminator. As we discussed under *Advertising propositions* (see page 83 ff.), however, it is not fair to let the creative department go off without any nuggets at all. They still require:

- An understanding of how consumers use the category.

- How they discriminate between brands.
- What advertising styles are used in the market and how successful they have been.

Do not be lazy and just cop out.

11 THE CREATIVE BRIEFING

This section deals with the actual creative briefing. Unless you have a magically charismatic personality, or know the creative team very well, it is not a good idea to catch them on the hop and just read the brief to them; they can read!

A reasonably formal meeting at which the teams are briefed fully, and time is given to eat/play with/wear/smell the product, to watch films, and for them to ask questions, is a very good idea.

Remembering our Nielsen presenter analogy, get to the interesting bits as soon as possible. What is it that the creative people are being asked to do? Start with the advertising objectives and proposition, and then bring in the support, market background and target market. Resist the temptation to show off your knowledge of the market but do make sure that they know what you and the client are expecting from this advertising.

Couch everything in positive terms and speak with conviction. All problems are intrinsically interesting. The more boring the subject matter, the more scope there is for the creative imagination to run riot. The more pedestrian the competitive advertising, the easier it is for them to produce distinctive advertising.

A meeting is a different medium to the written word and consequently you do not have to be tied down to exactly what you have written in the brief. If, for example, you have found it difficult to express your propositions as succinctly as you would have liked in the brief, then you can use analogies, film clips, magazines and so on in the meeting, to help flesh out your point.

There is the famous story of a JWT planner who used a pair of slippers and an alarm clock to describe the difference between one breakfast cereal and the rest. When we were trying to sum up the brand personality of Holsten Diät Pils to our creative department we used clips from *Butch Cassidy and The Sundance Kid*, *The Sting* and *Klute* to illustrate the idea of 'passive superiority'.

If you are not very interested in what you are talking about and express doubts and worries about the whole project then why should *they* try? On the other hand, be explicit and factual about any restrictions that do apply. These are not absolute barriers to good advertising, merely obstacles that we have to work around.

12 RECEIVING CREATIVE WORK

The next step in the creative/account-group dialogue is when they show you some work. Ideally you should try and develop the sort of relationship with your creative teams whereby you can help shape their work from the early stages so that you end up with a joint product that you are both pleased with.

If you are being presented with what the creative department regard as finished work then there are a number of points which may help you to make the meeting more productive. Try to cultivate a reputation for speaking your mind, even if what you have to say is not palatable. When creatives have written an advertisement, they are itching to find out what people think and in fairness you should tell them.

There are two types of reaction you will have to an advertisement, one intellectual, one emotional, and it is a good idea to separate them in your reponse. This can lead to four different possible responses:

a) You love the advertisement, it's on brief
b) You hate the advertisement, it's on brief
c) You love the advertisement, it's off brief
d) You hate the advertisement, it's off brief

For a) you say, 'Great, don't bother to wrap it up.' For d) you say, 'Sorry lads, it's not even close.' But b) and c) are much more difficult.

For b) you have to ask yourself whether or not it is relevant that you do not like the advertisement. It is worth expressing your opinion because in explaining why do you not like it, you may find ways of improving it, or come to appreciate it more. For c) you should try to find out why it is not on brief and whether or not it is salvageable. If it does not seem to be, then again it can be back to the drawing board (although their idea may be better than the brief).

Neither c) nor d) should happen very often if your brief is unambiguous and you have been involved in the creative process. If you do have to turn work down, to avoid damaging the relationship you should do it firmly but graciously. Always avoid leaping straight to negatives and problems; try to think of possible solutions to problems even as you are articulating them. Remember you are all trying to achieve the same end, namely good, effective, advertising, and you should work together.

6 *Creative development research*

Leslie Butterfield

WHY ADVERTISING RESEARCH IS A SPECIAL CASE

Creative development research is but the tip of an iceberg. Consideration of what might or might not be deemed 'good practice' in this area demands, of necessity, an examination of the context within which creative development research takes place. For, at the heart of the issues that surround the role of research at this stage of the process, are some fundamental questions about what advertising is *per se*.

In my view, implicit in the question 'how do you research advertising?' is the question 'how does advertising itself work?' Until you have a view on this, I contend, you cannot really have a view on advertising research.

Increasingly, in the UK in particular, there is a recognition of a 'new way' of looking at advertising and advertising research. Basically, it stems from a recognition that advertising works in a more subtle way than traditional models like AIDA suggest. Even more importantly, it recognizes that the consumer's relationship with advertising is a two-way process: the maxim of 'it's not just what advertising does to people, but what people do with advertising that matters'.

One also needs to think about the people who *create* advertising—and how to get the best out of them. It could be argued that if this 'new way' is really happening, why should creative people be nervous of research at all? The answer is that creative people are generally not nervous of research that helps them, only of research that does not.

In simple terms, most strategy development research helps, and some creative development research helps. When it does it is welcomed. When it does not, it is frequently rejected. But the difference between the two can often be the researcher or planner him or herself.

While there is in some senses a fairly fundamental antithesis between the logical, deductive, realistic, evaluative approach of the researcher, and the more intuitive, lateral, impressionistic and subtle approach of the creative person, this does not mean that research on creative work cannot be done; it just needs to be handled sensitively. One has to recognize that the creative person does not necessarily work to the same objectives or disciplines as the planner—yet it is the planner's job to 'bridge the gap'.

But why is *advertising* research a special case? Why shouldn't all the same disciplines that apply to other areas of research simply translate across to the area of advertising?

The answer is vitally important. It is precisely because people have often made the assumption that you can translate the 'notions' of research directly across, that so many advertising people are cynical about research.

Advertising research is a special case because the consumer's relationship with advertising is 'special'. It is, as we have already discussed, a two-way relationship. It also operates at two levels: rational and emotional—both equally important. In some ways, too, it is a very private relationship—advertising touches nerves with people that they may not even admit to: sexuality, greed, envy, love, childishness, and so on.

To complicate things still further, advertising works at both a conscious and a subconscious level. It may affect people in ways that they may not even recognize or understand. How then do you elicit their reactions, when they may not even realize that they are reacting?

One answer to this is by trying to better understand how advertising works in each unique case. By seeking to understand what advertising does or can do for 'my unique product in this unique market'. By thinking about it, rather than just accepting the derived myths of previous generations of researchers.

Having a view about creative development research demands not only that you have a view about how advertising works, but also of how people work. That can mean studying theories of buyer behaviour or personality theories—but it can also mean simply observing and thinking about the people around you—preferably outside the business. Look at how they watch television, how they are attentive or dismissive towards advertisements, how they talk about them, what they remember, what effect it has on them and the things they buy, how they explain why they bought the things they did, and so on. And then ask yourself: are the measures I use *really* giving me an insight into these things among buyers of my product?

More importantly still, think about creative development research not as just a simple process in which we 'test the advertisement' and consider only two parties (the advertisement and the consumer) but as a *complex* process requiring that we *understand* the advertisement and therefore a process that involves many parties and many influences:

- Advertisement.
- Consumer.
- Researcher.
- Environment.
- Research format.
- Other ads.
- Brand imagery.
- Other brands.
- Retail outlets.
- Other consumers.
- Recent experiences, etc.

The more complex the process, the more likely one is to acknowledge the 'uniqueness' of any particular research project on any particular advertisement. Ultimately, what this implies is that, rather than viewing advertising research as an evaluation or 'testing' process, one should view it as a development or 'learning' process. This means that one's *attitude* shifts from one of interest and concern about techniques, to one of interest and concern about *applications*, about *understanding* and about having a *point of view*.

It is this development or 'learning' process that I want to examine in this chapter. While a number of techniques will be described and discussed, the principal emphasis will be on *applications*.

DEFINING THE ROLE

Creative development research is research at the stage of initial creative ideas having been agreed, but BEFORE a finished advertisement is produced. This in itself is something of a limiting concept, since so much of what research can contribute to the end-result is learnt at earlier stages and hence is part of the 'creative development process'. The definition is important in two ways:

- It defines what we are *not* examining: creative development research is *not* to do with evaluating concepts outside those directly related to an agreed script or visual. So we will not be examining 'adcepts', concept boards, collages, projective techniques, etc. We are talking here of the examination of materials that seek to convey an advertising idea that has been agreed to a fairly detailed level, i.e. a script or press 'rough'. Equally, we are not talking about research on *finished* advertisements, either pre- or post-exposure.
- It helps to define the planner's unique and important role in the process, and how it differs from that of the account manager, or the outside researcher.

We have already discussed the importance of 'context'—the ability to investigate, learn and make judgements about advertising, within a framework of existing knowledge about the brand. It is the understanding of this context that makes the planner's role unique. Unlike the account manager, he comes to the creative development research process with the consumer's perspective firmly in mind. In the right environment he will be able to speak without fear or favour about what he already knows, and what he is about to find out.

Unlike the outside researcher, however, he will also understand the complexities of the business and marketing background against which the advertising is to be developed. This will allow him to pick up vital details and nuances of consumer response that may well be missed by the outsider.

It is, without doubt, *the* most crucial (and controversial) stage of advertising development. And by being *within* the organization that produced the idea, the planner is uniquely positioned to be at his most influential.

So how should a planner execute these responsibilities fairly and effectively? Perhaps the most fundamental aspect of the planner's role (especially in terms of his ability later to communicate his findings), is to be clear about the *objectives* of research at this stage. It is axiomatic that part of being able clearly to define what is and is not to be considered, is the ability also to define what can and cannot be 'found out'.

There is little point in researching what absolutely *cannot* be changed. Thus, if the planner finds himself in a situation where the production timetable has been agreed, and the director booked to start work on the shooting script the day after the research is completed, there may be little point in doing research at all. Indeed, this sort of scenario hints at a bigger problem of lack of corporate commitment to the research input that ought to happen—probably worthy of separate debate within that organization.

Even *in* this situation, however, it may be that script changes can be accommodated right up to the last moment—especially where these are to a post-shoot dubbed voice-over for example.

The basic maxim remains true, however: if it *cannot* be changed there is no point in researching it. Given that this situation does not pertain, what then of our original question regarding what can and cannot be found out? To answer this question one must observe the basic division between strategy and execution—or, in a sense, content and form (Figure 1).

This model begins to define our 'area of interest'. Thus, it is *not* the role of creative development research to define the advertising strategy or help us write the creative

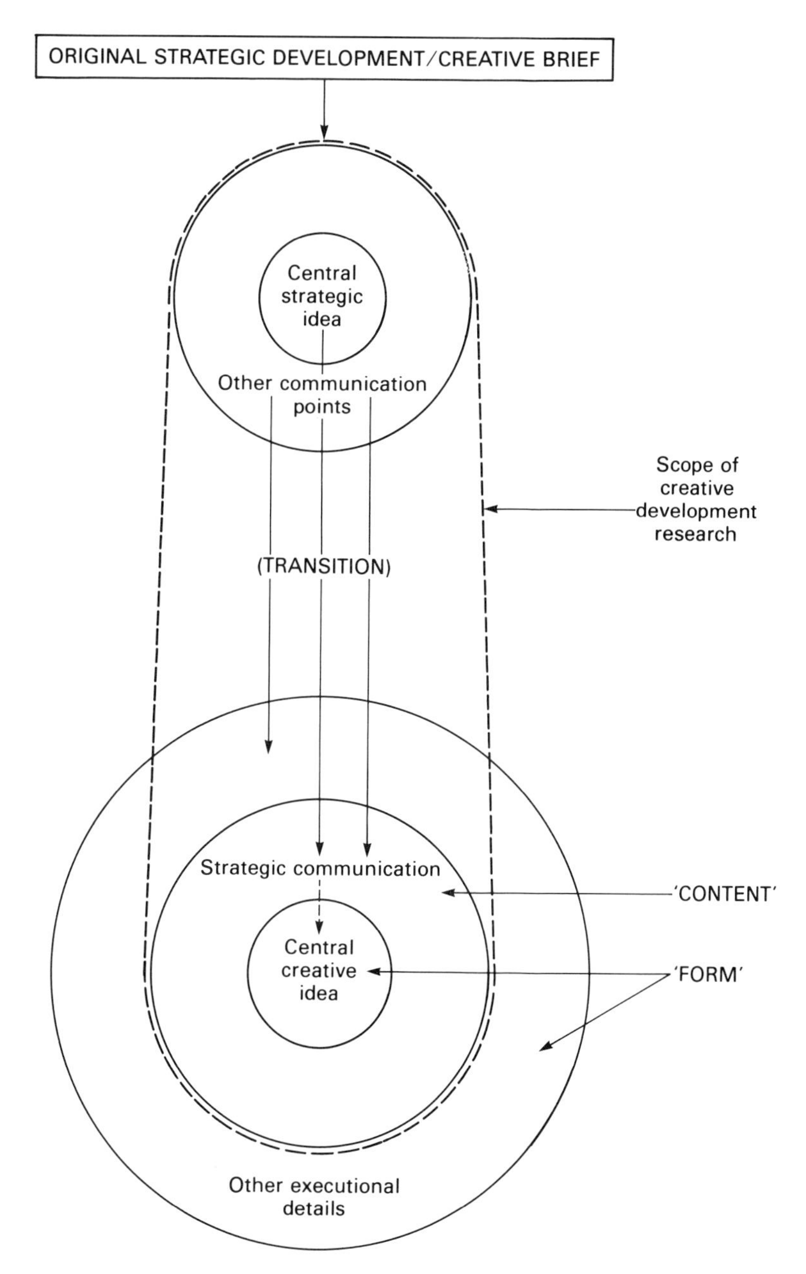

Figure 1: Scope of creative development research

brief—we should have got to that stage long before we have an animatic or press rough in our hand.

Equally, it is not the role of this stage of research to evaluate minor executional details. Anyone who works with rough advertising materials will know that there are *details* of execution (press or TV) that cannot be communicated—nor indeed should one attempt to do so. Arguably, an animatic that attempts to replicate every nuance or expression of the characters involved runs a severe risk of focusing the consumer's attention on those details and *away* from more important and central issues.

Even photomatics, while expressing visual appearances more realistically, cannot replicate flow and movement that may be critical to the final execution.

These issues of executional 'form' are of less interest to us here than are issues of 'content' (of the strategic communication) or the form of the *central* creative idea. While it may be that the research suggests solutions to problems connected with executional 'form' (e.g. the age of a character, the importance of 'surprise' at a particular point in a commercial, the serving of a product with particular accompaniments, etc.), this is not the principal purpose of the research.

If we refer back to the model above, we can see that the principal purposes (in order of priority) are as follows:

1 To examine comprehension of and reactions to the central creative idea.
2 To examine how well the central creative idea communicates the central strategic idea.
3 To examine comprehension of and reactions to the strategic communication of the advertisement.
4 To examine how well the strategic communication of the advertisement reflects the other communication points that we *intended* to get across.
5 To examine to what extent the executional details of the advertisement contribute to or detract from the overall communication of the advertisement.

This then is the scope of our investigation at this stage. In the rest of this chapter we shall examine each of the main media separately, and within each:

- The forms of stimulus materials.
- The ways in which they may be introduced.
- Order of questioning.
- The separation of content from form, etc.

before returning to examining interpretation and feedback and some of the other key issues.

RESEARCHING TELEVISION

Inevitably, some of the general principles discussed here will be applicable to other media. Nevertheless, television is not only the medium most likely to be researched, it is also the one where the range of techniques available varies the most widely. Let us start by looking at the available stimulus materials before moving on to a more general examination of the way in which these can be used.

Less 'finished'
More imagination required
Less expensive/time consuming

More 'finished'
Less imagination required
More expensive/time consuming

Figure 2: Television research stimulus materials

Television research stimulus materials in a sense lie along a spectrum as in Figure 2. Discussion of the relative merits of these different materials has been extensive. I present here a personal view, though it is based on extensive use of *all* of these techniques at one time or another, though with varying degrees of success. One thing that is worth saying, however, is that I would rather use any one of these methods than do nothing at all. Regardless of the technique, I have always learnt something. This is indeed a critical point, since I have also yet to meet anyone who can truly claim to have learnt nothing from such research—whether they then applied what was learnt appropriately is a different issue. The fact remains that the most important and irrefutable reason for doing research on rough advertising is that it works!

SCRIPT

Yes, it can be done! In fact, if you listen to a good creative presentation of a script you can see how an idea can be brought to life straight off the page. Indeed, it can avoid some of the problems that we will touch on later regarding animatics: respondents will be left in no doubt whatsoever as to what you are 'showing' them.

Essentially, it relies upon the ability of the presenter. A good presenter can convey an idea very well and conjour up all the right images and nuances. If you feel uncomfortable about presenting scripts, take someone along with you who *can* do it well. This is beneficial in any case since it distances you or the researcher from the idea in the eyes of the respondents—they won't think it's *your* idea.

Introduction of the idea in this case is relatively straightforward, you don't have to 'explain' the stimulus method as you do with (e.g.) animatics. Simply tell respondents that you (or someone else) are going to read out an idea for a television commercial, that they should listen quietly and carefully to what is said, but that they will get a chance to listen to it again. Then present the script; describing the total idea and sequence first and then going through the copy and vision elements in tandem. This, in effect, is a 'spoken' narrative tape and can usefully convey at least the key elements of a creative idea successfully.

It shares some of the same problems as narrative tapes (which we will return to) but is useful where time is of the essence—for example, before a new business presentation—where *some* feedback is needed prior to development or presentation of the idea.

Obviously though, it is a less than satisfactory method on any kind of permanent basis since the translation of the creative idea in the minds of respondents is much less 'controllable' than with more finished materials. Essentially, you are *hoping* for broad unanimity of interpretation by respondents, which may well not be the case, especially where the creative idea relies heavily on *visual* elements. Better than nothing though.

NARRATIVE TAPE

Narrative tapes certainly have the advantages of speed and cost relative to more finished material. Their proponents would argue that they have advantages, too, in limiting the degree of 'closure' of the creative idea, hence allowing respondents to imagine the described scene and action themselves.

One or two agencies even use these as their main technique for researching TV. However, having used them on a number of occasions myself (usually where time precluded production of more finished materials), I do feel that they are fraught with problems:

- Because they do not 'close' the idea, they suffer from problems of multiple interpretation by respondents. It is difficult enough even with an animatic to understand whether what you 'put in' is what respondents are 'taking out'. With narrative tapes the problems are multiplied still further by the lack of visual references—making the controllability of responses (and hence their interpretation) very difficult indeed.
- A further problem is that, even when well produced, a narrative tape may end up sounding like a mini-radio play and lasting anything up to three or four minutes to describe a 40-second commercial. Thus all sense of pace or delivery is lost and the creative idea becomes laboured and studied. Humour, wit and reactions generally are hard to convey in this format—while the very detail of the narrative often encourages respondents to be equally nit-picking and laborious in their reactions.

If you do use them (again, they are better than nothing), try to keep them short and concise, use a *lively* voice-over, *don't* try to describe every detail of the script and avoid the use of technical 'film' jargon (freeze, hold, optical, etc.)

TAPE AND BOARDS

This is (both on our spectrum and in fact) a good 'half way house'.

The key to good presentation of this material is rehearsal. Having selected the seven or eight 'key frames' from the commercial and recorded the voice-over (and music) on a separate tape, mark up your copy of the script carefully, allowing time for *each* frame to be taken in—and then practise flipping over the boards at the relevant points in the script. (Dropping them forward on to a flat surface is usually better than removing them one by one by hand.)

In the research situation, again only a minimum of explanation will be required since it will be clear to respondents that this is far from being a finished film.

The advantages of this technique are that it *does* contain a visual as well as an audio element and hence avoids the 'radio play' syndrome discussed above, and yet it does not 'close' the idea totally and thus does not allow respondents lateral response to the idea. On the other hand, it is *not* using the medium in which the idea will eventually appear—and hence can look a bit cheap or 'tacky'; a problem if 'style' or production values are an important element of the intended communication. Also, it is often impossible to make the whole method match up to the intended time length of the finished commercial without having unbearably long pauses on individual frames.

Also, because for respondents it will be such an unfamiliar way of seeing an advertising idea, there is a danger of their over-analysing elements of the visual presentation or simply not being able to make the imaginative leap from stimulus to the finished result. As with animatics, this can to a degree be avoided by showing an example of another commercial (which may be familiar to them) in both stimulus and finished form to illustrate the transition that occurs and hence defines the kind of imaginative leap that is expected of them.

Again, storyboards and tapes are a very 'staccato' way of presenting a creative idea—flow, movement and hence, to a degree, pace are lost in this format. Therefore, they are best suited to simpler creative ideas, such as demonstrations, simple 'slice of life' stories, etc.

Where time is of the essence, this is a 'good enough' technique, though having gone to the effort of drawing key frames and recording a voice-over, it is then a relatively small step to producing an animatic—and thus, in my view, obtaining an overall much better end-result.

CASE HISTORY 1: PRE-TESTING OF *THE ECONOMIST* TV COMMERCIAL 'INSIDE INFORMATION'

The commercial was written to position *The Economist* as 'the ultimate tool for being kept well informed on an all-round basis'. It was aimed at AB businessmen aged 25–45 years and was intended to encourage non-readers and convert irregular readers to becoming regular readers.

The commercial showed the heads of various well-known political and business figures being 'opened up' by a journalist from *The Economist* in the search for the truth. However, all the figures (Margaret Thatcher, Clive Sinclair, Ronald Reagan, Sir Freddie Laker and the *Economist* journalist) were drawn in the style of the *Monty Python* cartoons. The idea behind this device was to indicate that *The Economist* probed more deeply into issues than other publications but in an interesting and unusual way. When the script and key frames were taken out into research, it was apparent that there was little difficulty in comprehending the intended message. In fact, the entire execution was expected to have impact, to be fun to watch and to be humorous.

However, some problems were highlighted and the most crucial one concerned the nature of the *Economist* journalist. The original cartoon character was felt to be inappropriate. He was perceived as bumbling, disorganized, down-market—definitely not a city journalist. This was hardly a flattering image for the *Economist* readers or for *The*

Economist and by rejecting the journalist, there was also a tendency to dismiss the entire commercial.

After two groups it was realized that this could be a major problem and the planner asked for a new journalist to be drawn and developed so that he remained in the original Pythonesque style but looked less manic and less dishevelled.

The response to this new character changed the response to the entire advertisement. He was regarded as much more serious, organized and capable and thus far more in keeping with the expected image of *The Economist*. However, the tone and style of the commercial ensured that he was not too stilted or stuffy and therefore non-readers were able to re-evaluate their image of the magazine in a positive light (Storyboard 1).

THE ECONOMIST

'INSIDE INFORMATION'

VISION	*SOUND*
We open on a still photograph of the head and shoulders of Ronald Reagan. A reporter, with notebook and pencil, comes into frame next to him.	
He lifts the top of Reagan's head, as if it were a lid, and looks inside. He closes the head and scribbles something in his notebook.	*Brian Redhead VO*: Every week, *The Economist* lifts the lid on politics and current affairs.
Reagan moves out of frame and is replaced by Sir Freddie Laker. Our reporter opens his head, looks into it, and scribbles in his pad.	It brings you inside information on the latest events in the business world.
Sir Freddie leaves frame, and is replaced by Sir Clive Sinclair. Our reporter opens Sir Clive's head and puts his own head inside it. He reappears, impressed, and writes in his notebook.	In science and technology, too, it delves deeper than most.
Sir Clive exits frame and is replaced by David Steel. Our reporter opens Mr Steel's head and David Owen pops out. He then opens Dr Owen's head, and Mrs Thatcher pops out. Our reporter closes all the heads and writes in his notebook.	*The Economist* is always enlightening . . . . . . often provocative . . . . . . and never dull.
A hand enters top of frame and opens our reporter's head. The hand takes out a copy of *The Economist*.	*The Economist*. For the investigative reader.

PRODUCT: *ECONOMIST*

TITLE: INSIDE INFORMATION

MVO: Every week *The Economist* lifts the (MUSIC: American National Anthem) lid on politics and current affairs.

Brings you inside information on the latest events in the business world.

In science and technology too it delves deeper than most. (SFX: *Electronic beeps*).

The Economist is always enlightening, (SFX: "*Pop!*") often provocative (SFX: "*Pop!*") and never dull.

The Economist (SFX: *Chattering/Typewriter*),

for the investigative reader.

Storyboard 1

ANIMATICS

Animatics are probably the most widely used TV research stimulus material—and in my view *potentially* the best. Of course, as Wendy Gordon points out in her excellent review article ('Stimulus Material: Current Thinking & Development', *AQRP Conference Paper*, January 1986), 'animatics can be excellent or appalling'—but their strengths in my view far outweigh their weaknesses at this stage of the advertising development process.

The guidelines for good animatics are now well documented:

- Do not attempt to replicate every action and movement of the script, except where this is essential to the explanation of the idea.
- Do not over-caricature the depiction of people in the commercial.
- Do stick to the overall time length and sequence of actions actually intended for the finished film.
- Do think hard (and talk to the creative team) about the style of drawings that will best convey the intended mood and tone of the commercial.
- Do not be afraid to use quite coarse, pencil-sketch drawings of simple ideas in the animatic.

Good animatic production is not an exercise in superrealist painting. But it can be an enormously valuable 'dry run' for the creatives prior to producing a finished film—this indeed is one of the covert benefits of animatics—it gives creatives an opportunity to think about sequences, timings, storyline, logic flow, etc., before finally committing themselves on film.

The critics of animatics will claim that there are some ideas to which an animatic will not do justice. The answer to this is that ultimately no animatic will do justice to every detail of an idea—but that is not what is intended anyway.

Thinking back to our earlier model, it is not the role of the animatic to convey every executional detail, but rather to help the moderator to elicit consumer responses to a central idea and a strategic communication. If a creative idea *has* a central thought and a strategic intent (which hopefully all creative ideas will have!) then an animatic *can* help to elicit reactions to those elements.

The more complex, stylized or emotional the intended execution is, the greater is the onus on the moderator to be sensitive and judgemental in his or her interpretation of consumer responses to what will inevitably be a less than perfect rendering of that idea. Properly constructed and introduced, however, the animatic can be a powerful weapon in the advertising researcher's armoury:

- Animatics use the medium in which the finished film will actually appear.
- They bring together sound and vision in a realistic way and in an accurate time-frame.
- They can convey pace, flow, humour, scale and mood very effectively and are, in my view, the best balance between the 'real thing' and a script that currently exists.
- They are neither too 'rough' to preclude accurate conveyance of an idea (as with narrative tapes) nor too finished to preclude imagination on behalf of respondents (as is often the case with photomatics).
- They can even be easily supplemented with other visual or video references of particular scenes, techniques or people, to 'explain' a particular element to respondents.

In this area, I have myself used animatics in tandem with:

a) Finished films for other products to illustrate a particular style or mood (e.g. surrealism).
b) 'Scientific' films to illustrate particular techniques (e.g. reverse ultra-slow motion).
c) Casting tapes or photographs of one or more possible presenters 'reading' the same script.
d) Photographic references to particular scenes that might appear in a finished film (e.g. 'images' of America).

The key though to the successful use of animatics is the successful explanation of what they are to respondents. Remember that you may deal with animatics every day whereas respondents will probably be seeing one for the first time. It may be tedious for you to have to explain them to respondents, but it is essential that this is done clearly, carefully and repeatedly if one is to avoid the problems of respondents judging the animatic as a finished commercial. A full five minutes of explanation is *not* too long—and again one can usefully use examples of animatics and their transition to finished films for other products to illustrate the points.

In introducing the animatic it is vital to explain that what they are going to see is:

- 'Rough', and not finished.
- Something that is made *before* a finished film.

Both of these elements are crucial if respondents are to recognize that what they are about to see bears a *resemblance* to a finished advertisement, but is not the same as a finished ad.

Equally important however, is what *not* to say:

- Do not use the word 'animatic'—it will mean nothing.
- Do not call it a 'cartoon' (you will have enough trouble persuading some respondents that it is not a cartoon later, without planting the idea in their heads now).
- Do not ask respondents how it needs to be changed, how it could be improved, what *they* would have done or just for their likes and dislikes. In other words, avoid giving them an *evaluative* framework in which to judge the advertising. 'Evaluation' is *not* the way ordinary people approach advertising—they will either watch it and get involved in it or they will not. It is the *moderator's* job to evaluate the advertising by interpretation from consumers' reactions to the totality of the communication—and then by exploring the detail of their reactions to individual elements within the total.

With these caveats regarding the introduction and production of animatics, this medium still remains in my view the best option for creative development research on television—and well worth the time and money spent on producing a good-quality execution.

CASE HISTORY 2: PRE-TESTING OF A NEW TV CAMPAIGN FOR BRITISH TELECOM YELLOW PAGES (see pp. 110–119).

At the time of the pitch for *Yellow Pages*, the agency presented three scripts, subsequently made into animatics. The objective of the advertising was to encourage a very broad target audience to view the medium more positively, and use *Yellow Pages* in new and different ways ('Not just for the nasty things . . .').

In the series of group discussions that followed, the 'J.R. Hartley' script emerged virtually unchanged (see Storyboards 2 and 5).

The 'Pony' script, however, ran into serious problems relating to its 'up-market' humour, tone of voice and subject matter (Storyboard 3).

The 'Hungarian Band' script also suffered from the upmarketness (or 'marginality') of some of the examples used—and the fact that in addressing many subjects, it failed to communicate single-mindedly the strategic message that was intended (Storyboard 4).

One vignette, however, in 'Hungarian Band' was especially well received—that of the little boy admiring his new bicycle, and the suggestion was made that *this* subject could form a more 'down to earth' example to replace the pony in the second script. This thought was picked up by the creatives, and a new second commercial was developed retaining the birthday present idea of the original 'Pony' script, but substituting a bicycle as the actual present given, and setting the whole idea within the very much more 'mass market' context of a northern city (Storyboard 6).

The third script was dropped altogether, and subsequent commercials have maintained the 'single example' format of the first two executions in what is now an effective and well-liked four-year-old campaign.

PHOTOMATICS

To the far right of our spectrum come photomatics—literally an animatic using photographic 'stills' rather than drawings. While some creatives would say that this technique approximates far better to the finished result than a conventional animatic, my argument would be that it is precisely *because* of this that they are less effective. Photomatics leave almost nothing to the imagination of the respondent—and undoubtedly they will judge the photomatic as a finished film.

Though *you* may have selected a particular still of a character fairly arbitrarily, they will read that photo as being the intended character—and attach all their likes or dislikes of that character to the photo. Thus by 'closing' the area of imagination so far, you are actually restricting what might be usefully learnt from a less finished stimulus material—in effect they leave the moderator almost no 'room for manoeuvre' around particular elements of the commercial that may be problematic or offer potential. They are also very time-consuming and expensive to produce.

Arguably, they are only appropriate where it is impossible for a drawing to convey a particular visual element that is absolutely central to the creative idea (e.g. a very specific facial expression, a detailed food shot, etc.). In fact, experience shows that this is actually seldom the case—an animatic together with visual references of the kind discussed earlier will generally be a better option.

Before moving on to examine other media, it is worth discussing briefly at this stage the actual conduct of qualitative research on rough advertising—since the various media have a great deal in common in this respect. Having shown the animatic or other material, what form should questioning of respondents then take?

I have already hinted at what *not* to ask—and indeed personally I err very much towards open-ended non-directive questioning at the immediate post-exposure stage.

Having established that respondents *have* understood the form of stimulus material they have just been shown, I might ask: 'So what did any of you think of that?' I would then allow spontaneous comments to endure for as long as possible—even using my silence as a prompt for further comments. I do this because I put a lot of importance on the early reactions that people have, before they get into an analytical or critical mode—so I want to maintain spontaneity as long as possible.

I will step in though if I feel either that there is a fundamental misconception of the idea or if one or two respondents are heavily loading the overall response too positively or negatively.

When I do start talking again myself the next things I wish to establish are:

- Branding: it is amazing how often people cannot remember the advertised brand after having seen an advertisement.
- The 'main thing' that the advertisement was trying to get across (the central strategic idea).
- Recall of the storyline (the central creative idea).
- What the advertisement 'said' about Brand X (the strategic communication).
- The detailed things they noticed—and what if any significance these had (the executional elements).

This sort of sequence of questioning is important if one is sensibly to structure people's reactions at the stage of interpretation—and it is a sequence that can apply to rough executions in *all* media.

I would stress again the importance of 'front-weighting' responses—people's initial reactions are more likely to be their true reactions than later, more studied attitudes. Finally, beware too of 'order effect'. Rotating the exposure of two or more executions is vital, since respondents seem always to prefer the second execution seen to the first. (Indeed if this is *not* the case, it usually suggests to me that the first execution was particularly strong!)

RESEARCHING CINEMA

All that we have said above regarding TV applies equally to cinema commercials—the only qualification being that the moderator can allow for greater attention levels than might be expected for TV in the real world situation.

RESEARCHING RADIO

In a sense, radio is the easiest and cheapest of all media to research. Making a radio commercial in its finished form (unless it is extraordinarily complex) is cheaper than making an animatic—and well worth the effort. There really is little point in trying to make a 'rough' radio execution when a finished one will be just as cheap!

PRODUCT: *YELLOW PAGES*

TITLE: J. R. HARTLEY ANIM.

MUSIC/MAN: I don't suppose you have a copy of *European Butterflies* by J. R. Hartley, mm . . . It's rather old.

(SFX: *Shop bell*). (SFX: *Traffic*). (SFX: *Shop bell*). It's by J. R. Hartley. (SFX: *Door slamming*).

DAUGHTER: No luck dad? Here, try this half way down.

MVO: Good old *Yellow Pages*. We don't just help with the nasty things in life like a blocked up drain. We're there for the

nice things too. MAN: You do? Oh, that's wonderful. Can you keep it for me?

My name? . . . Oh yes, it's J. R. Hartley.

Storyboard 2

YELLOW PAGES/*40 seconds/15.3.83*

'J. R. HARTLEY'

PICTURE	*SOUND*
We see a tall old gentleman in a bookshop. He is talking to an assistant who is bored and negative. Even before he has finished talking the assistant is shaking his head.	*Old Man*: I don't suppose you have a copy of *European Butterflies* by J. R. Hartley . . . . . . it's rather old . . .
Cut to man leaving another bookshop closing door behind him.	*SFX*: *Doorbell jangling.*
Cut to man leaving yet another bookshop closing door behind him.	*SFX*: *Doorbell jangling.*
Cut to man seen through window, we see assistant shake her head.	
Cut to close-up of man's face in different bookshop—weary.	*Old Man*: It's by J. R. Hartley.
Cut to man closing his own front door and leaning against it.	*SFX*: *Door closing.*
Grown-up daughter helps him off with his coat and hands him open copy of *Yellow Pages*.	*Daughter*: No luck Dad? Here try this . . . half way down. *SFX*: *Yellow Pages* Theme
Cut to the old man in armchair with *Yellow Pages* on his lap. He is on the phone waiting. We cut to see close-up of entry 'Books—Rare and Secondhand'.	*MVO*: Good old *Yellow Pages*. We don't just help with the nasty things in life, like a blocked drain, we're there for the nice things too.
Cut to the old man's face as he talks on the phone. Super on righthand corner of frame the *Yellow Pages* logo.	*Old Man*: You do? Oh, that's wonderful. Can you keep it for me? My name? Oh yes . . . it's J. R. Hartley.

PRODUCT: *YELLOW PAGES*

TITLE: BIRTHDAY ANIM.

MUSIC/MUM: Want to talk about Cathy's Birthday? DAD: Mmm . . . MUM: You know what she really wants, don't you?

DAD: Ah . . . MUM: I'll give you a clue. It's got four legs and eats hay. DAD: A vegetarian dog.

MUM: No, a pony. DAD: Yes, I know . . . How do I buy a pony? I've never bought a pony. MUM: Here, look under livery stables. DAD: Can I find the money

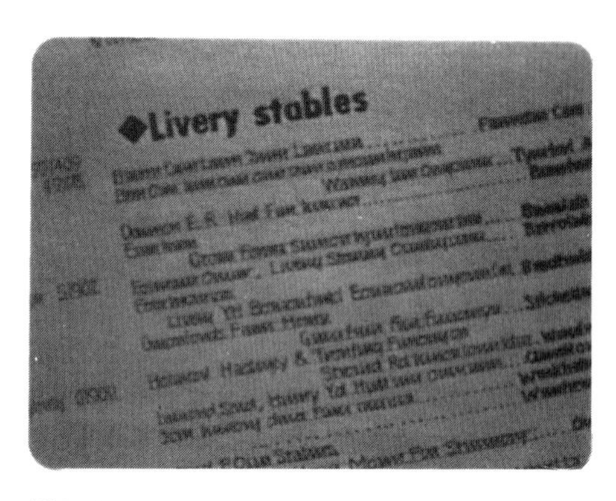

if I look under money? Hmm. No, no livery stable. MUM: Hey, let me see, Dan. DAD: Mmm . . . MVO: Good old *Yellow Pages*.

We don't just help with the nasty things in life like a leaking roof.

We're there for the nice things too. CATHY: Oh, thank you.

Storyboard 3

YELLOW PAGES/*40 seconds/15.3.83*

'BIRTHDAY'

PICTURE	*SOUND*
We see a man in his early thirties sitting at his desk in his study working. The desk is piled up with books. It is evening and the room is softly lit.	
His wife comes in and sits on the arm of his chair.	*Woman*: You want to talk about Cathy's birthday?
She engages him in conversation. He is initially reluctant to join in because he knows what it's about but gradually comes round.	*Man*: Mmm. Mmm. *Woman*: You know what she really wants, don't you? *Man*: Ah . . . *Woman*: I'll give you a clue. It's got four legs and eats hay. *Man*: A vegetarian dog? *Woman*: No, a pony. *Man*: I know. Where do I buy a pony? I've never bought a pony.
She fishes the *Yellow Pages* off the desk and gives it to him.	*Woman*: Here—look under livery stables.
He starts to look up livery stables and pretends it's not there—puts *Yellow Pages* on table.	*Man*: Can I find the money if I look under money. . . . no—no livery stables.
She slips onto his lap and sees the 'stables' in the book.	*Woman*: Hey, let me see . . . Dan?
They embrace. Camera goes in onto heading in book.	*SFX*: *Yellow Pages* theme.
Cut to girl of about eight on pony. We see her face in CU as she takes off cap and talks to her parents.	*MVO*: Good old *Yellow Pages*. We don't just help with the nasty things in life, like a leaking roof, we're there for the nice things too.
Super in corner of frame the *Yellow Pages* logo.	*Cathy*: Daddy. Thank you.

PRODUCT: *YELLOW PAGES*

TITLE: HUNGARIAN BAND ANIM.

HUNGARIAN MUSIC/MVO: They fled to England in 1956. Now their son is getting married here and *Yellow Pages*

helped find a Hungarian Band to bring back the old days. She always said she'd rather have one good thing than a room full of

rubbish. *Yellow Pages* helped her find her perfect Persian carpet. He wanted a bicycle so light he could

carry it on one finger. *Yellow Pages* helped his dad find it for him. In a world full of problems *Yellow Pages* brings

people together with the things they

want. It's a nice feeling.

Storyboard 4

YELLOW PAGES/*40 seconds/15.3.83*

'HUNGARIAN BAND'

PICTURE	*SOUND*
We see a wedding party. A Hungarian band is playing and people are dancing. We track through to see the father and mother of the groom dancing gently together.	(*HUNGARIAN MUSIC*) *MVO*: They fled to England in 1956. Now their son is getting married here and *Yellow Pages* helped to find a Hungarian band to bring back the old days.
Cut to room with large French windows. It is furnished with just one modern chair, a record player and a beautiful Persian carpet. A young woman in a raincoat walks around and leans against the fire place.	(*MUSIC: CHOPIN*) *MVO*: She always said she'd rather have one good thing than a roomful of rubbish. The *Yellow Pages* helped her find her perfect Persian carpet.
	(*SFX*: *Yellow Pages* Theme)
Cut to gleaming new bicycle inside garage. A young boy about 11 is looking at it. He goes up to it and lifts it on one finger. He smiles.	*MVO*: He wanted a bicycle so light he could carry it on one finger. The *Yellow Pages* helped his Dad find it for him.
Cut to close-up of *Yellow Pages*. We see pencil ticking off address under Kitchen Planners. Cut to husband and wife in kitchen showroom.	*MVO*: In a world full of problems, *Yellow Pages* bring people together with the things they want.
They embrace as we super *Yellow Pages* logo in righthand corner of frame.	*MVO*: It's a nice feeling.

PRODUCT: *YELLOW PAGES* TITLE: J. R. HARTLEY

MUSIC/MAN: I don't suppose you have a copy of *Fly Fishing* by

J. R. Hartley. It is rather old. SHOP ASSISTANT: I'm sorry.

MAN: It's by J. R. Hartley.
DAUGHTER: No luck Dad? Never mind there's still a few more

to try.
MVO: Good old *Yellow Pages*. We don't just help with the nasty things in life

like a blocked drain. We're there for the nice things too.
MAN: You do,

oh, that's wonderful. Can you keep it for me. My name . . . oh, yes, it's J. R. Hartley.

Storyboard 5

YELLOW PAGES/*50 seconds/27.7.83*

'J. R. HARTLEY' (Post production)

VISION	*SOUND*
We see a tall old gentleman in a bookshop. He is talking to an assistant who is bored and negative.	(Music under) *Old Man*: I don't suppose you have a copy of *Flyfishing* by J. R. Hartley ...
Even before he has finished talking the assistant is shaking his head.	... it's rather old ...
Cut to man leaving another bookshop closing door behind him.	*SFX*: *Doorbell jangling.*
Cut to man leaving yet another bookshop closing door behind him.	*SFX*: *Doorbell jangling.*
Cut to man seen through window, we see assistant shake her head.	
Cut to man walking up steep hill towards another shop.	
Cut to close up of man's face in different bookshop—weary.	*Old Man*: It's by J. R. Hartley.
Cut to man closing his own front door and leaning against it.	*SFX*: *Door closing.*
Cut to grown-up daugher who hands him open copy of *Yellow Pages*.	*Daughter*: No luck, Dad? Never mind, there's still a few more to try.
Cut to the old man in armchair with *Yellow Pages* on his lap. He is on the phone—waiting. We cut to see close-up of entry 'Books—Rare and Secondhand'.	*MVO*: Good old *Yellow Pages.* We don't just help with the nasty things in life, like a blocked drain, we're there for the nice things too.
Cut to the old man's face as he talks on the phone.	*Music starts to swell finally revealing* Yellow Pages *Theme.*
	Old Man: You do? Oh, that's wonderful. Can you keep it for me? My name? Oh yes ... it's J. R. Hartley.
He puts receiver down on cradle and smiles in relief.	
We super *Yellow Pages* logo in corner.	

PRODUCT: *YELLOW PAGES*

TITLE: BICYCLE

MUSIC/DAD: Hello Richard?
RICHARD: Hello.

DAD: You're not still on about that bike are you? I remember when bikes were bikes, proper mudguards and a cover for the chain. Look

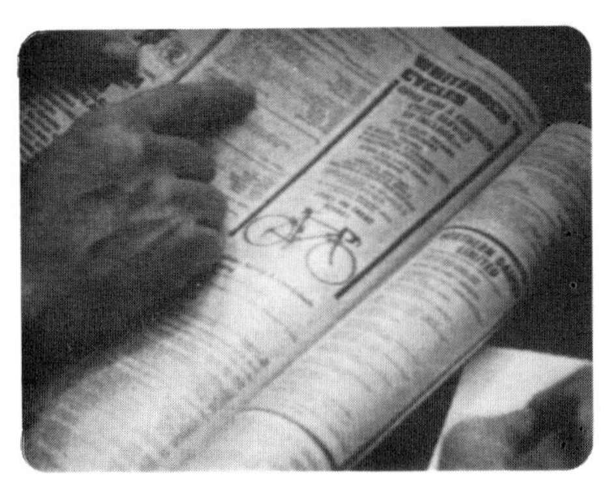

at the saddle, it's like sitting on a razor blade . . . Maybe next year, ay?

RICHARD: Yeah.
DAD: How d'ya get on love? MUM: Found one.
DAD: Great. MUM: Roper's say they'll keep

it till weekend. DAD: You better give us the address then. MVO: Good old *Yellow Pages*. We're not just there

for the nasty things in life like a leaky roof, we can help with the nice things, too. DAD: I were right about that saddle though.

Storyboard 6

YELLOW PAGES/*50 seconds/27.7.83*

'BICYCLE' post production

VISION	*SOUND*
We see father coming home along alley at back of terraced homes.	(Music under)
He is about 40 carrying a bag of tools.	
He turns into a back yard of one of the houses.	
He sees his son, about 12, sitting in yard reading a bicycle brochure.	*Father*: Hello Richard. Eh, you're not still on about this bike, are you?
He takes brochure off son.	
We see the boy's growing disappointment and silent concern.	
	I remember when bikes were bikes.
	Proper mudguards and a cover for the chain.
	And look at that saddle—be like sitting on a razor blade.
The father gets up and hands brochure back to the boy.	Maybe next year, eh? (He enters house)
Cut to him coming through door. He winks at his wife. We see his wife at the table with open copy of *Yellow Pages*.	How did you get on, love?
Cut to CU of *Yellow Pages*.	*Wife*: I think I've found one—Ropers—says he'll keep it till weekend.
We see heading Bicycle Shops and Repairs. We see several listings have been ticked.	*Father*: Give us the address, then.
Cut to father at table writing address on edge of newspaper. He tears it off and puts it in top pocket.	*MVO*: Good old *Yellow Pages*. We're not just there for the nasty things in life like a blocked drain, we can help with the nice things, too.
Dissolve to hallway of house. We see boy in cycle gear wheeling his bike out of front door.	*Music becomes more positive revealing* Yellow Pages *Theme at the end.*
Cut to father at bedroom window watching son take bike out. He is pleased.	
Son senses someone looking and gazes up at window—father ducks back.	
Cut to son cycling up hill. He stands on his pedals to cope with the slope.	
Cut back to father's face at window. CU of his face as he says his line.	*Father*: I were right about that saddle though.
Super *Yellow Pages* logo in corner of frame.	

The major difference from television, in my view, is that radio as a medium is more passive and 'background' than television. Thus, unlike TV where I would generally not place a TV animatic in a reel with other animatics, with radio I would simulate a proper commercial break (at least for first exposure) by placing the 'test' commercial in the middle of a group of five to play to respondents—even with a very short (10–15 seconds) extract of programme either side. With that reel, and a good quality tape player (*not* the one you are recording the group with), introduce the advertising by saying that you would like the respondents to listen to a 'typical' commercial break. Having played the tape, elicit spontaneous reactions to each commercial *in the order in which they appeared*, before returning specifically to probe further the 'test' commercial.

After this, questioning can following very much the same lines as for television discussed above.

RESEARCHING PRESS

Whereas the majority of the debate regarding research on TV advertising has related to stimulus materials, the majority of the debate here relates to research methodology.

Given that we are researching press advertising *prior* to exposure, there really is only one stimulus form: the 'rough' press advertisement itself. 'Rough', of course, can cover a multitude of different degrees of finish:

- Hand-drawn rough layout with written headline and no copy.
- Artist-drawn visual and headline but no copy.
- Artist-drawn visual, set headline, pack shot photograph.
- Highly finished rough: set headline and copy, artist-drawn visual, etc.

Regardless of form, the task of explaining to respondents what it is they are seeing is generally easier than for television—and choice of 'state of finish' of the rough is more to do with the decision as to the research method, as we shall see.

The conventional wisdom is that one researches television in group discussions, and press advertising in depth interviews. The argument in support of this is that in so doing, one is replicating the 'natural' situations in which people use the medium (TV at home with family; press on one's own). While there is clearly truth in this, it is something of an oversimplification.

Furthermore, the selection of the research method on this basis overlooks a number of important points:

- Depth interviews are generally more intimidating for respondents than group discussions.
- They are extremely expensive and time-consuming.
- They do not offer one of the key benefits of group discussions, namely the cross-fertilization of ideas between respondents.

On the other hand, conducting full group discussions (of seven or eight people each) on press advertising does present problems of its own, primarily that of the moderator not being able to analyse the responses of *individuals* within the group to a particular execution. For all these reasons, I have found that mini-groups (of four or, at most, five respondents) are a very good compromise method.

The mini-group format allows the moderator to dwell on the reactions of each individual in turn, without letting the other respondents become impatient that their 'turn' will not come for a long time. It also allows for individuals in the room to discuss each other's points of view, without that debate becoming unmanageable—the moderator can restrict the discussion to just two respondents for example. Because of the smaller number of people, it also allows time for each *individual's* reactions to the whole campaign to be explored in considerable depth. At the same time, because of the size of the group, respondents tend to develop a greater degree of rapport *between themselves* than would be the case in a larger group or with an interviewer in a one-to-one situation. This generally eases the flow of the conversation and reduces the degree of intensity that accompanies so many depth interviews.

How, then, to expose the advertising? A number of possibilities exist in this area that are worth touching on briefly:

Where only a single rough layout of each advertisement is available, then usually some simulation (either one-to-one or in a mini-group) of a brief exposure can work very well. Having told the respondent(s) what form the material is in, literally show them the advertisement for 5 to 6 seconds and then take it away.

Questioning can then relate to what if anything was noticed during that brief exposure—hence giving some clues as to the main things that the advertisement was or was not conveying, including branding again. After exploring these initial reactions, the advertisement can then be shown more fully and discussed in greater detail.

Where a number of prints of a rough layout are available, respondents can go through the same process themselves, turning the advertisement face down when you ask them to do so.

Where one press advertisement in a campaign has been finished up to a high degree (perhaps even using a test photograph), or where previous advertisements in the same campaign have been run, these can be used to illustrate the 'style' or look of the campaign before less finished roughs are exposed in the way described above.

The 'folder test' method is perhaps one of the best techniques of all, though generally more appropriate in the depth interview situation.

Here, recruitment of relevant people is disguised among questions relating to a specific medium in which the advertisement might appear (e.g. the *Sunday Times* magazine). Respondents arrive in the belief that they are going to be talking about that magazine, and indeed when they arrive they are asked to wait a few minutes and given a copy of the magazine to look at. This 'copy', in fact, is a constructed magazine, the pages of which are inside plastic wallets, bound in a folder. Among the pages will be the test advertisement (in a highly-finished rough form), plus examples of other advertising in the category, plus other advertisements and editorial features.

If a highly-finished (photographic) rough cannot be produced, then other advertisements can be 'mocked-back' to a semi-finished form to maintain comparability. Either way, although the respondent will realize he is not looking at a 'proper' magazine, he *will not* realize that it is in fact only one advertisement you are interested in.

After allowing, say, 10 minutes for him to browse through the magazine (in a separate room), the interview then begins, and the moderator asks about *all* that has been read or looked at in the folder (including editorial), perhaps asking the respondent to go through page by page pointing out what was or was not looked at.

Then questioning begins to focus on the category of products (and advertisements for these) that are actually of interest, before alighting on and discussing in detail the test advertisement itself.

This technique is about the closest one can get to the replication of 'real world' readership behaviour and can be extremely effective in eliciting spontaneous reactions to an execution. Again though, regardless of the stimulus material or methodology chosen, the order of questioning with regard to press advertising will be very similar to that for television discussed above.

It cannot be stressed enough that consumer's respond to advertising holistically rather than atomistically. If you or the moderator encourage the atomistic examination of individual elements of the advertisement, or create a clear evaluative framework for respondents to judge the advertising by, you are seriously distorting the way in which consumers might *actually* respond in the real world.

This is why the majority of quantitative techniques are so inappropriate at this stage of the advertising development process. The very fact of their structured approach leads to an ordering of responses that is a long way away from helping us to understand how our unique piece of communication actually works.

Qualitative research allows respondents to find their own vocabulary and 'structure' to describe their reactions—often in ways that cannot be predicted when writing a questionnaire or even a discussion guide. A good moderator will encourage this kind of spontaneity, no matter how tenuous the associations or how diffuse the stream of ideas is, rather than seeking all the time to impose logic and sequence on the discussion.

That imposition can take place later when listening back to tapes or just thinking about all that has been said. It is at that stage that the pieces of the jigsaw can be slotted together and structured, not while the interview or discussion is in progress.

Press advertising is uniquely complex—and the degree of 'take out' from a press advertisement may vary enormously between respondents. This is not the place to discuss how press advertising *actually* works. Suffice it to say that it cannot be assumed that the reader will necessarily do more than look at the visual, glance at a headline and perhaps register a brand name. It is very often the case that body copy will not be read at all. Certainly it is unrealistic to expect that confusion or contradictions in headline or visual can be 'resolved' by respondents being expected to read the copy—generally they will not! Press advertisements should communicate *most* of what they are intended to communicate without the assumption that copy will be read; that is why press roughs without copy *are* generally sufficient as a research stimulus. If they 'fail' at that level, they will almost certainly fail in the real world.

Finally, if you are interested in testing the above theory yourself, try getting respondents in the research situation to read long copy advertisements. More often than not they will either do so reluctantly, or refuse to do so at all. If that is the reaction in the comparative unreality of the research situation, gauge for yourself the likelihood of the same advertisement being read in full in a non-forced situation!

There will, of course, be exceptions to this (high-interest categories, new concept products, etc.)—but it is these very exceptions that illustrate the general 'rule' that I have described.

CASE HISTORY 3: PRE-TESTING OF A PROPOSED PRESS CAMPAIGN FOR SEAGRAM'S 'MASSON LIGHT' WINE

Seagram (UK) were launching Masson Light, a dealcoholized wine, primarily to health-conscious or socially conscious women who would welcome a socially acceptable good-tasting alternative to alcohol. The advertising communication was to be a very simple, confident and stylish introduction of the product.

The agency's creative treatment consisted of full-page press advertisements, each featuring a personality and a witty quote about the wine or its benefits. The endline summed up the proposition; 'Masson Light. Wine with everything but alcohol'. The personalities ranged from Paula Yates and Oliver Reed, to the weightlifter Liza Lyons.

Given the 'social' nature of wine-drinking occasions, the agency researched the concepts in mini-groups of four to five people, in preference to in-depth interviews. The concepts were presented in rough form, with one highly finished layout to demonstrate the intended look of the campaign. Photos of the personalities featured were also used as stimulus material.

The groups threw up all sorts of issues. Respondents were sensitive to every executional element, and tried—in some cases in vain—to fit them all together. If any element was not right, such as the personality in the setting, or the tone of the quote, the whole communication tended to be lost.

The Paula Yates concept held together nicely. She was right because she was respected and admired as an individual, and her endorsement of something unusual like Masson Light was credible. The proposition in the quote was amusing and appropriate both to her and to the product. The layout and the tone of the execution was confident and stylish. Every element enhanced every other and contributed to the message about Masson Light.

Things did not click so easily for the Frank Bruno idea. The problem was the choice of personality here. Sports celebrity endorsement is something of a cliché, and people tended to take the health/sports association out of this as the main idea. Though this was appropriate for a dealcoholized wine, they found Frank Bruno a misfit; a boxer doesn't wear a black tie or drink wine from delicate glasses.

Perceptions changed radically if the advertisement successfully communicated that these contrasts were deliberate and that Bruno was in on the joke. His endorsement became valid and the black tie was an amusing 'hammed' pointer to style and sophistication. The whole advertisement became a witty variation on the 'sports endorsement of health product' theme.

Finished rough: Liza Lyons

Press rough: Frank Bruno

One general finding was a need for more product information. People are used to and enjoy reading descriptions of a wine's taste and looked for them here. On the basis of such a description they would slot a wine into their mental repertoire. When debriefing the research the agency recommended adding a line about the wine's taste, which would support Masson Light's claim to proper wine status.

The first execution in the series to run was the Paula Yates advertisement, to which only minor changes were made.

RESEARCHING POSTERS

In general, the comments above for press apply here, too. Obviously though, techniques such as the 'folder test' are inappropriate to this medium—whereas, for example, showing the poster large and 'remote' (such as via 35 mm slides shown on a wall) become more relevant. This latter technique can be enhanced by surrounding the test poster slide with 'environmental' shots of other posters or road/traffic scenes.

After initial exposure in this way, questioning can proceed as for press or TV, though recognizing that posters *must* communicate quickly, hence the 'studied' situation is in a sense less relevant than the initial exposure period.

With posters, too, in my view, the depth interview is still less essential than for press.

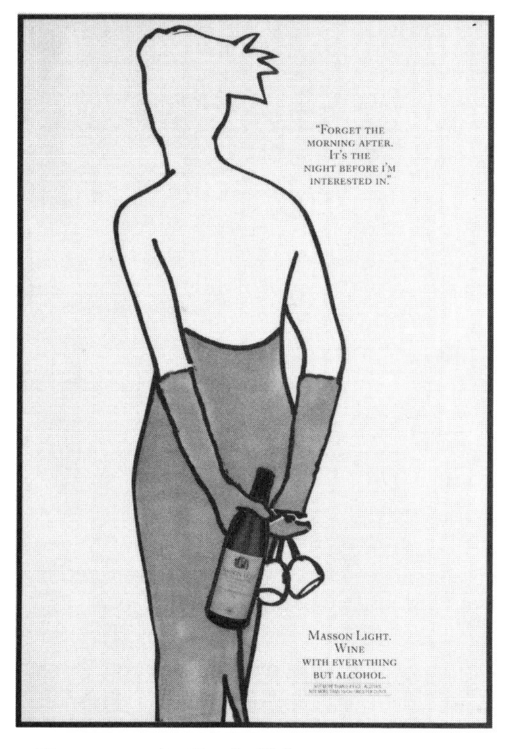

Press rough: Paula Yates

Finished advertisement: Paula Yates

Particularly if the poster is to be exposed in the way described above, full group discussions may well be perfectly appropriate.

Finally, and again only in my personal view, posters are the one medium where I would feel a lot happier to use some quantitative measure of how the advertising is working. This is partly a result of observing so many recessive or indecipherable posters that manifestly fail to deliver any message at all, and partly a function of the availability of some quite good filmic techniques for superimposing a highly finished poster rough on to blank 'hoardings' within a piece of film shot, for example, around a specific town. This seems to me to be quite a good approximation to the way in which posters are actually seen, lends itself to a research situation quite well, and allows for important questions regarding stand-out, impact, brand registration and main message communication to be elicited quantitatively relative to other campaigns or executions, and at a stage where action can still be taken to redress any failings in respect of these measures.

It is because posters *have* to be relatively simpler, quicker and more impactful in their environment that a quantitative measure of this medium might, on occasion, be desirable. With press or television, the role of creative development research is much less to do with measures such as these, much more to do with understanding a complex piece of communication and a surrounding set of images. This, then, is perhaps a good opportunity to move on from the consideration of specific media to a more general discussion about the approach to creative development research and some of the specific issues that arise in this area.

THE ROLE OF QUANTITATIVE VERSUS QUALITATIVE RESEARCH

It will not have escaped the reader's attention that quantitative methods have not figured highly in the preceding discussion. With the exception of the poster research situation, it is the author's view that quantitative methods are significantly less appropriate to creative development research in most cases than are qualitative methods.

The reasons for this relate back to some of the earlier discussions in this chapter regarding the way in which advertising works. Advertisements in the various media discussed do themselves lie along a spectrum of complexity (Figure 3).

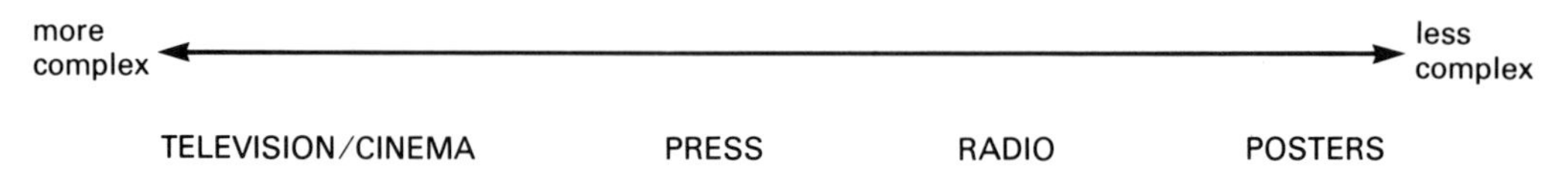

Figure 3: Spectrum of complexity for media advertising

The nature of the *potential* for communication in each of these media varies significantly, with posters being the simplest, television advertising being the most complex.

In my view it is this 'potential for complexity' that defines both the role of research *per se* and the nature of that research. The more complex the medium or the specific communication, the greater the onus on research as an aid to *judgement*. The less complex the medium or the communication, the more the research can play a role in its own right as a guide to impact and communication of a simple message.

This observation has two important outcomes:

- The role of the *planner* becomes increasingly important as one moves towards the more complex end of the spectrum, since what he 'brings to the party' is precisely the contextual judgement that is necessary to put the research into some sort of perspective, relative to everything else that is known about the brand and its consumers.
- As one moves towards these more complex media and communications, the role of research is much more to do with understanding than with measurement. As such, quantitative research becomes increasingly less appropriate, while the greater degree of insight, diagnosis and flexibility provided by qualitative methodologies becomes more important. Then, the task of research is to help the planner and the creatives understand how and why the advertising is working in the way that it is, and how this can be built upon and developed. Qualitative research uses much looser constructs to allow this understanding to be gained.

Of course, quantitative research can be used to evaluate animatics or press roughs either solus or relative to other advertisements or norms. In these cases, the general principles discussed above will still prevail regarding order of questioning, key areas to be covered, etc. But my argument is that the very nature of quantitative research makes it so often an inappropriate or even misleading method of examining the subtleties of consumer reactions to advertising.

There may well be good reasons (impact, branding, etc.) when one comes on to examine reactions to a finished film or press advertisement to use quantitative measures. But at this stage the emphasis is on creative *development*, not evaluation. To develop advertising requires sensitivity, diagnosis, contextual understanding, the ability to pick up and make sense of subtleties and nuances and the ability to feed back such knowledge in an actionable way. Qualitative research, done well by someone who understands the brand and its advertising (best of all the planner himself) can provide precisely those attributes. This is a lesson that has been learnt in this country over the last ten years or so, and the quality of UK advertising stands as testimony to its benefits. It is a lesson that the US agencies are just about to wake up to.

INTERPRETATION

All that has been written so far should indicate that creative development research, especially in the more complex areas of press and TV advertising, is a developmental and highly judgemental process. It should be clear also that the reporting of qualitative research findings from advertising research is a matter of interpretation. It is the moderator's and planner's job to interpret consumers' responses in order to make them actionable within the creative development process.

How do we do this if consumers do not themselves have an evaluative framework or even, on occasions, a suitable vocabulary for discussing advertising? The answer to this, unfortunately, is 'experience'! Over time, one develops a good understanding of the kind of responses and 'models' that consumers *do* operate with, and what these mean. Let us examine just a couple of these here.

The first and most important consumer 'construct' that the moderator or planner has to deal with is that 'people expect advertising to *sell* them something'. In research situations, consumers frequently respond to advertising as though they were at the point of purchase. Hence they expect the advertising to tell them: how big, how many, what taste, what colour, what price, etc.—almost like point of sale material or packaging. Yet, very often, the job of advertising is simply to *get* people to the point of purchase—and the barriers to this may be image-based rather than product-based.

More often than not advertising has to interest consumers in the 'idea' of the product, rather than the product itself. Yet because it is the latter that people buy, it is the product itself about which they feel they *should* be informed. Understanding this consumer model is crucial to one's ability to interpret the all too-frequent 'why don't they show me/tell me more about the product' type of response.

Second, and connected with the first point, is consumers' tendency to emphasize the rational response. Not only will consumers portray their own purchase decision-making as highly rational, they will claim that this is what they want the advertising to be telling them, too. Connected with this is the tendency (among men especially) to resist emotional appeals; a resistance, it has to be said, that is heightened by being in the company of seven or eight other men. Both sexes though, at the more general level, generally find it difficult to talk about *imagery*. It is not something they talk about much in their daily lives; they often feel uneasy about being thought to be influenced by it—hence they try to avoid discussion of it.

Once again, it is the job of a good moderator to get behind the rational response, explore the emotional reaction, observe the body language—or specifically probe for the *feelings* that the advertisement conveyed—or even ask about 'the kind of feelings that *other* people might get from that advertising', or 'the things that the person who made the advertisement was trying to get across'.

Interpretation is also about making the most of the research situation itself. Qualitative research is *not* about head-counts. The thought that comes up in, say, a group discussion that *really* moves an idea ahead might only be raised by one person. Yet it may be such a powerful or lateral solution to an apparent problem as to outweigh the negatives of all the other respondents.

Finally, in interpretation, the moderator must have his or her *own* conceptual framework for analysing consumers' response. The kind of model that I outlined earlier can be really helpful in this respect: it allows you to sort out reactions to the central creative idea from those to the peripheral executional elements; the *key* communication points from the minutiae—critical if everything consumers say is not to be taken at face value, or given equal importance.

FEEDBACK

Here too, in a sense, we are referring back to some of the general attitudes and principles dealt with earlier. The planner's job (whether he or she conducted the groups or not) is to act as the 'bridge' between the research and the creative team. As well as understanding *their* approach to the advertising, the planner has to communicate to them his interpretation of what consumers took out of it.

We wrote earlier of the need for sensitivity in this area; we have also written about the need for interpretation. What is most obvious from this is that the very *least* effective feedback is simply reportage of what people said—especially given the vehemence of people's language about advertising they *do not* like! It is unnecessary and unhelpful simply to tell creatives a whole series of negative comments from research. By all means summarize the problem areas—but dwell more on the opportunities or ways round these problems.

It also makes good general sense to start the debrief with what is good rather than what is bad, defining the strengths of the creative idea before talking about the weaknesses that need to be addressed. The creatives will need to be motivated to re-think an idea they may by now have passed on from weeks ago. You are hardly going to get them to be constructive and enthusiastic again if you start by reeling off a whole set of negatives.

The final point here is very simply, to tell the creatives *first*. It can be pretty demotivating to hear how your idea went down in research third hand, after the client. It is *their* idea... they have a right to be first to know the news: good or bad!

THE CONDUCT OF CREATIVE DEVELOPMENT RESEARCH

Throughout this chapter, I have tried to address the perspective of the account planner at this most crucial stage of advertising development. Once again though the word 'moderator' also crept in when we were discussing the conduct of qualitative research on advertising.

To a degree, I have used the words 'planner' and 'moderator' synonomously when discussing conduct since even though the planner may not be the moderator of such research it is clearly his role to act as 'mediator' between the research and the creative process. This apparent confusing of terms is worthy of further explanation.

In UK agency planning circles there has for some time been a debate regarding whether planners should or should not conduct their own research.

Those against this way of working claim that planners are not recruited to be qualitative researchers—that there are others (freelancers generally) better qualified to do this. Planners, they argue, cannot be 'objective' about the conduct of research on advertising they themselves have helped produce—and anyway an outside researcher will carry more 'weight' with the creative team and the client.

Those in favour of this way of working (including myself) would argue that the planner's job is to be the 'representative' of the consumer within the agency. As such the most vital part of their job is the understanding of the consumer. The best way to understand consumers is to talk to them—and the best way to talk to them is first hand. If a planner is not good at talking to consumers first hand, he probably is not a very good planner. Therefore, a good planner ought to be a good qualitative research moderator. In this view of the job there is no substitute for first-hand enquiry. The planner is the person closest to the brand and its advertising on a continuous basis; he understands the context within which the advertising has to work better than anyone else. Thus, by definition, no outsider will ever be as well briefed to tackle creative development research, since no briefing can substitute for the accumulated knowledge of the brand that resides in the planner.

In this view of the job, 'objectivity' is a non-issue. The very thing that makes a good planner good at creative development research is his *proximity* to the total creative process. It is because he does identify with the creative work that he will be best placed to see how it can be developed and improved. Remember, we are talking about advertising development, not evaluation. In the latter case objectivity may be an advantage; in the former it is almost certainly a disadvantage. Qualitative research is about participation and ideas, not distance and observation—it is *not* an objective method, and neither should it be so.

As to the argument about 'weight'; it is the job of the *agency* to create a climate within which the consumers voice is heard, listened to and acted upon both within the agency and by clients. If the planner cannot command 'weight' with creatives when he himself has done the research, in what other situation can he possibly be expected to do so? So, too, with the client. The agency has to have sufficient confidence in itself to support the planner and his findings, whether good or bad, in debriefing the client. Only by being totally honest about its own work can the agency hope to build and maintain good, long-term relationships with its clients. The planner's role—and the role that research itself can play—is critical within this climate of trust between agency and client.

For all of these reasons, I would hope that the day will soon come when *all* planners take pride in being outstanding qualitative research moderators themselves—since this means simply being outstanding at that skill which lies at the very heart of the planner's job: communicating with and understanding consumers.

What then of the situation where the planner does not or cannot do the research himself? The answer is that the planner has to ensure that the person who *is* going to moderate the research gets as close as possible to the brand and its advertising before the research takes place. This means:

- Reviewing the brand itself, its performance in the market, its users and its competition.
- Reviewing the brand strategy and the creative brief for this advertising specifically.
- If possible, using the same researcher who did any strategic development research on the brand, again at this stage.
- Briefing the researcher *thoroughly* on this advertising specifically—if possible with the creatives there, too, to talk about why *they* think the advertising is the way it is.
- Giving the researcher *lots* of opportunities to look at the advertising him or herself before the research takes place.
- The planner attending the research and, if possible, working together with the researcher on the debrief, even (maybe) doing some of the debrief.

All this boils down to one word: involvement. If the planner is proud of his job, he will want to make sure he does do all these things. Equally, if the researcher is any good at his job, he will want the planner to do these things too. (But how much easier, and better, if they were one and the same person.)

SOME CONCLUDING REMARKS

What I have tried to illustrate in this chapter is that 'using research in creative development' is not simply about listing techniques, but rather about having an attitude or a 'point of view'. It is an attitude that, I believe, should start with a view about how advertising works and about the role of research. This sequence of approach leads to not one theory of advertising but many and, from this, an attitude to advertising research that is to do with understanding, learning and developing, rather than measuring, testing and evaluating.

I hope I have also illustrated the importance of defining clearly what can and cannot be found out in research—and hence also provided a model for understanding the scope of creative development research and for prioritizing responses when interpreting consumer reactions.

Also I have tried to illustrate the ways in which consumers' responses to advertising differ from advertising peoples'—and why.

I have suggested that, generally, qualitative methodologies are a better way of understanding those responses and indeed that such methodologies offer the planner a unique opportunity to be involved himself at the very heart of the process by personally conducting such research.

I end with a quote from what I believe still remains the best dissertation on advertising research, Alan Hedges' 'Testing to Destruction':

> We are not *testing* the advertising since we do not have, and cannot have, any such machine. We are *studying consumers* in order to gain some better understanding of the way they are likely to react to ... advertising ideas. Since both the stimuli and repertoire of possible responses are highly complex (and since the research situation is a highly unusual one) we know that we cannot make any precise and simple formulation of what a given advertisement will achieve—but we *can* improve our understanding to the point where we are better able both to produce relevant and effective ideas and to judge when we have a campaign which is adequate for our purposes.

REFERENCES

1 Daniel Starch: 'Measuring the Effect of Advertising on Sales' (five articles), *Printer's Ink*, March–May 1964.
2 Mark Lovell: 'Advertising Research' in *Consumer Market Research Handbook*, ed. Robert Worcester, Van Nostrand Reinhold 1978.
3 Gary Duckworth: Unpublished speech to Account Planning Group, London, 1985.
4 David Cowan & Ross Barr: 'Guiding Creative People—The Vital Link', ESOMAR Seminar paper, Monte Carlo, 1983.
5 Wendy Gordon: 'Stimulus Material: Current Thinking & Development', AQRP Seminar paper, London, 1986.
6 Alan Hedges: 'Testing to Destruction', IPA, 1974.

7 Testing advertisements

Mary Stewart-Hunter

A CONTROVERSIAL AND THORNY SUBJECT

Whatever the theoretical or practical objections advanced by the agency as a matter of policy, or by the individual planner in response to a particular brief, almost all of us will at some time find ourselves involved in a pre-testing study.

Pre-testing is a technically difficult subject and one full of minefields for the planner. The literature is extensive but not usually very helpful at the practical level, consisting of either very well-argued cases against pre-testing or papers from research companies generally in support of their own particular technique. While the endless debate on qualitative versus quantitative research is useful theoretical background, it rarely provides much guidance on how to do it.

Pre-testing is also a highly political issue, arising at a point when clients are about to commit large sums of money on production or even larger sums on media expenditure. Handled badly, pre-testing can become extremely divisive, threatening the hard-won trust between client and agency and, at a more personal level, between client researcher and agency planner.

Also, pre-testing will often release a great deal of internal agency emotion. However much the client may have dictated the technique, it may appear to account handlers that the planner has not argued strongly enough against it or to creative people that the planner is not on their side. Even though we are rarely blamed if something goes wrong, we will always feel bad about it. Even when things go swimmingly, we rarely get any thanks. Few planning reputations are made in this arena.

You could be forgiven for expecting, as a result of this chronicle of woes, that I am about to argue against pre-testing. That would, I believe, be both unrealistic and unhelpful for it is likely that all of us will be involved in such a study at some time and will need to know how best to set about it.

Until now, I have referred to 'pre-testing' as if it were one technique with one set of objectives, one set of advantages and one set of problems. Clearly this is not the case. Nor is there one simple and widely agreed definition of what it actually is. For example, there are at least three ways pre-testing can be defined:

- *Structured quantitative research into advertisements.* Perhaps the most commonly used definition. Thus, pre-testing could include research into rough, as well as finished, advertisements.
- *Research to evaluate the likely effectiveness of a finished advertisement prior to exposure.* This definition distinguishes between research on finished advertisements and research on rough advertisements (generally called creative development research); *and* between research prior to exposure and that done during or after exposure (often called post-testing).

- *Research to check specific issues, generally impact and communication, rather than to evaluate the appropriateness of the creative idea* or provide guidance on its development. A more controversial definition since the distinction between the idea, its communication and impact can be regarded as overly mechanistic.

A further definition could be argued around the use of the word *testing*, which some planners will assert signifies all that is bad about pre-testing. Whereas creative development research recognizes overtly that advertising works as a complex two-way process between advertisement and consumer, pre-*testing* can seem to assume a much more simplistic one-way effect that can be accurately measured. Similarly, while creative development research recognizes that creative ideas are vulnerable and need sympathetic handling to get the best out of them, pre-*testing* seems to imply that an advertisement will be subjected to certain rigorous standards until it proves it has nothing wrong with it. Put simplistically, it often appears that, whereas in creative development research, the advertisement is held to be innocent until proved guilty, in pre-*testing* it is held to be guilty until proved innocent.

While this is not a very helpful definition, there is clearly a lot in these distinctions that is central to avoiding the pitfalls of pre-testing.

Returning to the three definitions; because each of them is perfectly valid, the scope of this chapter is necessarily rather broad. Although I will be concentrating on research to evaluate impact and communication at post-production stage using quantitative techniques, I will discuss pre-testing with rough materials as well. Most of what I have to say will be about television commercials, but I will pay attention to other media.

Before examining specific objectives and methods of pre-testing let us look at some of the broad issues relating to the circumstances when pre-testing arises.

1 PRE-TESTING VERSUS CREATIVE DEVELOPMENT RESEARCH

Many of the misconceptions about pre-testing arise because people tend to regard these two things as alternatives. In reality, they are capable of providing different kinds of information at different points in the campaign development process and should be regarded as complementary, not competitive.

In Chapter 6, Leslie Butterfield defines the objectives of CDR as being to assess the extent to which the *central* creative idea is capable of gaining the desired response from the audience *and* to build an understanding of how the responses arise, so that the creative team can see how best to develop and improve the idea. Thus, CDR represents an early check on the creative direction and a means of improving the end product.

In many cases the results of CDR will be sufficiently clear-cut to suggest a strong and effective commercial. Using their experience and based on their trust in the Agency, many clients will then judge that no further research need take place, until the commercial is monitored in the campaign tracking study. However, there are a number of circumstances in which the client and/or agency may feel the need for further confirmation:

- Where the results are equivocal, pointing to a *potentially* strong idea requiring amendment to help it achieve full potential.

- Where the original execution has been substantially changed in the process of production (for example, for ITCA reasons).
- Where the use of rough material was judged to be a poor approximation to the real thing.
- Where the qualitative technique is not considered to be sufficiently robust to base major financial decisions on.

You may regard this last point as a bit of a let-off for those clients who have insufficient experience and understanding of the creative and research processes, who are too nervous to make major decisions without 'belt and braces' evidence, or simply do not trust their agencies sufficiently. But however much you and your agency may dislike it, there are many clients who are like this, often with good cause.

For all these reasons, the need for pre-testing may emerge, either on an *ad hoc* or routine basis. The really important thing in these situations is not to let the desire for pre-testing take over and displace the use of CDR. Apart from the obvious risk of conducting a pre-test on a film that has not already been checked out at rough stage, the loss of CDR may have disastrous results on the creative product. Without it, all that insight and understanding will be lost to you and to the creative people, as will be the opportunity of making a good idea better. Without the early intervention of sensitive consumer feed-back, original and perhaps apparently risky ideas may be brushed aside in favour of more tried and trusted techniques.

2 TIMING PROBLEMS

The pre-testing of finished films creates enormous problems since, in all but the most perfect of situations, the period between the end of production and on-air dates is generally very short. Not only is there little time for research, but much more importantly there will be even less time to implement any changes that might be indicated by the research.

This time pressure is more than just inconvenient however, it is also the mechanism that tends to force the black and white, 'go – no go' framework on the research findings which is at best unhelpful and at worst dangerous. Commercials that might otherwise be highly effective run the risk of being rejected because there is no time, for instance, to re-shoot certain scenes, to re-edit or to improve lip-synch dialogue.

It is sometimes tempting to steal time by agreeing to research the commercial before it is complete, for example before colour grading has occurred, before optical effects (like dissolves) have been applied or before the final soundtrack has been laid. This temptation should be resisted wherever possible because if the objective is to test a finished film then it makes no sense to use something less than perfect. When respondents are shown an animatic they can usually be persuaded to allow for the fact that it is rough, but when a film appears to be finished they will find it much harder to make that allowance.

Given these problems, what are the possible benefits to clients of routine pre-testing of finished films? For a large client company with big brands generating huge budgets with multi-execution campaigns there can be some real benefits. If, say, three commercials are shot, they can generally afford to scrap one if it does not appear to work as well as the others. The research might suggest that the three commercials have differing appeals to various sectors of the target, in which case the media rotation plan can be amended accordingly. Other advertisers may take the view that provided the commercial does not appear totally ineffective they can afford to run it as it stands, while the agency makes the necessary amendments in time for the second burst.

This kind of pragmatism was typical of the big packaged goods companies of the 1960s and 1970s, when production costs were a lot smaller than today and when the real value of media budgets was a lot higher. Thus advertising executions were more 'disposable' and so finished film testing made more sense. In the USA, where media budgets are much greater in relation to production costs, the same view is still prevalent and today it is mainly those UK companies with US parentage that follow this practice.

But whether or not this pragmatism exists among clients, the pre-testing of finished films remains a very anxious time for the agency and represents a major problem for the planner to manage. Of course all the usual wise advice about careful design, thorough briefing and sensitive interpretation applies. Having already conducted a CDR study will pay dividends, because the planner can then use these findings as parameters for the pre-test.

3 PRE-TESTING ANIMATICS

So far the discussion has assumed that pre-testing necessarily entails finished films but, as stated earlier, it is possible to include certain forms of research into animatics within the broad definition of pre-testing. Typically, this would be done as a final quantitative check on a commercial prior to production.

The benefits of pre-testing animatics are clear. The research happens prior to production and thus can avoid the situation of costly finished commercials being scrapped. It also allows the creatives to work out in advance of production what needs to be done to the film to improve its performance.

The problem is also obvious: some commercials cannot be easily replicated in an animatic, though if the client is prepared to pay for a top-quality production, even the most difficult subjects *can* be translated into animatic form.

4 PRE-TESTING OF OTHER MEDIA

The pre-testing of print media and radio is much less common than for television, presumably because the financial stakes are generally much lower. However, where it does take place, most of the issues discussed above (e.g. timing problems, rough versus finished material) apply as much as they do to television.

PRE-TESTING OBJECTIVES

Advertisements are designed in particular ways to achieve certain predefined aims, and the objectives of advertising research should be designed in relation to these specified aims. It is in relation to this simple and non-controversial proposition that the theoretical problems of pre-testing emerge.

First of all, what do we mean by 'certain pre-defined aims'? Well, the advertising strategy should make it clear what these are, but in reading or writing any advertising strategy, one soon becomes aware that it consists of a series of layers. Take this simple model, for instance (Figure 1).

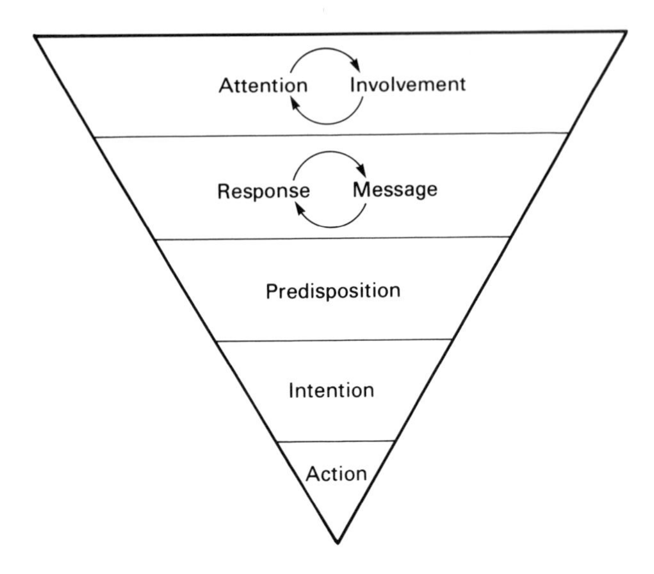

Figure 1: Layers of advertising strategy

At its most direct level, an advertisement is designed to gain the attention and involvement of the target audience, and they are intended to extract a certain message. This message is designed to affect their existing predispositions in such a way that their intentions may be altered in favour of the advertiser. Given the circumstances of a particular market, this intention has the potential to be translated into a particular action.

Which of these layers should pre-testing be measuring? I think that most people these days would agree that the last layer, that is whether or not the target audience will *act*, is not something that advertising can directly affect and is therefore not a legitimate objective for pre-testing.

Where it becomes more controversial is in the areas of *intention to act* and *attitude change*, which many practitioners believe are legitimate objectives for pre-testing. In certain markets it is possible to argue against this on the grounds that attitudes and intentions follow, rather than precede, behaviour. Whether or not you believe these effects are legitimate objectives, all your real world experience will tell you that there are enormous practical problems in attempting to measure these kinds of effect.

By observation, we believe that a great deal of advertising works in a non-rational or even unconscious way. If that is so, how does someone know what their intention is until faced with the need to make a decision? Even if they do 'know', do *we* have the right way to ask them about it or do *they* have the ability to articulate? What happens if they see another competitive commercial after they have been exposed to ours? How long does it take for attitudes to change? How do we take account of the duration and frequency of the advertising?

Many of these problems surround all pre-testing objectives, but are especially acute when attempting to predict the effects of advertising or when attempting to measure something that probably happens some time after the measurement was taken. However, as we move up through the layers of the simple model (Figure 1), the more we are dealing with straightforward 'real time' communication issues that can be observed.

Many researchers, planners and clients believe that only these 'real time' responses are legitimate and practical objectives for pre-testing. The legitimacy of communication testing is further argued in the context of the whole process of strategy definition. Developed in the context of the client's and agency's understanding of how a particular market works, backed up with rigorous analysis of consumer data, the strategy identifies what needs to be communicated to bring about the desired marketing goals. Most planners would argue that, having agreed the communication objectives and later having ensured in CDR that the creative idea is capable of delivering them, the role of pre-testing is to check that they are being delivered.

However, other people (particularly on the other side of the Atlantic) have come to quite a different point of view. Taking a 'black box' approach, they do not believe that the test needs to replicate reality, provided that the measurement can be validated in the real world. If, say, an intent to purchase measure can be shown to correlate with actual sales levels, then they believe that the experimental measure must be a good predictor of likely advertising effectiveness. By conducting many such tests over time, experience will be built up that will help to identify a potentially ineffective commercial from an effective one. Such experience is generally known as 'normative data'. I shall talk more about 'norms' in the concluding section of this chapter.

In the remainder of this section I will discuss in more detail the specific measures that are encountered in pre-test techniques.

IMPACT

So far, impact has only been mentioned in passing, and then only in the context of communication testing. In fact, impact is very different from communication and much more problematic in research terms.

At its most direct level, an advertisement is designed to gain the attention and involvement of the target audience—unless an advertisement is noticed it stands no chance of achieving any of its objectives. I think it also goes without saying that unless that attention is active, involved and interested, these objectives will be only partially achieved.

You will have noticed that I have introduced at least two separate ideas into this discussion of impact and used a number of different words as though they were interchangeable. This is the problem with impact; it is a concept made up of a number of component factors, that do not have a commonly agreed terminology. But because it is crucial to know what is being measured, it is necessary to define what these components might be:

- The ability of an advertisement to capture the attention of its audience. This is sometimes called 'stopping power'.

- The ability of an advertisement to hold that attention long enough for the audience to take in the message. Anyone who has moderated or observed a group discussion will know that there are many ways in which one can gauge whether an advertisement has captured the respondents' attention. It will be apparent from their body language, from the tone in which they respond and from what they say. However, in quantitative research none of these responses is at all easy to measure.

  Recognizing that physical response is an important indicator of attention, various researchers have experimented with direct observation techniques but, because of the complexity of the physical response, these techniques were only ever able to measure isolated aspects of it. Various bits of hardware, like the eye camera and skin-galvanometer, have been borrowed from the psychology laboratory but have never proved commercially useful, at least on this side of the Atlantic.

  With direct observation thus ruled out, we are left with what people say and how they say it. In quantitative research, it is possible to record verbal responses (though not tone of voice) but often people don't *say* very much and the very act of asking them to verbalize draws their attention to the advertisement in an unrealistic way. Thus concentration on verbal responses can run the risk of over-estimating the attention value of an advertisement.
- How well an advertisement gains attention *relative* to the other advertisements in its media environment. Advertisements that appear to generate an attentive response when examined in isolation can sometimes prove to be weak on attention when having to compete for that attention. Thus, testing for impact sensibly involves some form of comparative appraisal. This is done by showing the test commercial in a reel composed to replicate a programme break (or a press advertisement in a mocked-up magazine) and recording the respondents' recall of what they saw.
- Memorability. We should not assume that attention and memorability are the same thing. (A psychologist would state that they are definitely not the same.) It is theoretically possible for an advertisement to gain attention, communicate an instant and memorable impression about the brand and then be forgotten. We know that recall levels decay over time, but since most pre-testing takes place within minutes of seeing the advertisement, this cannot be a very common occurrence. Thus, it is generally accepted that remembering having seen an advertisement is a useful surrogate measure of the attention value it originally generated. For some advertisers, remembering having seen an advertisement is also important in its own right. So called 'famous advertising' is now recognized as indicating a high level of involvement with the advertisement and the potential for effective communication.
- Branding. However, it is possible to have highly memorable advertising that is ineffective, because it is not well branded. Evidence from advertising tracking studies reveals that many advertisements lack 'impact' in the sense that they have low advertisement awareness and recall levels. In effect, this means that whether or not such advertisements gained attention at the time of showing, they are not well linked to the brand name. Although I have heard people argue that remembering the ad/brand link does not matter provided the advertisement has rubbed off positively on the brand, experience suggests that the ability to link explicitly the advertisement with its brand is an important indicator of its communication ability. Thus 'branding' is another of the components of this broad concept called impact.

In summary, 'impact' is a highly complex notion and therefore hard to measure precisely in quantitative testing. Although these problems are widely acknowledged, the generally accepted view is that impact should be measured, in a comparative way, in terms of the ability of the audience to remember seeing the advertisement at all *and* their ability to link the advertisement with its brand.

INVOLVEMENT

Although involvement is inextricably linked to impact, it is sufficiently important to be discussed also in its own right. Moreover, the means of measuring involvement are different from those of measuring impact and so need to be dealt with separately.

Involvement is best defined as the quality of impact. An advertisement that involves its audience is one that is watched, read or listened to more carefully; thus it will be better remembered *and* will communicate its message more powerfully. The type of involvement will vary from advertisement to advertisement, but it is always a matter of striking some chord with the audience. For example, involvement can arise from personal identification, or from being amused or entertained, or from being touched or inspired by the emotional or sensual values emanating from the advertisement.

As with 'attention', involvement is much easier to assess in qualitative rather than quantitative research: from body language and from tone of voice as well as from what is actually articulated. Thus quantitative pre-testing can only ever give a partial, one-sided view of involvement. However, whereas probing can dangerously exaggerate the attention being paid to an advertisement, the right kind of questioning can be quite revealing as to the advertisement's ability to involve.

The right kind of question is one that encourages people to use their own words to describe their responses: in terms of what they saw or heard, their thoughts and feelings and their likes and dislikes. By examining the content of their response, and the quantity of it, a great deal can be inferred as to how involved they were and whether that involvement was working in a positive direction.

The major problem with this technique is that of research quality. Any open-ended questions, but particularly those designed to assess involvement, depend on:

- Being administered by sensitive interviewers trained to record *everything* that is said.
- On thoughtful and well-briefed coders who can put some kind of structure on responses without losing their richness.
- On the interpretative ability of the researchers themselves. (Prompted questions are also used to assess involvement.)

Various other means of assessing involvement have been tried in the past but are now rejected. These either involved some kind of physiological observation, or systems that rely on the respondents themselves to indicate their degree of involvement (such as the theatre test 'Clapometer').

COMMUNICATION

In this context, communication is usually defined as the ability of an advertisement to deliver the desired message, in an understandable and believable way. Although apparently simple, the whole area of communication is full of pitfalls for the unwary:

- First, this definition tends to imply a simple one-way process: that of a receptive consumer waiting to be delivered the right message. All our experience suggests that communication is a far more complex, two-way process, to which consumers bring the benefit of all their own beliefs and experience, which, in turn, may cause them to reinterpret the message in terms that make sense to themselves rather than to us. So the way in which a message is intended to be delivered may be very different from the way it is received, which may be different again from the way it is relayed back to the researcher.

  So that the research can anticipate this process, it is very important that the researcher is furnished with a brief that clearly distinguishes between the objectives of the advertising, the way these have been interpreted in the advertising (the stimulus) and the desired or expected consumer response to them.
- Advertisements can range from those that work at a purely rational level to those that work at a totally non-rational level. This means that they will vary enormously in the degree of processing the consumer has to do to extract the message (or series of messages) and, even more crucially, to be able to articulate that message back to us. Where we expect respondents to have legitimate difficulty in describing the message or point of an advertisement, it is very important to allow them to express their feelings in a totally open-ended way, rather than force them to deliver us a neatly packaged, but artificial, conclusion.

  As with involvement, open-ended questions have a large part to play in communication testing, though it is possible to additionally check on the communication of specific points through the use of prompted questions.
- Comprehension and credibility are important concomitants of communication, but great care needs to be exercised to sift out the real and important problems from the chaff of over-rational 'research response'. For instance, many effective advertisements work via the use of analogy, metaphor or symbol which, at a purely rational level, may be 'hard to understand'. Similarly, many effective campaigns use hyperbole to dramatize their point which, at that purely rational level, may be 'hard to believe'.

ATTITUDES AND ATTITUDE SHIFTS

Some of the problems associated with attitude shifts have already been raised in an earlier context:

- How long and how much weight of exposure is required for attitudes to change?
- At what point do favourable attitudes coalesce to form an intent to purchase?
- What happens to our brand's attitudes when competitors advertise on the same dimensions?
- Does attitude always precede behaviour or are there circumstances where behaviour affects attitudes?

Although there may be answers to these questions for individual brands, at a generalized level most of these questions remain largely unanswerable.

It has always been the received wisdom that attitudes take a long time to change, even in response to consistent heavyweight campaigns, though recent evidence from continuous tracking suggests that there can be considerable volatility in attitudes, indicating a degree of short-term effect. However, the extent to which this is due to sheer advertising presence stimulating the consumer to think more about the brand than hitherto, *or* the direct result of advertising communication is extremely hard to assess. I favour the view that advertising communication is at least part of this measurable effect and that attempting to look at attitude shifts in pre-testing *can* be a useful evaluative tool.

However, there are considerable technical difficulties in attempting to measure such shifts in the space of an interview. Various techniques have been devised, such as pre-interviewing (as in twenty-four-hour recall) or using a control sample that has not been exposed to the advertising. Some techniques make no attempt to measure change and simply collect attitudes in an absolute way, providing no evaluative, though possibly some diagnostic, measurement.

PERSUASION (INTENT TO PURCHASE)

Although the stated objective of such a measurement is to assess the persuasive or motivational power of an advertisement, the actual question is generally formulated in terms of intent to purchase.

Most of the problems raised in relation to attitude shift attach to 'persuasion' as well, only more so. As far as its proponents are concerned, its major advantage is that as a single measure it can be interpreted against a bank of normative data, thus dispensing with the need to measure a 'change'.

Apart from the theoretical problems, its major practical danger is that, as a single measure, it is too readily seen as the summary score or bottom line of an advertisement's likely effectiveness.

DIAGNOSTICS

So far, the discussion has concentrated on evaluative measures designed to help clients and agencies decide whether they should be spending large sums of money behind a particular advertisement. However, there are other important issues beyond just whether an advertisement has an acceptable level of impact or message communication. If the advertisement seems to be achieving these levels, it is usually helpful to understand why (or to confirm the understanding gained in CDR). Even more significantly, if the advertisement appears deficient in some way, it is essential to be able to pinpoint the reasons. If they are relatively minor reasons, perhaps they can be dealt with before the air-date. If the problems are more intractable this understanding needs to be built into any future creative brief.

PRE-TESTING TECHNIQUES

Because of all the theoretical and technical problems encountered in pre-testing, the short history of the subject is littered with techniques, many of them now dead and buried. It is not my intention to review these in detail, but before discussing the most commonly used approach it will be helpful to touch on a few of the better known:

THEATRE TESTING

This is a generic name for a group of techniques (e.g. Schwerin, ASL, AAL) that involved the showing of a test commercial to a large audience, drawn to represent the target audience for the advertisement. The interview was administered centrally by a 'compère' with respondents self-completing a questionnaire. Generally, the questionnaire would cover brand and advertisement recall (from a reel of five or more commercials) and some simple message communication questions.

An added refinement was the use of an electronic dial (or 'Clapometer') to indicate the degree of interest experienced throughout the test commercial. Persuasion scores figured significantly, usually with a hidden pre-exposure brand preference being elicited at the recruitment stage and a further brand preference question asked at the end of the interview session.

CLUCAS

Whereas the typical theatre test took an entirely holistic (even black-box) approach to pre-testing, the Clucas technique attempts to look at a commercial in a bit-by-bit, atomistic way. The underlying theory was that any commercial is a series of separate (but linked) devices, each with its own particular purpose in terms of attracting attention, generating involvement, gaining sympathy or communicating a message.

The first step was for the agency to predefine exactly what each small section of the commercial was trying to achieve. In the research, the respondents were shown the commercial and then asked to:

- Underline on a copy of the script what they remembered having seen and heard.
- What they liked and disliked.
- To indicate what each section was communicating to them about the product.

Each of these elements was then graphed with time on the x axis and percentage response on the y axis, which demonstrated how attention, involvement and communication waxed and waned throughout the commercial. By overlaying these graphs on one another the researcher would then attempt to demonstrate the relationship between the various elements and to identify where any problem areas lay.

Whether or not television commercials really do work in this way, it certainly is not the way that most creative people design them and thus this technique was always extremely difficult for agency people to work with.

TWENTY-FOUR-HOUR RECALL

This approach, in widespread use in the United States, is relatively rare in the UK except among some of the major US-owned packaged good companies. Like theatre testing, it is a generic name for a number of specific techniques based on the on-air exposure of a test commercial. By showing the commercial in a realistic way in the home environment, twenty-four-hour recall attempts to overcome some of the major pitfalls encountered in the unrealistic 'hot-house' research environment.

The sample is either recruited in advance or after the test exposure. If recruited in advance, the sample is asked to watch the programme in which the commercial is to be shown. At this point a pre-exposure brand preference question is asked which is then repeated when respondents are reinterviewed the day after the commercial has been shown. In this way a persuasion shift measure can be added to the other recall questions. In other techniques, the sample is recruited the day after the commercial has been shown, and qualifies on the basis of claiming to have watched the programme (or time slot) in which the commercial was aired. A brand preference question will normally be asked, but since no 'shift' can be measured, this and other measures can only be evaluated against a normative data bank.

This is obviously a very expensive technique involving not only fully finished film but media costs as well, though these are usually minimized by showing the commercial in off-peak times in a restricted area. These days almost all interviewing is conducted by telephone.

The proponents of twenty-four-hour recall believe that this technique offers the most realistic appraisal of how effective a commercial will be in the real world. Much of the interpretation is made on the basis of comparisons with normative data and the heavy users of the technique will tend to have many years' worth of data in identical product fields against which they can make their judgements.

Critics of twenty-four-hour recall have a number of other problems:

- It is a very expensive study to mount and this is exacerbated by the huge contact sample required to identify enough people who can remember seeing the test commercial.
- There are many criticisms related to the quality of data yielded by twenty-four-hour recall. Even among those remembering the advertisement, the content recall is usually very superficial, which means that both its evaluative and diagnostic ability is limited. Inevitably this is a technique that puts more emphasis on crude numbers than it does on the more qualitative aspects of effectiveness.
- The technique assumes that all commercials work in the same way, requiring only one showing to achieve a level of impact and recall.

IMPACT AND COMMUNICATION TESTING

As a result of all the theoretical and practical problems associated with pre-testing, most clients and agencies (and thus research companies) tend to favour simple impact and communication tests. Although such studies are by no means free of problems, they do have the advantage of being flexible enough to take account of the requirements of differing market categories, brands and advertising styles. Although some kind of normative assessment may often be present, the study is usually complete in itself and the interpretation is generally made by taking an overall view of all the data and its internal relationships.

THE TYPICAL IMPACT AND COMMUNICATION TEST will be a central location (or hall test) study, recruiting its sample by prior invitation (relatively rare) or from passers-by in the adjacent streets and shopping centres. The sample can be as tightly defined as required, though of course too obvious a recruitment questionnaire may give prior warning to the respondents about the topic of the study, with detrimental effects on the impact question.

Once inside the location, the respondents will be shown the reel of commercials to establish advertisement and brand recall levels (impact). The number of commercials in the reel is a subject of some debate. Five commercials is the general rule (roughly replicating the number in a commercial break) but some practitioners argue that this makes it too easy for respondents to recall all of them, regardless of their relative success at gaining attention. It is certainly true that in a reel of five test commercials, it is unusual for any commercial to be recalled by less than 60 per cent. Increasingly, therefore, research companies are recommending that the reel should consist of seven or even ten commercials.

The composition of the reel is worthy of considerable discussion as the precise selection will determine the interpretative context for the test commercial. Most people seem to agree that all the commercials should be aimed at a broadly similar audience to the test commercial, otherwise the latter will stand out by default. Beyond that, they should ideally be selected to provide a range of likely impact levels, against which the test commercial can be compared. However, interpretation is extremely hard unless some kind of experience (on the researcher's behalf) or normative data can be applied.

This is why many clients who do a lot of pre-testing tend to use a common reel across all their tests in the same product field, which they update from time-to-time. This provides the combined advantages of a stable context and a range of test scores that can be compared with the one in hand. Some agencies put their own house reel together, though this can be an uncomfortable experience as, by definition, one of the agency's clients always has to come bottom!

In some cases, especially where there is a lot of competitive advertising, the reel may be composed only of competitive commercials. While I can see the attractions to the client of comparing his impact score with that of his competitors, in reality those competitive commercials will never compete side by side in a break. Furthermore, the fact that they are all, say, lager commercials, will make it easier for respondents to recall all the commercials.

A word should be said about *animatics* here. By definition impact testing on animatics is difficult because they are often devoid of all the production values that make a commercial attention-getting. However, if such a comparative impact test is judged essential, then it is important that the remainder of the reel is composed of other animatics, which almost certainly means that the choice will be limited. If you have any choice at all, try to vary the style and pace of them, because watching a reel of five or more animatics can be a very boring experience.

THE QUESTIONS USED TO ESTABLISH IMPACT will vary by research company, by client or by agency, but here are some examples:

- What commercials do you remember seeing? What others? What else?
- If commercial mentioned but not brand name ask:
  You mentioned seeing a commercial for ....
  Can you tell me what brand of .... was being advertised?

In this way it is possible to look at the level of those remembering the advertisement and the proportion of those linking the advertisement to the brand name.

Before the remainder of the interview takes place, the test commercial is generally shown again, in order to focus respondents' attention on it. The next section of the interview generally includes all the open-ended questions designed to elicit involvement and communication levels. The precise questions will obviously depend on the commercial and the research objectives, but for example, questions to establish 'involvement' levels could include one or more of the following:

- What thoughts or feelings went through your mind as you watched that commercial?
- How would you describe that commercial to someone who had never seen it?
- What, if anything, did you particularly like in that commercial?
- What, if anything, did you especially dislike?

In evaluating the answers, one is looking for the quality and intensity of response, rather than necessarily the actual points being made (though these may be useful in evaluating communication). Again, experience is necessary in order fully to interpret these findings; for instance an involving commercial will generally have a significant level of dislikes (about 20 to 30 per cent) as well as a high level of likes (about 70 per cent or more).

The open-ended questions can often be supplemented with pre-coded questions, for example:

- Here is a list of things that other people have said to describe this commercial. Can you tell me which of them you agree with? You can choose as many or as few as you wish.
  Witty
  Eye-catching
  Not very funny
  Pleasant to watch
  Boring
  Attractive people
  Old fashioned
  Original
  Up-to-date
  Informative

(The descriptors should include those you think are important to generating involvement, plus some 'blinds'.)

The approach to the communication questions is usually along these lines:

- What do you think was the main thing that commercial was saying about the product?

- What else was it saying?
- What reasons did the commercial give you for buying/using the product?

In the case of a new product, you might ask:

- How would you describe that product to someone who knew nothing about it?

Again, pre-coded questions can be used to supplement the open-ended questions, for example:

- I'm going to read out some things that other people have said that this commercial was saying about the product. How well (show card) do *you* think the commercial was making the point that:
  It is a high-quality product.
  It is soft to the touch.
  It is made only from natural materials.
  It resists stains.
  It is better value for money than man-made products.

(The attributes would contain the copy points you want to communicate plus some 'blinds'.)

You will notice that this question was formulated in communication terms (i.e. 'how well do you think it was making the point?') but frequently you will see this kind of question formulated in terms of attitudes to product (i.e. 'how much do you agree with this statement?'). As mentioned earlier, there does not seem much point in asking attitude questions unless some kind of comparison can be made, for example, based on a data bank drawn from previous studies in the same product field or by interviewing a matched control sample. In the latter approach, the respondents are recruited to match the main sample precisely, but are not shown the commercial and are only asked the brand attitude questions.

The same comparative procedure can be used for a persuasion or intention to purchase question.

The final issue to tackle is diagnostic information, though it may not be necessary to add extra questions for this; the explanation may be only too obvious from the involvement and communication questions. However, sometimes there may be specific issues you need to probe, because you (or the client) suspect there may be a problem. For example:

- You will remember that there was some music playing in that commercial. How appropriate was the music in your view? (Show card. 5 point scale.)
- And how much did you personally like the music? (Show card. 5 point scale.)

TECHNIQUES FOR PRE-TESTING RADIO

The fact that media budgets for radio are considerably lower than those for television and other media probably explains why relatively little quantified pre-testing of radio commercials appears to be done. However, if pre-testing is required, few methodological problems arise since radio can be treated in exactly the same way as television. It is theoretically as possible to conduct a twenty-four-hour recall study on a radio commercial as it is on a television commercial though all the same interpretative problems exist. Some form of impact and communication test will be the more usual choice.

TECHNIQUES FOR PRE-TESTING PRESS

Pre-testing press is rather more difficult, if some form of impact measure is required. The normal way of doing this is to insert the test advertisement into a mock-up magazine, composed of other advertisements and editorial. Generally this is done using a folder with clear plastic sleeves—hence the name 'folder-test'. The interview procedure would then normally follow the direction outlined above under *Impact and communication testing*. 'Reading and noting' is a rather different technique, in which the interviewer takes the respondent through the magazine asking them to say what they remember noticing. This technique is generally used for post-testing an advertisement *in situ*.

TECHNIQUES FOR PRE-TESTING POSTERS

Again, the poster pre-test will usually be based on the *Impact and communication test* format, though the impact measure should be designed to reflect the special way people experience the poster medium. Ideally, the poster should be seen *in situ*, thus allowing for the scale of the image to be apparent. This can be done (but with some difficulty) by photographically superimposing the test poster over a photograph of an existing site. The test poster can then be shown with others to gain some kind of comparative impact measure. Whether the poster is shown solus or in a 'reel', it should only be shown for a few seconds, again to reflect the generally fleeting view that the passer-by gains. Communication can be examined by this technique or simply by using miniature proofs, but again the poster should only be on view for a few seconds.

TECHNIQUES FOR PRE-TESTING ROUGH MATERIAL

The question of pre-testing animatics has already been dealt with (see page 135). As far as rough radio, press or posters are concerned, the broad impact and communication procedure can be used, though comparative impact testing will always be difficult unless you are prepared to go to the cost of reducing competitive materials to a similar rough finish.

MANAGEMENT OF A PRE-TEST

Anyone with experience of pre-testing, and, I hope, most of those who have read this chapter, will agree with me that pre-testing is an extremely inexact science dependent to a large extent on the theoretical context in which the data is collected and upon a large degree of subjective interpretation. There is nothing inherently wrong with an inexact science, provided that this is acknowledged by all concerned. The real problems of pre-testing emerge when the inexactitude and subjectivity are not recognized.

This is why the management of a pre-test is such an important role for the planner. Although in many agency/client relationships, the specific responsibility for administering the study may lie with the client research department, there can be very few situations where the planner does not have the opportunity to advise or comment on the design or to be involved in the briefing and interpretation processes.

TIMING is the first critical 'management' issue. As we know only too well, the time available for pre-testing a finished advertisement is usually very brief, but in most situations there is ample time to anticipate the need and plan in advance, in terms of setting the objectives and determining the research design. In particular, there should always be time to select and then brief the right research company.

THE CHOICE OF RESEARCH COMPANY is the second—and one of the most significant variables in a pre-test. A sensitive researcher who acknowledges the inexactitude and subjectivity of the task can produce a very different conclusion from one who is convinced of the precision and universality of the technique. There is no easy solution to the problem of finding the right researcher, other than to beware those who offer panaceas and glib answers.

BRIEFING is the third major plank in the management of the pre-test. Whether or not the planner is writing the research proposal, it is always worthwhile providing a written statement of the objectives of the advertisement. Ideally, this should cover at least four topics:

- The role the campaign must perform to achieve the defined marketing goal(s).
- The particular communication objectives of the advertisement.
- The way the advertisement has been designed to elicit its response.
- The response we expect and/or desire the audience to make.

It generally helps to set these points in a context that explains the reasons for the strategy and for the development of the particular execution.

In my mind, the more the researcher is informed of the complexity of the particular communication model, the more sensitive his or her interpretation will be. *Interpretation* itself is a more difficult issue for the planner to manage in the active sense, without appearing to be attempting to 'fix' the results. Other than ensuring that a thorough briefing has taken place, the planner's contribution is generally restricted to the debrief, though even here room for manoeuvre is circumscribed by the need not to lose credibility in the eyes of the client. Nonetheless it is important that the planner plays an active role in commenting on and questioning the conclusions being drawn.

There are two broad approaches to the interpretation of pre-test data which I have categorized (perhaps even caricatured) as the 'external action standards' and 'internal health check' approaches. In the 'external action standards' approach, the underlying assumption often appears to be that the test advertisement is 'guilty till proven innocent' (which, indeed, it often is, since this attitude frequently goes hand in hand with only light usage of creative development research). The implicit (and sometimes explicit) objective is to ensure that the test advertisement reaches a certain standard, usually one that has evolved out of a series of similar tests conducted over a period of time, and based on measures (e.g. impact scores, main message communication scores, and persuasion scores) that have, in the past, been observed to correlate with advertising effectiveness in the real world. Although this approach may have been demonstrated to work well for certain brands in certain markets, there are a number of problems and objections associated with it:

- The issue of applicability of norms from brand to brand, market to market and time period to time period. For instance, a score that may be predictive in the detergents market may not be in the shampoo market and almost certainly will not be in the fragrance market. What is predictive for a functionally positioned brand may not be for an emotionally positioned brand in the same product field. What is predictive among down-market older ladies, may not be among young working women. What has worked for a brand in the past may not be applicable to that same brand in a changed and more competitive market place.
  If these (and many other) limitations are conscientiously applied to the normative data bank, they can often result in the normative assessment being made on the basis of a mere handful of observations, which can render any conclusions, *drawn on these terms alone*, distinctly shaky. It is always wise for the planner to enquire as to the provenance of a 'norm'.
- The reliance on a single measure (or small number of key measures). Not only does this approach assume that all advertisements work, and ultimately can be measured, in exactly the same way, it also pre-supposes a receptive consumer eager to react in a formularized way, to suit the convenience of the research technique.
- The effect it may have on the creative team and on the planner's relationship with them. It *may* be a bit of a myth that demoralized creative teams cynically set out to beat the 'norms' at the expense of creativity, but it is easy to see how they can unconsciously slip into a formularized solution to get their work through. If this does occur, it then becomes increasingly difficult for the planner to exert any constructive influence on them. The creative team are faced with an alien research technique that bears little resemblance to their experience of the real world and so any attempt to provide constructive guidance from the real world is regarded as irrelevant to the main task of surviving the next pre-test, which anyway the planner has had a hand in foisting upon them. And so the spiral descends!

However, pre-testing cannot be conducted without the use of some kind of normative assessment, because it is impossible to put a value on a research finding without having some kind of external guide as to what it means. From other kinds of research, we all know that a 60 per cent spontaneous awareness figure is good, but that when 75 per cent say they are likely to buy regularly this will rarely be translated into anything more than a 10 per cent four-weekly penetration. But what about a 70 per cent brand recall figure? And is it bad if only about 40 per cent can precisely play back the main communication point?

The answer to the 'norms' issue lies in the sensitive application of a broad normative framework as part, *and only part*, of a thorough investigation of the data as a whole. It can be very reassuring for a client to hear that experience suggests that a 70 per cent brand recall figure is good going, but equally reassuring to be told that although only 40 per cent bothered to mention the main point in a specific question, the responses to other questions demonstrate that they have clearly understood the message. Likewise, it may be necessary to point out that a higher than average impact score should be tempered by a low level of involvement with the advertisement as a whole, demonstrated by the paucity and blandness of the open-ended responses. It is only through looking at the data as a whole, and by examining the links between the consumer's responses that the real state of health of the advertisement can be evaluated and any problems diagnosed in a way that can be treated.

Where the advertising strategy has been grounded in thorough analysis of existing data and when it has been exposed to the consumer in a rough state in creative development research, it is reasonable for this alternative interpretative framework (the 'internal health check') to assume that the advertisement is effective until proved otherwise.

8 Campaign evaluation

Jeremy Elliott

WHY EVALUATE

All the previous chapters have been about planning, that is, looking ahead. But campaign evaluation is retrospective. It looks at what is past. So is it an account planning function at all?

If we believe (as most planners surely do) that relevant and well-executed advertising is an investment which, by adding value to a brand, brings the advertiser a profitable return, then we should be prepared to evaluate campaigns as investments rather than costs, and to compare their returns with those of alternative investments. Advertising and marketing should be accountable.

But simply measuring the effect, without learning from it and then putting that knowledge to use, is to miss out on the major benefit: gaining a better understanding of *how* the advertising stimulus led to the observed response. The more we can understand that, the better our planning will be next time. Making the past continue to work for the brand is as good a definition as any of the planner's job. Close observation of just which effects a campaign produces, and the size of these effects, helps us to set more accurate and realistic objectives for the future.

That in turn tells us what to look for when setting up and interpreting the appropriate research, and helps us to judge performance. For if we do not set the criteria and standards of judgement *before* the campaign runs, we cannot prevent subjectivity creeping into the evaluation. And unless we have a realistic view of what effects may be achievable, we cannot judge the actual performance:

- If a target is met, is that success, or was the target too low?
- Is failure really failure, or over-ambitious target-setting?

Too often, we do not routinely measure results because we cannot properly evaluate advertising performance because we do not know how to set realistic objectives because we do not routinely measure results.

Campaign evaluation is a learning process. There are techniques, which will be described later in this chapter. But evaluation is essentially a discipline, not a set of techniques. It demands:

- Setting up a hypothesis about how the campaign will work, based on the role and strategy assigned to the advertising.
- Setting specific targets for the campaign: *which* effects do we expect to see, among *whom*, and how large will they be?
- Setting up the research to monitor these effects (or adapting existing research).
- Evaluating the results, against the preset criteria and standards.
- Reviewing the targets: were they the right ones? was the scale realistic?

- Revising, where appropriate, our previous hypothesis of how the campaign would work, into a view of how it did work.
- Applying the knowledge gained to the next campaign, to improve the hypothesis about how it will work, and to set more apt and realistic targets.

The starting point for this process has to be a general theory of how advertising works, which we particularize for each brand and campaign.

HOW ADVERTISING MAY USUALLY WORK

Advertising theory abounds with the idea that advertisements *do* something to people. Hence what have been described as the linear sequential or transportation models of advertising effect: in which advertisements act on an inert consumer audience, to propel them step by step through a series of stages from, for example, awareness to comprehension, to interest, to desire, to purchase.

Apart from the acute over-simplification of such models, they assume that advertising's function is just to implant factual messages at a reasoned level in order to persuade a customer (who is deemed to be making a considered and rational choice between brands) to be converted to the one advertised. Occasionally this may be true. But it is patently not true for most consumer goods most of the time. Firstly, we are not passive receivers. Perception, communication, learning and memory are—consciously or unconsciously—active processes of the mind. Furthermore, we could not possibly find time for a considered judgement of every single purchase choice. In most fields we simply ring the changes between a repertoire of acceptable brands, within which our choice for today may be habitual, superficial, non-rational or mere impulse.

For established repeat-purchase goods, most marketing effort is devoted to maintaining or enlarging a share of this repertoire purchasing. Getting on to the repertoire in the first place—winning initial trial and subsequent repeat purchase—is usually a secondary aim. (The priorities are reversed for new products, but only during the early launch phase.) Consequently, most advertising for repeat-purchase goods is aimed at existing buyers or users of the brand, whereas the conversion logic of the linear sequential models would require that the target be non-users.

The way advertising affects consumers' choices, in totality, is not a neat sequential and mechanistic system, but a hugely muddled, often irrational and essentially *human* process. And unless those of us who are advertisers comprehend this, we are unlikely to be able to persuade effectively.

There is one general model which not only fits most of what we know, but has amply stood the test of time. It was first proposed by Timothy Joyce nearly 20 years ago (17), and it remains equally valid today (see Box 1). It says that advertisements modify or reinforce attitudes by bringing the brand into focus and investing it with favourable associations. Favourable associations in turn arouse or reinforce interest in buying the brand. Advertisements and purchasing can also be linked directly, since one of advertising's roles, where the brand habit is already strong, is to act more directly through a reminder or memory-jogging function.

At the same time, having bought a brand can heighten attention to its advertisements

BOX 1
How advertisements may work (after Joyce, 1967)

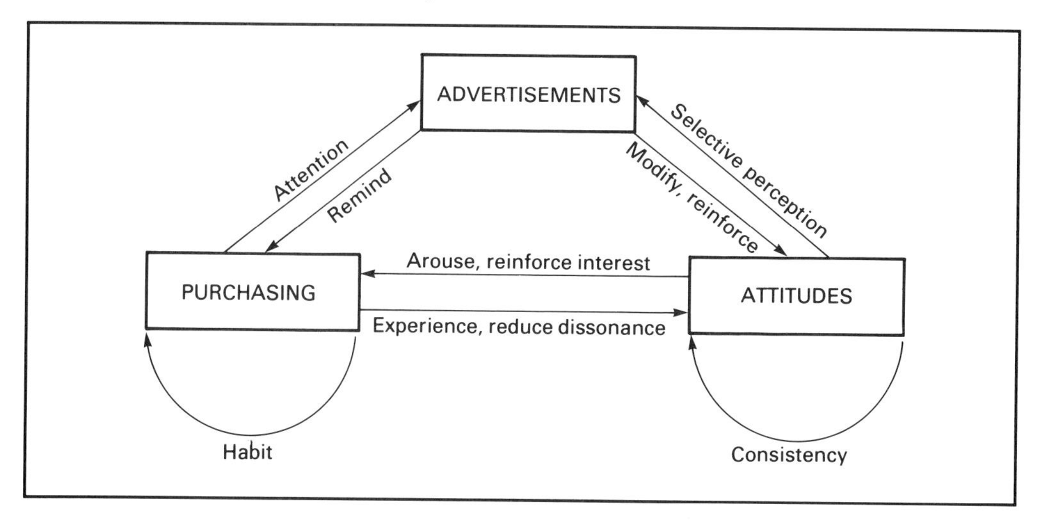

seen subsequently, so we can also draw in a reciprocal arrow from purchasing to advertisement. Similarly, purchasing also influences attitudes, either through direct experience of the product or because the psychological drive to reduce dissonance leads to more favourable brand attitudes in order to justify and support the purchase choice. Hence the often observed phenomenon of attitudes shifting after purchase rather than before. Finally, attitudes affect preconceptions which, in turn, affect the selective perception of, and attention to, advertisements.

So it is two-way traffic throughout the triangular relationship between advertisement, attitudes and purchase. Additionally, there are two important loops in the system. The strong drive for consistency which exists in our structure of feelings and beliefs will tend to put order and conformity into the attitude box, even without the stimulus of advertisement or purchase. And a similar drive—habit—governs purchasing behaviour to such an extent that it can remain unaffected by advertising or by attitude shift if these fall below some minimum threshold level.

The whole system is non-sequential. There is no clearcut chain of cause and effect, which makes it all the more difficult to distinguish and quantify the effects of a campaign. But this general model is closer than other theories to a reality we, as marketers and consumers, can recognize. From it flows an implication that is crucial to campaign evaluation:

- Different advertising campaigns, fulfilling different roles, will produce different *kinds* of effect.

KINDS OF EFFECT

The most useful conceptual framework for examining these is the direct/indirect scale of advertising response, proposed by Stephen King some years ago (18). In this, he drew up a scale of immediacy; at one end, the direct end, are those campaigns whose effects will be almost immediate. At the other end of the scale are those whose effects will take longer to emerge. It is helpful to use this scale in considering what kinds of effect we can expect to see and measure (Box 2).

- Starting at the *direct* end of the scale, we have what is commonly called 'direct response advertising'. The consumer sees the advertisement, decides to buy, and reaches for pen or phone. Results are measurable, in fine detail, from replies and orders. No need for attitude research; you can vary the advertisement or the medium, directly observe the effects, and infer what went on in people's minds.
- Second in the scale is the 'seek information' role, where the advertisement is offering, say, a catalogue as a step towards the end sale. The response in the consumer's mind is 'Tell me more' and the ensuing action is to send off a coupon or enquiry. Again, effects can be directly measured and even followed through to end-sales.
- In the third response the advertising is not directly offering something, but presenting new information about a brand or reinterpreting old information in a way that is new and relevant to the consumer. If it is effective, the consumer's response is 'What a good idea'. And its effect should fairly swiftly be visible in increased purchasing and in a change either in attitude or in the salience or importance of the relevant attribute.
- Fourth is the role often assigned to campaigns for established repeat-purchase brands: to recall satisfactions. It elicits the 'That reminds me' response that triggers an extra purchase of the brand within the consumer's shortlist or repertoire. Such an

BOX 2
Advertising roles and measures of effect

	Direct/indirect scale of response	*Expected measures of effect*	
		Behaviour	*Attitudes*
Direct ↑	Direct response	Orders, replies	
	Seek information	Coupons, enquiries	
	Relate to own needs, wants, desires	Purchasing	Attitude change Salience change
	Recall satisfactions, reorder shortlist	Purchasing	Brand salience/ brand awareness
	Modify attitudes		Attitude change User image change
↓ Indirect	Reinforce attitudes		(No change) Added value tests

effect tends to be short term and small. Some behaviour effects may be discernible in purchasing, using econometric models. But since no rethink is involved, attitude shifts are not to be expected. We may, however, expect to see a lift in brand awareness or, more likely, brand salience (i.e. front-of-mind brand awareness), provided the research is conducted sufficiently often to detect what is likely to be a temporary blip in the graph.

- Next is another common role for advertising: to modify perceptions of the satisfactions offered by the brand. This we know to be a slow business. So tracing the effects via purchasing behaviour becomes increasingly difficult; the cause-and-effect chain is too long. We have instead to rely on looking for changes over time in what people think: their attitudes towards using the brand and their image of who uses it.
- Lastly, the most indirect of roles is aimed at protecting a brand from erosion by its competitors, by maintaining and reinforcing its added values. Another classical role of advertising, but one which presents peculiar difficulties for the evaluator, since the objective is to *prevent* change. How, then, to measure the effect? It is difficult to prove that no change is a successful result, at least by any of the usual short-term measures. Success may be judged only over lengthy periods of time, using methods that measure added value (e.g. blind/named preference tests or demand curves).

Two general conclusions emerge from this analysis:

1 Different campaigns, with different ends, need different monitoring techniques. No single method can cover it all. Monitoring research needs to be tailored to need, according to the campaign's role and strategy and the effects it is expected to yield.

2 Campaigns whose roles are towards the direct end of the immediacy scale can be evaluated satisfactorily on behavioural measures: sales, enquiries, etc. But the more indirect the response, the less likely that even the most sensitive measurement technique will be able to detect effects in behavioural data. In these cases we necessarily have to turn towards intermediate variables about what consumers think and feel, variables that are notoriously more difficult to interpret and to measure with as much precision as behavioural factors. This is not to say that such measurement should not be attempted, only that its shortcomings should be well appreciated.

WHAT TO MEASURE

The choice of what to measure depends on the campaign's role and objectives. It is better not to rely on a single measure. Several appropriate measures will not only improve confidence in the answer, provided they corroborate one another (so use more than one data source, if possible), but are also more likely to explain why the campaign worked as it did.

Nearly all advertising aims to persuade people to *do* something (buy the brand, shop at so-and-so's, accept the share offer). Obviously, the most direct way of assessing results is to measure these behavioural effects, and this should always be the first choice. But it may not always be possible, either because reliable data are absent, or because cause and effect are too far apart in time. Then it will be necessary to fall back on intermediate variables. These, however, are very much second best, because they depend on the assumption that they reliably predict ensuing behaviour—an assumption that is not supported by the evidence. The relationships between intermediate variables and end behaviour are, to say the least, inconsistent.

Nevertheless, these intermediate variables can shed light on how the advertising brought about the behavioural change—a valid and valuable role. But when, as sometimes happens, the attitudinal and behavioural evidence do not agree, then the data on what people *did* should be preferred. It is easier to infer what went through people's minds from the behavioural evidence (as in the example in Box 3), than it is to foretell what they would have done from the evidence of attitude data.

The more commonly used measures, and their research sources, are:

MEASURE	SOURCE
Intermediate variables	
Brand awareness/salience	
Brand attitudes/image	
User image	Tracking studies
Claimed brand usage:	Usage and attitude (U&A) studies
– ever tried	Qualitative research
– regular use	Advertising research
– occasional use	
Purchase intention	
Advertising awareness	
Advertising content recall	
Brand preference	Blind/named preference tests
End variables	
Sales volume and value:	
– ex-factory	Manufacturer's records
– trade sales	Retail audit
– consumer purchases	Consumer audit
Market share	
Penetration:	
– periodic	
– cumulative	Consumer panel
Rate or volume of purchase	
Repeat purchase	

MEASUREMENT TECHNIQUES

Having pre-set the campaign objectives and decided on the particular measures to be applied, the next question is:

- How to do the measuring?

Since campaign evaluation is still a relatively underdeveloped area, the range of

BOX 3

Purchasing information explains how advertising affected brand consumption

In 1981, Kellogg's Corn Flakes was advertised on 1 million milk bottles distributed by Unigate in London and the South. A question on AGB's TCA determined which dairy served each panel home, so before-and-after comparison was made for Unigate-served homes versus the rest who did not receive the advertisement.

The advertising's aim was to stimulate extra consumption of the brand, *among existing users*, by the evocative association of crispy flakes and cool milk. This is what analysis of the panel data revealed had happened: penetration was unaffected, but frequency and volume of purchase increased in Unigate homes. Furthermore, the volume increase occurred only in those Unigate homes which stocked Kellogg's Corn Flakes in the larder. So it must have been Corn Flakes in those extra bowlfuls. And the brand got the lion's share of extra purchasing that followed.

BEFORE/AFTER PERCENTAGE CHANGES IN VOLUME PER BUYER

	Unigate homes		*Non-Unigate homes*	
	Kellogg's Corn Flakes	Other cereals	Kellogg's Corn Flakes	Other cereals
All homes	+10	+2	−5	−2
Homes buying Kellogg's Corn Flakes	+10	+6	−5	−3
Other homes	—	−1	—	−2

(Condensed from Jeremy Elliott, 'How advertising on milk bottles increased consumption of Kellogg's Corn Flakes', *Advertising Works 2,* IPA, 1983).

currently available methods is neither widely known nor used, and is undoubtedly incomplete. New techniques will be invented. Research methods will be improved. So what follows in this section does not claim to be an exhaustive list of methodologies, but simply a list of techniques (Box 4) that have been found useful.

For reasons of space, it is not possible to illustrate all these with examples. Instead, references are given to particular papers in the first three IPA *Advertising Works* volumes of advertising effectiveness award-winners, which demonstrate the technique in action. (In any case, aspiring campaign evaluators should regard these books as essential reading.)

RUNNING GRAPHS

The simplest method of looking at the effects of advertising and other marketing variables is to maintain running graphs of sales, penetration, brand awareness or attitudes (or whatever other continuous data are available), showing the timing of advertising, promotions or other marketing actions. It is surprising how much one can

BOX 4
Methods of measurement

Technique	*What it measures*
Running graphs	Any continuous quantified data
Tracking studies	Intermediate variables
U & A studies	Intermediate variables
Blind/named preference tests	Added value
Consumer panel analyses	Purchasing behaviour
Qualitative research	Explanatory, mainly attitudes
Advertising research	Response to advertisements
Pre/post analysis	End variables (sales, etc.)
Demand analysis	Perceived brand value
Econometric modelling	Separate contributions of different marketing factors
Area tests	Effect of changing a marketing factor

learn from such graphs, updated and maintained over several years, so much so that it is well worth the effort of keeping them even if there is no formal plan of campaign evaluation. Simple observation will often reveal detectable effects. A burst of advertising may be swiftly followed by a rise in penetration (for fast-moving consumer goods, the short-term effects follow almost immediately). A new TV commercial may lift one or more of the attitude graphs. A price change can be seen to affect sales volume. And so on. All of which adds immeasurably to one's general understanding of the market and of the manner in which its consumers respond to marketing stimuli.

TRACKING STUDIES

Data collection is frequent or continuous, with small weekly samples which accumulate to moving monthly or bi-monthly averages. These show up short-term fluctuations in the variables being measured, which can reveal a lot about consumer response to the advertising, promotions, etc. (though care should be taken to remain alert to the margins of error in the data, to help distinguish between fluctuations that probably represent a real change and those that are random noise).

Tracking studies usually cover advertising awareness, recall and recognition; and brand awareness, attitudes and, to a limited extent, usage. By examining intervening variables between advertisement and brand purchase, their aim is to trace the cause-and-

BOX 5
Use of a tracking study, Lloyds Bank personal loans

TV advertising for Lloyds Personal Loans ran nationally during late February and March 1984, following a press campaign.

Claimed awareness of any Lloyds advertising rose when the TV advertisement appeared.

	Advertising awareness		
	Any %	TV %	Press %
Dec 1983	33	24	14
Jan 1984	32	24	12
Feb 1984	34	25	13
Mar 1984	47	37	17
Apr 1984	41	29	18
May 1984	38	n/a	n/a

(Source: Millward Brown Tracking Study)

Image data showed coincident rises of 4 to 5 percentage points for a number of attitude statements:

General 'Sort of bank I would be happy to join.'
'Provide helpful advice to customers.'
'Sympathetic to customers' problems.'

Specific 'Readily provide loans.'
'Offer a wide range of services.'
'Attracting new customers at the moment.'

It was considered that the advertising had contributed positively to the promotion of loans in the short term, and in the longer term to more general image changes for the bank.

Condensed from Jane Fiori, 'The Lloyds Bank Personal Loan', *Advertising Works 3,* IPA, 1985.

effect links between the two, thus explaining *how* the advertisement worked. An example of the use of a tracking study is in the Lloyds Bank Personal Loan paper (12), which shows how advertising recall and brand image scales moved in relation to advertising (Box 5).

This sort of information is invaluable in helping to detect advertising's contribution and, in particular, how the communication affected attitudes towards the brand. Such information—especially when combined with content recall—can usefully supplement other data to provide a diagnostic evaluation of the advertisement itself. Comparison with other commercials for the same brand may reveal differences, often quite subtle, in what they communicate, implicitly as well as explicitly, which are pointers for further brand strategic creative development. (See Box 6 for an example.)

The experience of a number of tracking study users, however, is that the evaluative

BOX 6
Impressions of a food brand conveyed by its advertising

A change of brand positioning for a food brand led to a change of campaign. The previous campaign had emphasized the substantiality of the product and its ability to satisfy hunger pangs. The new campaign concentrated on its nutritional and energy-giving qualities. The tracking study showed that it communicated them successfully. But it did not improve the brand's perceived value.

	Campaign [A]	Campaign [B]
Impressions of the brand given by the advertising:		
Substantial and filling	51	29
Healthful	32	24
Gives energy	21	63
Nourishing	19	24
Natural ingredients	2	24
Good value	32	24

Tracking research demonstrated that the campaign achieved the objectives set for it in the strategy. It did not prove that the strategy was right.

and explanatory value of this type of research, and consequently its ability to contribute to planning, has been less than hoped for. It produces diagnostic evidence about what different commercials communicate (at least, at the verbal rational level) and how well they do it. But the wider aim of tracing the links between advertisement and product purchase has not been generally met, partly because the relationship is not a simple one-way affair, and partly because it differs from brand to brand. Consequently, making use of the results relies heavily on interpretation, and that in turn depends on having sufficient data (which means you need at least a year's run) and being thoroughly conversant with the market.

It also requires familiarity with what the measures actually measure.

BRAND ATTITUDES/IMAGE As measured, usually by a battery of statements, this tends to be limited to a restricted number of formal beliefs at a verbal level rather than a full brand image comprising knowledge, beliefs and feelings. These restrictions limit the sensitivity of attitude data.

Evaluative attitudes are known to correlate fairly well with brand usage, so shifts in such attitudes can be used as a surrogate for behavioural measures, though such movements tend to be small. Descriptive attitudes, being more closely tied to the nature of the product, are even less sensitive to change.

One valid role for advertising is to focus on a product attribute and make it more desirable. In these cases, what is more likely to move is consumers' perception of the *importance* of this attribute, and thus their disposition to purchase, rather than the strength of the brand image itself.

When the benefits of fibre in the diet first began to be talked about, bran cereal advertising concentrated on the fibre aspect. Sales rose very rapidly. Yet the number of people saying that All-Bran, for example, was high in fibre did not change: they knew this already. What changed was the value that consumers put on fibre. But when tracking studies do not include a measure of the salience or importance of the various attributes, such changes go undetected.

USER IMAGE It is generally easier for advertising to modify perceptions of *who* buys and uses a brand (which indirectly conveys something about the brand's own personality) than to shift brand attitudes directly. Changes in user image provide additional explanation, but since it begs many questions about the relationship with purchasing behaviour, user imagery is a weak measure of overall campaign effect.

BRAND AWARENESS/SALIENCE Spontaneous awareness of a brand, particularly the extent to which it springs to mind first (salience), appears to be related to the brand's ranking within the purchasing repertoire. It correlates to some extent with purchasing. (Box 7).

BRAND USAGE Answers to questions like:

- Which of these brands have you bought in the past *x* months?
- Which do you buy regularly?

bear little relation to the actuality as revealed by panel purchasing data. Nor is there any good reason to suppose there should be. People do not keep records of commonplace activities such as buying groceries. So they can only answer such questions with an estimation of how they feel, currently and in the recent past, about purchasing the brand. In other words, such so-called usage questions in fact measure something rather different, an attitude towards purchase which probably represents the brand's current or usual ranking within the purchasing repertoire. As such, these measures are a useful barometer of brand health, particularly where previous experience has shown some correlation between them and actual consumer purchasing.

PURCHASE INTENTION Ostensibly the most useful measure, intention to purchase is nevertheless not much help. Analysis has shown that purchase intention questions get answers that correlate with respondents' purchasing behaviour in the *past* rather than in the future (13). It is a measure of what people have done, rather than what they will do. As a predictor of buying behaviour, it has no value beyond the level of history repeating itself.

ADVERTISING AWARENESS, ETC. Often used as a surrogate measure of the effectiveness of a campaign, largely because it is a measure that has been found to respond more directly and sensitively to advertising. Simon Broadbent has pointed out that advertising elasticities on awareness are generally higher than on sales (14).

BOX 7
A correlation between penetration and brand awareness

The graph below shows an example of a close relationship between the four-weekly percentage of homes buying a food product (penetration) and the percentage naming the brand in answer to an unprompted awareness question (spontaneous brand awareness). The correlation is impressive, given that the two indices come from different sources. They corroborate each other well.

Which is cause, and which effect? The awareness index appears to lag behind penetration, suggesting that it moves as a result of purchase. But this cannot be, because the awareness level is five times as high as penetration. Many more people can name the brand than buy it, even on a cumulative basis. Therefore awareness cannot just be a function of purchase. Both indices move together in response to some other stimulus. The advertising, perhaps?

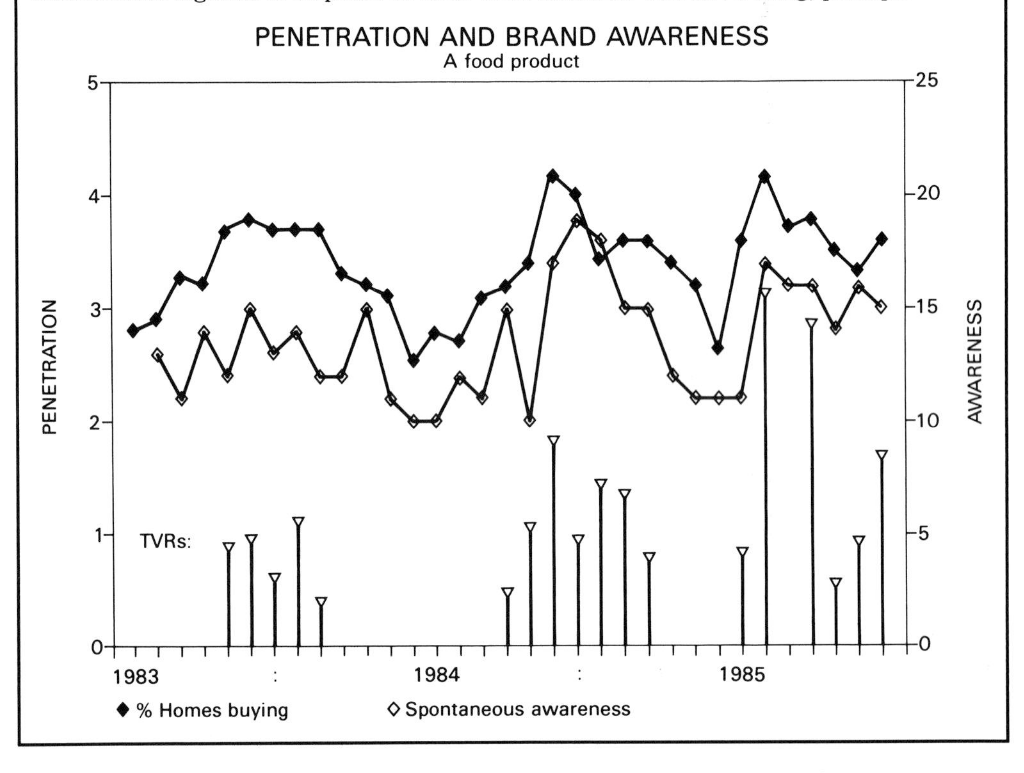

However, it has been well demonstrated that advertising awareness does not necessarily correlate with sales effectiveness (15). It does not necessarily imply effective advertising, any more than remembering a messenger implies remembering, still less acting upon, his message. Nor does low awareness necessarily mean the campaign is a dud. An award-winning case history for Cadbury's Fudge (7) reported on a campaign that was highly liked and highly sales-effective in spite of a low advertising awareness index, and concluded that it was possible to have a campaign that was enjoyable and effective without being 'top-of-mind'.

The debate about what these awareness measures really mean would be helped if it were accompanied by a consistent differentiation between the terms used (a lot that has been said and written on the subject does not make the distinction):

- Advertising *awareness* usually refers to a measure of remembering seeing any advertisement(s) for a brand.
- *Recall* measures what content of an advertisement is remembered.
- *Recognition* measures the prompted memory of an advertisement after being shown a representative frame of it.

Recall says something about the particular communication of an advertisement (though implicitly limited to the visual and verbal elements which can more easily be put into words when answering the question, rather than the emotional overtones) and as such can be useful as a diagnostic evaluation of the advertisement itself. But as surrogate measures of overall campaign effectiveness, none of the advertising awareness measures can be relied on.

USAGE AND ATTITUDES STUDIES

Generally fairly large-scale research surveys, U&A studies are conducted intermittently (e.g. quarterly or yearly) over quite long periods of time, since what they aim to measure is expected to show only slow movement. Typically, they may cover awareness, attitudes and usage for a number of brands, with samples sufficient for sub-division into user groups or by demographics.

U&A studies are essentially for the medium to long term. The Zanussi case history (8) shows, over no less than six years, a sustained build-up of brand awareness and imagery which would have been difficult to detect with as much certainty over a short run (Box 8).

In the case of Dettol (5), U&A research revealed, over a two year-span, shifts both in the frequency of product usage and in its usage occasions, which reflected the effects of the advertising campaign, even though there was virtually no change in the brand's image. Similarly, research for Kellogg's Bran Flakes (10) uncovered important changes in consumers' reasons for buying it.

But while U&A studies are useful for monitoring longer-term shifts and trends, they are nevertheless snapshots separated by intervals of time, and as such cannot say what fluctuations may have occurred in these intervals. Intermittent checks cannot capture the exact timing of shifts in the variables being measured and if, as often seems to be the case, some of advertising's effects occur quite swiftly, then U&A research will not be able to report the close association between advertising and effect as fully as continuous tracking studies.

U&A and tracking studies are both major research projects. They are expensive because they use large samples and need to be sustained over lengthy periods of time, before and after the advertising that is being evaluated. So they have to be planned in great detail and with foresight, because they represent a considerable commitment by marketing management.

BOX 8
Zanussi's appliance of science

Until 1976, Zanussi was almost unknown to the British consumer, despite being Europe's largest manufacturer of white goods. After building a distributor network for Zanussi-branded products, the company embarked in 1980 on the 'Appliance of Science' TV campaign, in which unseen beings from a technically advanced planet applied their science to constructing and delivering to Earth the most advanced appliances in the universe.

Annual U & A studies showed what resulted.

Zanussi	1979 %	1980 %	1981 %	1982 %	1983 %	1984 %
Spontaneous brand awareness	8	20	20	27	33	39
Brand imagery:						
Technically advanced products	20	31	34	39	44	48
Reliable products	14	13	13	22	26	25
Reputation for quality products	12	9	12	18	23	22
Good value for money	10	9	12	14	18	17
One of the biggest companies	6	6	7	8	12	16
Sales index (1979 = 100)						
Zanussi	100	93	126	138	162	n/a
Total market	100	93	91	104	113	n/a

(Condensed from Roger Clayton, Estelle Williams and Rick Bendel, 'Building a business through advertising: Zanussi', *Advertising Works 3*, IPA, 1985.)

BLIND/NAMED PREFERENCE TESTS

Blind/named testing is also a long-term measure of brand value, but less expensive and more limited in scope. A simple but effective technique, it measures the added value in a *brand*, over and above the value of the product itself to the consumer. And since one of advertising's key roles is to add value to a brand, over time, such tests can be an indirect means of assessing long-term effects.

The test employs two samples of target consumers, matched by demographics and product usage, consisting of 100–200 respondents in each sample (the number depends on the degree of accuracy needed). Each sample tastes or otherwise tests, in hall or in home, the brand in question compared to one or two closely similar products, and answers a questionnaire on which they prefer and why. The test is identical for both samples except that in one the brands are in blank packs, unidentified except by a code letter (blind), whereas in the other the brands are identifiable by being in their normal packs.

The blind test measures *product only* preferences, unaffected by any perceptions of the brand. The named test measures *brand* preferences, and the difference between the two tests represents the competitive added value built into the brand by past marketing and advertising, an effect that can be considerable (Box 9).

BOX 9
A blind/named preference test

A food product (Brand A) was taste-tested against two direct competitors. In blind test (i.e. with nothing to identify the brands), A emerged as the clear winner, preferred by nearly half the sample. The rest were evenly divided between B and C.

Among a matched sample of respondents who underwent the identical test, save only that on this occasion the brands were identified by name, preference for Brand A was significantly increased. The products were the same in both tests, so this difference can only be ascribed to the *added value* invested in the Brand A's reputation by past advertising and marketing actions.

In this case, Brand B turned out to have the weakest reputation.

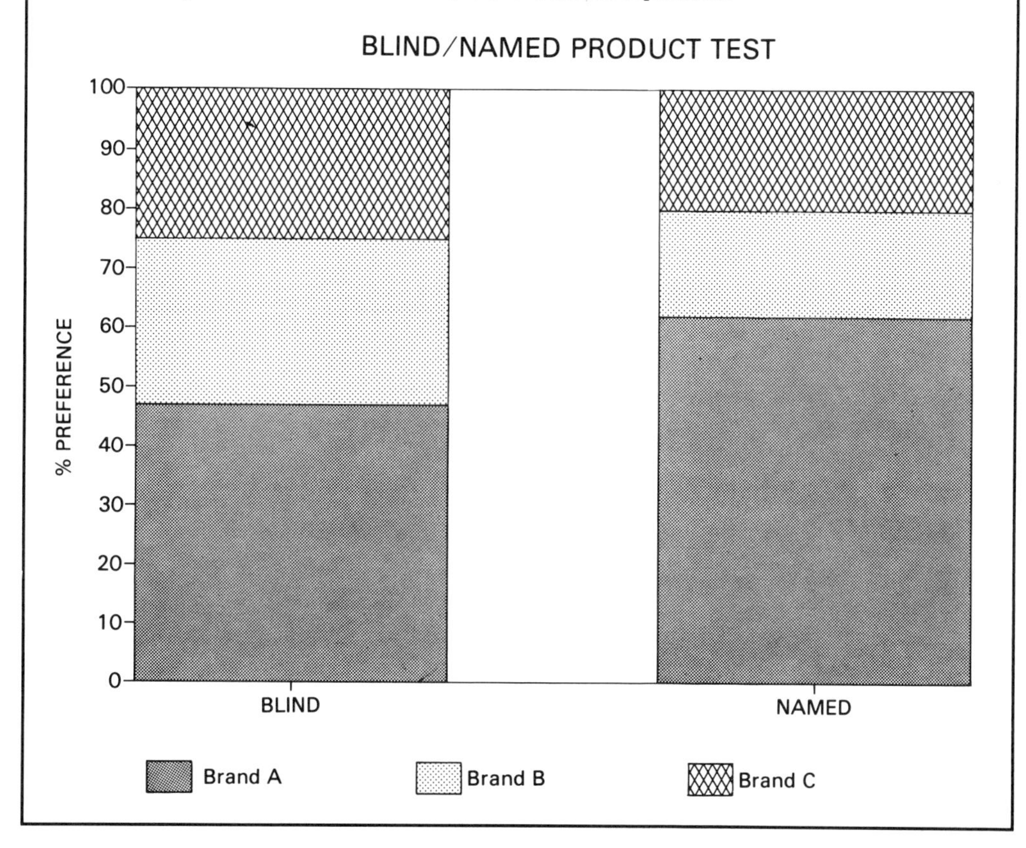

Repeated at intervals, blind/named preference tests will show up changes over time, either in consumers' perception of the comparative value of the brands in question or in the relative quality of the products themselves. Not all products are suited to such a technique. Unique formulations which are readily identifiable even without their pack, cannot satisfy the 'blind' requirement. But where two or more similar products exist, the technique is probably applicable.

CONSUMER PANEL ANALYSES

Consumer panels provide an unrivalled source of information about purchasers' behaviour through time, as further explanation of how advertising has exerted an influence. Useful analyses include:

DEPTH OF TRIAL Particularly applicable to new product launches, this measures the build up of trial (penetration) and repeat purchase through time, and provides a basis for estimating how the advertising influenced these two factors.

REPEAT BUYING Measures the turnover between consecutive periods of time in who buys a brand, their weight of purchase and their use of other brands, to provide a dynamic picture of how an advertising burst or a promotion affects a brand's position within the purchasing repertoire.

GAINS/LOSS This examines the switching flows between brands across comparable periods of time, to show how much of a brand's gains are due to switches from other brands, to increased rates of purchase among existing brand buyers or to new buyers coming in to the product field.

MIGRATION ANALYSIS This takes as its base those households who buy a brand at all in a specified period (e.g. during the early phase of a new campaign, or while a consumer promotion is current, or as trialists of a new product) and compares brand purchasing behaviour for periods before and after. It shows how the purchasing repertoire was altered by the marketing action, and whether this effect was temporary or lasting.

QUALITATIVE RESEARCH

The strengths of qualitative research are diagnostic rather than evaluative, but that does not mean it has no place in campaign evaluation. Even when we have lots of quantitative data, on attitudes as well as behaviour, there can still be gaps in our understanding. It is these gaps which qualitative studies can best fill, because they can more sensitively explore those areas of response and motivation, particularly the emotional and non-rational, which do not lend themselves readily to the question-and-answer techniques of the quantifiable study.

The Hofmeister case history (11) summarized in Box 10 is an example. It helped to explain *how* the advertising produced the result it did. And it clarified, evidently, the way forward:

- Which elements of the advertisements to keep.
- Which to drop.
- Which to amend.

Fine tuning relies on fine playback. This does not mean that qualitative can replace quantitative as the evaluative method. But it can amplify it.

BOX 10
Qualitative research aids understanding

Hofmeister lager set out to create a new image for the brand which was not only distinctive, a characteristic it had previously lacked, but of genuine appeal and relevance to younger drinkers. The creative solution was the invention of a stylish, street-wise character, George the Bear, to reflect the aspirations of these young drinkers. He became at once both brand and drinker.

With the launch of the new campaign, sales rose dramatically, as did trial and the numbers claiming to be current drinkers of the brand. Brand and advertising awareness also went up. Yet quantitative brand image data from the tracking study, mostly related to product qualities, showed no significant change.

Qualitative research, on the other hand, found that the advertising had altered consumers' perceptions of a hitherto faceless brand by giving it the desirable identity of George the Bear—confident, popular and enviable—an identity that drinkers readily identified with. They were happy to drink Hofmeister now because they saw it as popular and trendy rather than because it was a superior product. It was the non-functional side of the image that appealed, rather than the functional characteristic covered by the tracking study. It was qualitative research that revealed this.

(Condensed from Peter Field and Adam Morgan, 'Hofmeister: a study of advertising and brand image', *Advertising Works 3,* IPA, 1985)

ADVERTISING RESEARCH

Qualitative research often asks people directly how an advertising campaign influenced them. Quantitative research seldom does. But, as part of a monitoring programme, it can illuminate our understanding of whom the advertising influenced and how, as shown in the Kellogg's Bran Flakes case history (10).

PRE/POST ANALYSIS

Whereas the previously mentioned methods employ specially commissioned research, this next group involve any market data available from any source, new or existing (e.g. ex-factory data, retail or consumer audits, published general statistics, etc.). However limited it may be, something usually exists to work with.

In essence, pre/post analysis uses time series data to imply cause. That is, if advertising is followed by a sales increase, we assume that the first may have caused the second, not the other way around. At its simplest, to claim that, because we did so-and-so and sales then did such-and-such, the one *caused* the other, is naive. Other factors may have been at work. So it is logical to examine all other possible causal factors, if only to eliminate them. What is not eliminated, we can then be reasonably sure, was a cause.

The most straightforward method is, first, to collect the data on all the factors which the marketer thinks may have been influential. This is likely to include:

- Product quality (was there any change to product or pack?).
- Price (deflated, or expressed as price relative to its competition or market).

- Retail distribution.
- Seasonality (e.g. summer, school holidays, Christmas, etc.).
- Advertising weight.
- Other marketing actions (promotions, etc.).
- Competitive activities.

Possibly, too, one might want to include measures, say, of disposable income, or of ownership of a relevant durable, or of stock pressure in the trade—it all depends on the individual market circumstances.

Having collected the data, each factor should then be plotted on a separate graph, using a common time frame. Examine how sales or market share vary with each of the explanatory factors in turn, looking for first-order correlations:

- Does there appear to be a relationship, at least for part of the time? If none appears to the naked eye, the chances are that any correlation is unimportant.
- Does the apparent relationship make marketing sense? If not, it is probably misleading, so look for something else. The All Clear Shampoo case history (3) illustrates how various factors were examined, and discarded, in turn, until it could be concluded that the TV campaign had been the most important factor affecting sales.

If this approach sounds simplistic, remember that this is exactly how one embarks on the sophisticated techniques of econometrics. The important first step is to look at the data, then build your hypothesis about which factors to put under the microscope on the basis of that inspection.

DEMAND ANALYSIS

In its classical form, demand analysis plots a measure of *demand* (usually best expressed as the brand's share of market) against a comparable measure of its price to the consumer (e.g. relative to the market). If there is a reasonably strong and consistent relationship between the two, plotting a graph of the price/share points for a series of observations through time will show that the points are grouped more or less in a straight line. The expected relationship is negative. That is, *the higher the price*, the lower the demand; so the line is expected to angle down to the right.

The steeper the angle, the greater the brand's sensitivity to changes in price. *The closer the points approximate to a straight line*, the more certain that a price/share relationship exists. Using simple regression (calculable on a computer or even some pocket calculators) we can work out the formula that best fits the observed data, which will be in the form of:

$$\text{Expected share} = b \times \text{price} + \text{constant}$$

Here, b will be a (negative) coefficient which, multiplied by the price—and with the addition of the constant—gives the expected share at that price. It can be used to plot a straight 'best fit' line through the points on the graph. (To be punctilious, it should really be a curve, to relate proportionate changes in price to proportionate changes in sales, calculated from the logarithms of the variables. But the increased accuracy of fitting such a curve to a fairly narrow range of price differences is not significant, and a straight line in the natural values is a lot easier to calculate and use in practice.)

The formula can also be used to plot, on a sales graph, the *expected* share derived from the price in each period, for comparison with the actual. This can often point up where other marketing action, such as advertising, has lifted sales above the expected level.

The case history of Kellogg's Rice Krispies (1) illustrates the procedure, and also shows how—from the start of a new campaign—the demand line shifted abruptly up and to the right, thus demonstrating that the new advertising had added value to the brand, enabling it to command a higher share of demand at a given price. Sudden shifts like this in the demand curve are by no means unusual. Characteristically, there are periods of stable relationship between price and sales, separated by abrupt discontinuities when the line shifts upwards or downwards. (See Box 11).

These shifts sometimes occur at the time of a marketing change such as a new advertising campaign. Sometimes they reflect a latent change in consumer demand which is held back by the force of habit in purchasing, until a change is triggered off by some outside event: a supply shortage, for instance, or a promotion, or competitor action. It seems entirely likely that these discontinuities—reflecting as they do changes in the brand's perceived value to the consumer—may tell us something about advertising's long-term effects.

Demand analysis is an example of modelling: a simple, single-variable model but a model nonetheless. It is usually based on price as the explanatory variable, because price so often is the major factor affecting demand; but the technique is equally applicable to the relationship between sales and other factors. But as a single-variable model it seldom explains enough about a brand's performance to be satisfactory, and furthermore the single variable may 'grab' too much of the explanation for itself to be a reliable indicator of, say, the price elasticity. For that, it is necessary to turn to multiple-factor modelling.

ECONOMETRIC MODELLING

To explain the techniques of doing econometric modelling fully would take more space than is available in this book. What *can* be covered here is a brief outline of method and approach, plus some practical tips that may be found helpful by the non-statistician who is a 'consumer' of modelling. Those who themselves wish to become practitioners are advised to take an apprenticeship with an expert.

Modelling is used to:

- Improve our understanding of consumer (purchasing) behaviour in the market under examination.
- Identify the key factors affecting brand and market sales.
- Evaluate their relative importance.
- Assess the likely effects of altering those factors that are within the advertiser's control (e.g. price, quantity of advertising).
- Provide a means of monitoring ongoing brand performance, compared to that 'predicted' by the model.

In fact, the model will be a mathematical formula taking the following form:

BOX 11
The discontinuities in demand curves

Characteristically, demand curves reveal periods of stable relationship between price and sales, separated by sudden shifts upwards or downwards.

When these discontinuities occur is not predictable, nor are they obvious from a cursory look at the data. So plotting a series of price/share points can well produce a 'star chart' containing no apparent relationship at all, as in graph A. But all may not be lost. In such cases, try numbering the points in time order and then drawing lines between consecutively numbered points, like a child's join-the-dots picture puzzle. (John Davis dubbed this the Rupert Bear technique). One or more series of near-straight-line sequences are quite likely to appear, thus pinpointing *when* the discontinuities happened (graph B). In other words, fit the model to the observed data, rather than try to force the data into the straitjacket of a preconceived notion about how the brand and market must work.

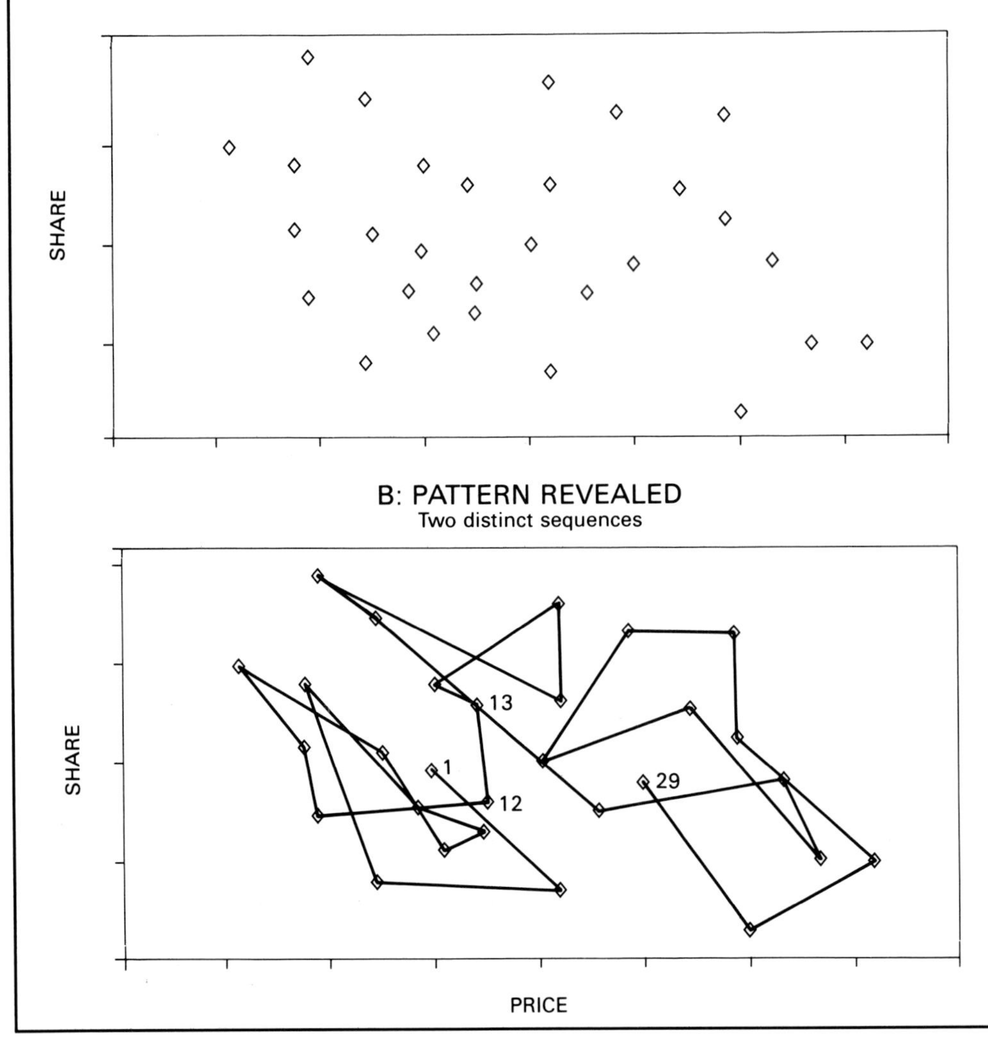

Dependent variable (e.g. sales) = constant
+ b × first independent variable
+ c × second independent variable
+ d × third independent variable
etc.

In this formula b, c, d, etc., stand for the coefficients which, multiplied by the values of each explanatory variable, and summed together with the constant, given the expected value of the dependent variable.

But a formula, however extensive and however good statistically, remains an over-simplified version of reality. Like a caricature, it will be a recognizable representation, but one which overemphasizes the more salient characteristics at the expense of the detail. And, like a caricature, it only portrays part of the truth—and that which it does depict may be exaggerated. This is not to deny the usefulness of modelling. As a practical marketing tool for untangling the complexities of markets its value is unquestionable, and goes well beyond a mere evaluation function. But we should always retain a healthy level of scepticism about models. They are not Holy Writ. And if a model does not make sense to the experienced marketer, then the marketer is right and the model wrong.

Model-building is a painstaking process. It starts with data collection, for the chosen dependent variable (usually sales, or market share) and for all the other factors which may be thought relevant. In practice, it is advisable to collect data for at least 30–40 periods, that is, about three years of monthly figures. It is also advisable to inspect the data very carefully for possible errors or inconsistencies, and to start by looking separately at each variable, as described above under *Pre/Post Analysis.*

Having collected the data and loaded it in to a computer, the modeller makes an initial selection of the most likely explanatory factors and runs a multiple regression. This examines all the factors simultaneously and picks the mathematical solution that best 'explains' the data. The resulting statistics tell him how well the total formula fits the actual data for the dependent variable, and how significant is the contribution of each of the explanatory variables. His next step is to drop or add a variable, and rerun the regression to see if he has been able to improve on the model's fit. This trial-and-error process continues (it may take 40 or more trials) until the modeller feels that his model is satisfactory. This process of building a model is well illustrated in two case histories, for Dettol (5) and for Kellogg's Super Noodles (6), and briefly explained in Box 12.

A model is satisfactory when:

- It makes marketing sense.
- It 'explains' a large proportion of the observed variance in the dependent variable, say 70 per cent or more (i.e. the R^2 is at least .70).
- The unexplained residuals are small and randomly scattered, so that there is no reason to suppose that a significant part of the explanation has been missed.
- Adding a further explanatory variable makes for little or no improvement to the overall fit, and adds nothing useful to our understanding of what makes the brand tick.

All this is no more than a bald outline of a complex but fascinating subject. Those who would like to pursue it further are strongly advised to look up Tom Corlett's comprehensive and lucid paper (16).

BOX 12
Building a model

Preliminary examination of the data has suggested that three factors in particular have influenced sales of a brand: its price, its level of distribution in retailers, and its advertising. The data are shown in graph A. Each factor appears to have affected sales, but by how much?

It helps to construct one's model in steps. As a first step, we look at the effect of price alone. The computer uses regression analysis to compare movements in the explanatory variable (price) with movements in the dependent variable (sales) to produce the formula that most closely fits the observed sales data. The result, illustrated in graph B, has an R^2 of .27, i.e. the single factor model 'explains' 27 per cent of the variance in sales. This is inadequate as explanation.

Next, we add a second variable (advertising). The computer now relates movements in *both* explanatory variables to sales movements and the result (graph C) is a much better fit ($R^2 = .67$). But inspection shows that the model overestimates sales in the earlier periods, and underestimates them later. It is missing out some other growth factor.

Inclusion of the third explanatory variable (distribution) produces a satisfactory fit (graph D). The R^2 is .86, and the coefficient attached to each variable is significant.

The formula of this final model reveals, after further calculation, that the brand has a high base level of sales (i.e. it has a strongly 'loyal' following); that advertising and distribution are strong contributors to additional sales above the base level; and that although price is a factor the brand is not particularly price sensitive. Quantified, these findings are valuable pieces of information when planning future marketing strategy.

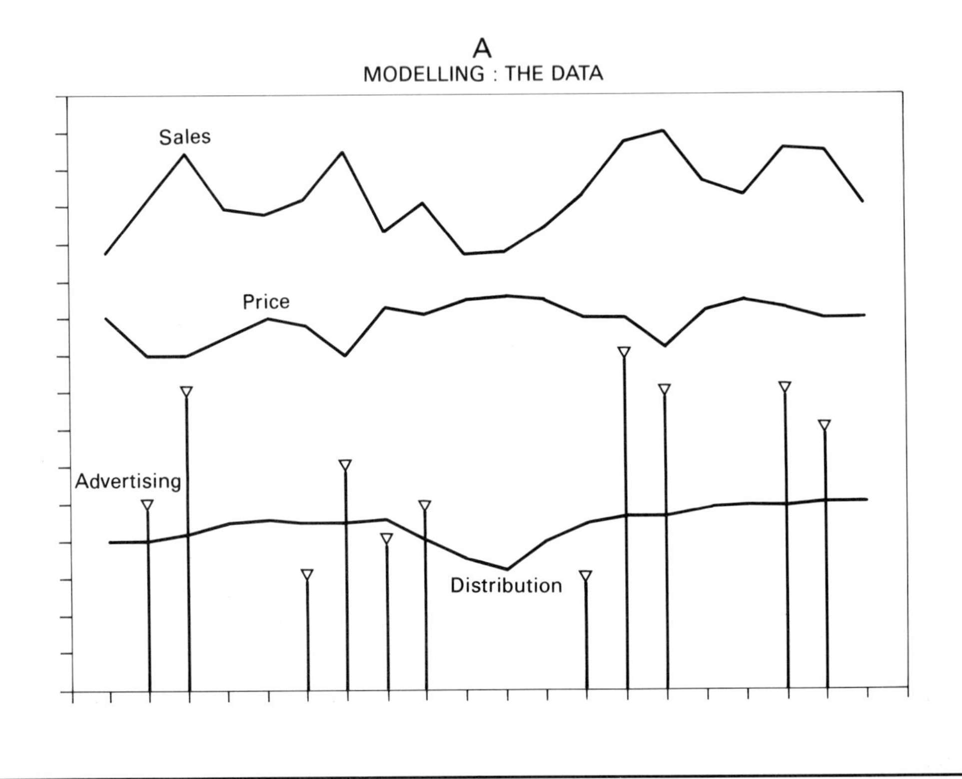

BOX 12 cont'd

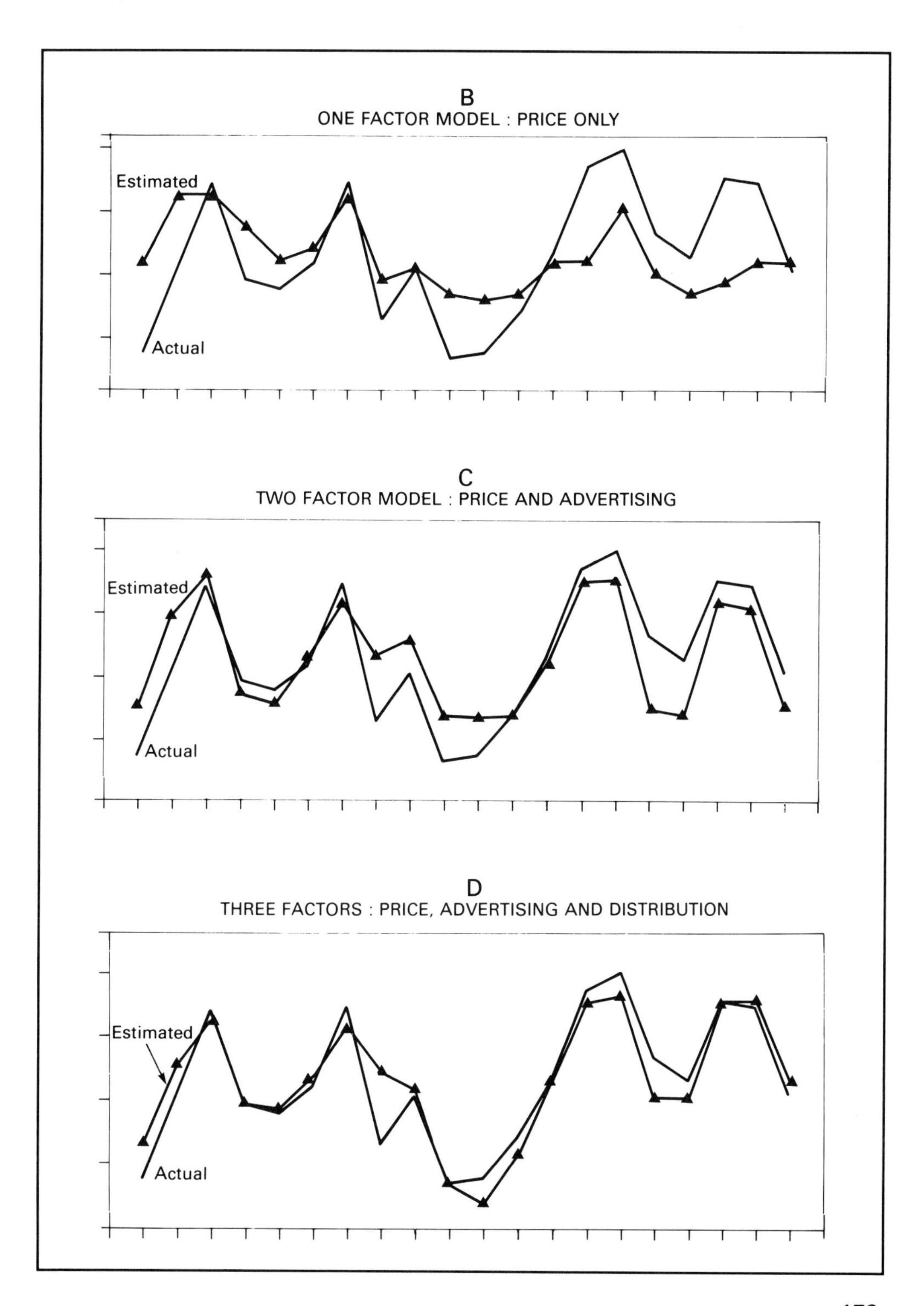
B
ONE FACTOR MODEL : PRICE ONLY
Estimated
Actual
C
TWO FACTOR MODEL : PRICE AND ADVERTISING
Estimated
Actual
D
THREE FACTORS : PRICE, ADVERTISING AND DISTRIBUTION
Estimated
Actual

AREA TESTS

Area tests of advertising usually take one of three forms:

- Weight tests.
- Schedule tests.
- Copy tests.

In all, however, the principle is the same: to reproduce in the test area all the marketing conditions that exist in the control area, apart from the single variable (advertising weight, or frequency and timing, or content) that is being examined. In reality, of course, such purism is impossible. No marketer can control all the conditions. But as far as it is possible to do so, he should try. This means that:

- The test area(s), and the control area(s) with which they will be compared, should be chosen for their representativeness on purchasing or consumption and demographics.
- The size of area to test in, and the duration of the test, should be determined by (a) the size of the change needed or expected in the dependent variable and (b) the margins of error in the data source to be used. (Standard error estimates should be obtainable from the research suppliers.) If an upweight test must achieve a sales growth of 5 per cent to justify the extra spend, there is no point undertaking a test that is too small to be able to tell whether a 5 per cent gain is real or random error. In practice, this usually means testing in two to three areas for six to 12 months.
- It is prudent, in any case, to test at least two areas, in case some element (a competitor's new product test market, for example) ruins the representativeness of one of them.
- As far as is humanly possible, the conditions of the test, once embarked on, should be adhered to. If it calls for a given number of TVRs, or a particular burst timing, the lure of special deals that would alter the schedule should be manfully resisted.

Even so, it is unlikely that conditions in the test and control areas will end up precisely as planned. So although it is possible simply to compare test with control results, without reference to other factors, this may be misleading.

A more accurate approach is to build a model of test area sales, for a period prior to the test, in which the relationship between test area and national (or control area) explanatory variables is fitted to the corresponding area: national sales relationship. This model is then applied to the actual explanatory variables that obtain during the test period to yield an estimate of what the test area sales *would have been* had the test not occurred. The difference between expected and actual is a measure of what the test has achieved, after making due allowance for other factors. (For illustrations of this approach, see the Lucozade (4) and Shloer (2) case histories.)

A further refinement of area testing is a crossover test, as described in the Shakers Cocktails paper (9), in which test and control areas are switched over for a second period of time, to eliminate some of the biases created by the inherent differences between our limited number of television transmission regions. This is particularly helpful where there are difficulties in applying econometric techniques to area data.

APPLYING EVALUATION TO PLANNING

Information gathered in monitoring research has two main strategic applications:

- To guide us in answering the 'how much' questions, which relate particularly to pricing strategy, and to the size and media deployment of the advertising budget. This is where the techniques of econometric modelling are at their most useful, by providing a model of the brand in its market which we can use in forecasting. No model, of course, can predict. But by removing some of the uncertainty about the future, it can valuably act as an aid to predictive *judgement*, by telling us what, on past evidence, is likely to be the outcome of certain actions. What if we raise or lower the price by a given proportion? What if we alter the advertising budget? Or what if we spend it in a different way?
- The second application is to do with the content of advertising. Here what we need is diagnostic evaluation, to help our understanding of *how* the advertising worked. In this sense, especially, evaluation is comparative rather than absolute. It cannot tell us what the advertising's content should be, but it can point us in the right direction. To do so, the research has to monitor the appropriate consumers' responses to the campaign and to the brand. In the eternal triangle between consumer, brand and advertisement, it is the relationship between consumer and brand that is key, and on which tracking research should focus.

In collecting evidence with which to answer the 'what content' questions, the emphasis is on improving our understanding of how a campaign worked, by examining how consumers responded to the brand and its advertising, so that next time round we may be able to set better-informed strategies. The evidence needed is diagnostic, the data may be hard or soft, and its application in planning is quite unlike the mathematical-logical approach to the 'how much' questions. Rather, it demands an empathetic understanding of how consumers think and feel about the brand and its advertising. That is, the planner uses his evaluation results just as he uses all his other evidence—to prompt and answer questions:

- Where is the brand?
- What is happening to purchasing behaviour?
- What are the factors affecting behaviour?
- Which of them can we do something about?
- What could we do with them?
- How could we achieve that?
- What would be the likely result?
- Is that good enough?
- Within all this, what is the role for the advertising?
- How do we expect it to work?
- What do we expect it to achieve?
- How are we going to evaluate the results?

If this sounds like a recipe for starting the planning process again from the beginning, it is.

IN CONCLUSION

Four general precepts to end with:

- Evaluation is a learning discipline. Set the evaluation criteria and standards before the campaign starts. Use them to evaluate. Then take another look at the criteria and standards. Were they the right ones?
- Try to use more than one evaluation method and more than one data source. Corroboration is invaluable.
- Remain scrupulously impartial. Any sign of bias in the evaluation will rightly lead to its rejection by the client. Look at all the evidence. Make as good a case for dropping some bits, as for including others. Play devil's advocate: try to knock holes in your argument.
- Apply what you learn in planning the next campaign and setting better objectives. *Go back to Chapter 1.*

REFERENCES

ADVERTISING WORKS, IPA, 1981

1 Jeremy Elliott, 'Kellogg's Rice Krispies: the effect of a new creative execution'.
2 Elizabeth Leffman and Michael Stewart, 'Shloer: increase in sales as a result of a media change'.
3 Gil McWilliam, 'The case for All Clear shampoo'.
4 Mike Soden and Michael Stewart, 'The repositioning of Lucozade'.
5 Angus Thomas and others, 'Dettol: a case history'.

ADVERTISING WORKS 2, IPA, 1983

6 Peter Croome and Jocelyn Horsfall, 'Advertising: key to the success of Kellogg's Super Noodles'.

ADVERTISING WORKS 3, IPA, 1985

7 Peter Carter, 'Cadbury's Fudge: how advertising has built a brand'.
8 Roger Clayton and others, 'Building a business through advertising: Zanussi's appliance of science'.
9 Simon Clemmow and Damian O'Malley, 'The effect of advertising on the launch of Shakers Cocktails'.
10 Jeremy Elliott, 'Breaking the bran barrier—Kellogg's Bran Flakes 1982–84'.
11 Peter Field and Adam Morgan, 'Hofmeister: a study of advertising and brand image in the lager market'.
12 Jane Fiori, 'The Lloyds Bank Personal Loan—accessible borrowing'.

OTHER SOURCES

13 Michael Bird and Andrew Ehrenberg, 'Intentions-to-buy and claimed brand usage', *Operational Research Quarterly,* Vol. 17, No. 1, 1966.
14 Simon Broadbent, 'Price and advertising: volume and profit', *Admap,* November 1980.
15 Simon Broadbent and Stephen Colman, 'Advertising effectiveness: across brands', *JMRS,* January 1986.
16 Tom Corlett, 'Modelling the sales effects of advertising: today's questions', *Admap,* October 1985.
17 Timothy Joyce, 'What do we know about how Advertising works?', ESOMAR paper 1967, reprinted as JWT booklet no. 25.
18 Stephen King, 'Practical progress from a theory of advertisements', *Admap,* October 1975.

Index